The Politics of Food Sovereignty

Food sovereignty has been a fundamentally contested concept in global agrarian discourse over the last two decades, as a political project and campaign, an alternative, a social movement, and an analytical framework. It has inspired and mobilized diverse publics: workers, scholars and public intellectuals, farmers and peasant movements, NGOs, and human rights activists in the global North and South. The term 'food sovereignty' has become a challenging subject for social science research, and has been interpreted and reinterpreted in a variety of ways. It is broadly defined as the right of peoples to democratically control or determine the shape of their food system, and to produce sufficient and healthy food in culturally appropriate and ecologically sustainable ways in and near their territory.

However, various theoretical issues remain: sovereignty at what scale and for whom? How are sovereignties contested? What is the relationship between food sovereignty and human rights frameworks? What might food sovereignty mean extended to a broader set of social relations in urban contexts? How do the principles of food sovereignty interact with local histories and contexts? This comprehensive volume examines what food sovereignty might mean, how it might be variously construed, and what policies it implies.

This book was originally published as a special issue of the journal *Globalizations*.

Annie Shattuck is a PhD candidate in Geography at the University of California, Berkeley, USA.

Christina Schiavoni is a PhD researcher at the International Institute of Social Studies in The Hague, in the Netherlands.

Zoe VanGelder is a Researcher and a Yale Fox Fellow currently based in Mexico City, Mexico.

Rethinking Globalizations

Edited by Barry K. Gills, University of Helsinki, Finland and Kevin Gray, University of Sussex, UK.

This series is designed to break new ground in the literature on globalization and its academic and popular understanding. Rather than perpetuating or simply reacting to the economic understanding of globalization, this series seeks to capture the term and broaden its meaning to encompass a wide range of issues and disciplines and convey a sense of alternative possibilities for the future.

Dialectics in World Politics
Edited by Shannon Brincat

The Redesign of the Global Financial Architecture
The Return of State Authority
Stuart P. M. Mackintosh

Markets and Development
Civil Society, Citizens and the Politics of Neoliberalism
Edited by Toby Carroll and Darryl S.L. Jarvis

Occupying Subjectivity
Being and Becoming Radical in the 21st Century
Edited by Chris Rossdale

Globalization and Global Citizenship
Interdisciplinary Approaches
Edited by Irene Langran and Tammy Birk

The Politics of Food Sovereignty
Concept, Practice and Social Movements
Edited by Annie Shattuck, Christina Schiavoni and Zoe VanGelder

Time and Globalization
An interdisciplinary dialogue
Edited by Paul Huebener, Susie O'Brien, Tony Porter, Liam Stockdale and Rachel Yanqiu Zhou

From International Relations to World Civilizations
The contributions of Robert W. Cox
Edited by Shannon Brincat

Global Insurrectional Politics
Edited by Nevzat Soguk

Time, Globalization and Human Experience
Interdisciplinary Explorations
Edited by Paul Huebener, Susie O'Brien, Tony Porter, Liam Stockdale and Yanqiu Rachel Zhou

Localization in Development Aid
How Global Institutions enter Local Lifeworlds
Edited by Thorsten Bonacker, Judith von Heusinger and Kerstin Zimmer

The New Global Politics
Global Social Movements in the Twenty-First Century
Edited by Harry E. Vanden, Peter N. Funke and Gary Prevos

The Politics of Food Sovereignty

Concept, Practice and Social Movements

Edited by
Annie Shattuck, Christina Schiavoni and Zoe VanGelder

Routledge
Taylor & Francis Group
LONDON AND NEW YORK

First published 2017
by Routledge

2 Park Square, Milton Park, Abingdon, Oxfordshire OX14 4RN
52 Vanderbilt Avenue, New York, NY 10017

Routledge is an imprint of the Taylor & Francis Group, an informa business

First issued in paperback 2018

British Library Cataloguing in Publication Data
A catalogue record for this book is available from the British Library

ISBN 13: 978-0-415-78729-1 (hbk)
ISBN 13: 978-0-367-13929-2 (pbk)

Typeset in Times New Roman
by RefineCatch Limited, Bungay, Suffolk

Publisher's Note
The publisher accepts responsibility for any inconsistencies that may have arisen during the conversion of this book from journal articles to book chapters, namely the possible inclusion of journal terminology.

Contents

Citation Information

The chapters in this book were originally published in *Globalizations*, volume 12, issue 4 (August 2015). When citing this material, please use the original page numbering for each article, as follows:

Chapter 1
Translating the Politics of Food Sovereignty: Digging into Contradictions, Uncovering New Dimensions
Annie Shattuck, Christina M. Schiavoni and Zoe VanGelder
Globalizations, volume 12, issue 4 (August 2015) pp. 421–433

Chapter 2
The Land Question in the Food Sovereignty Project
Philip McMichael
Globalizations, volume 12, issue 4 (August 2015) pp. 434–451

Chapter 3
Food Sovereignty and the Recognition of New Rights for Peasants at the UN: A Critical Overview of La Via Campesina's Rights Claims over the Last 20 Years
Priscilla Claeys
Globalizations, volume 12, issue 4 (August 2015) pp. 452–465

Chapter 4
Competing Sovereignties, Contested Processes: Insights from the Venezuelan Food Sovereignty Experiment
Christina M. Schiavoni
Globalizations, volume 12, issue 4 (August 2015) pp.466–480

Chapter 5
Sovereignty at What Scale? An Inquiry into Multiple Dimensions of Food Sovereignty
Alastair Iles and Maywa Montenegro de Wit
Globalizations, volume 12, issue 4 (August 2015) pp. 481–497

Chapter 6
Food Sovereignty in Everyday Life: Toward a People-centered Approach to Food Systems
Meleiza Figueroa
Globalizations, volume 12, issue 4 (August 2015) pp. 498–512

Chapter 7
'Quiet Food Sovereignty' as Food Sovereignty without a Movement? Insights from Post-socialist Russia
Oane Visser, Natalia Mamonova, Max Spoor and Alexander Nikulin
Globalizations, volume 12, issue 4 (August 2015) pp.513–528

Chapter 8
Return to Freedom: Anti-GMO Aloha 'Āina Activism on Molokai as an Expression of Place-based Food Sovereignty
Clare Gupta
Globalizations, volume 12, issue 4 (August 2015) pp.529–544

Chapter 9
Broadening the Land Question in Food Sovereignty to Northern Settings: A Case Study of Occupy the Farm
Antonio Roman-Alcalá
Globalizations, volume 12, issue 4 (August 2015) pp. 545–558

Chapter 10
A Recipe for Change: Reclamation of Indigenous Food Sovereignty in O-Pipon-Na-Piwin Cree *Nation for Decolonization, Resource Sharing, and Cultural Restoration*
Asfia Gulrukh Kamal, Rene Linklater, Shirley Thompson, Joseph Dipple and Ithinto Mechisowin Committee
Globalizations, volume 12, issue 4 (August 2015) pp.559–575

Notes on Contributors

Priscilla Claeys is a Postdoctoral Researcher in Social and Political Sciences at the University of Louvain (UCL), Belgium. Her research interests include peasant movements, food and agriculture, human rights, and economic globalization.

Joseph Dipple is a MA student in Native Studies at the University of Manitoba working on the implications of natural resource extraction and exploitation on Indigenous communities, particularly the construction of hydroelectric generating stations in northern Manitoba.

Meleiza Figueroa is a PhD candidate in Geography at the University of California, Berkeley. She was formerly a radio journalist and lead researcher on the film 'Wal-Mart: The High Cost of Low Price.'

Clare Gupta is a National Science Foundation SEES (Science, Education and Engineering for Sustainability) Postdoctoral Fellow at the Yale School of Forestry and Environmental Studies. Her dissertation work in the University of California Berkeley's Department of Environmental Science, Policy and Management examined the implications of wildlife conservation for the livelihoods of rural communities living near protected areas in northern Botswana.

Alastair Iles is Associate Professor in Environmental Policy and Societal Change at the Department of Environmental Science, Policy and Management at the University of California at Berkeley. He researches green chemistry science and politics, participatory approaches to governing technologies, and policies for diversified farming systems and for food sovereignty.

Asfia Gulrukh Kamal is a PhD candidate at the Natural Resources Institute, University of Manitoba. She has a Masters in Cultural Anthropology from University of Manitoba and a Master of Social Science from Women's Studies, Dhaka University, Dhaka, Bangladesh.

Rene Linkalter is the Director of Health of Tommy Thomas Memorial Health Complex and Community Care in O-Pipon-Na-Piwin Cree Nation. He is the Vice Chair of community food sovereignty program Ithinto Mechisowin (Food from the Land). He has a Bachelor of Arts degree with a focus on Sociology and Native Studies.

Natalia Mamonova is a PhD candidate at the International Institute of Social Studies (ISS) of Erasmus University, the Netherlands. Her PhD research is on land grabbing in the post-Soviet countryside, land conflicts, responses by the local population, and rural social movements in Russia and Ukraine.

Philip McMichael is Professor and Chair of Development Sociology, Cornell University, and is a member of the Civil Society Mechanism in the CFS/FAO. His current research is on agrarian movements, land questions, and food regimes.

Ithinto Mechisowin Committee has seventeen community food champions, youth, elders who came together to establish O-Pipon-Na-Piwin Cree Nation's community-based food sovereignty program, Ithinto Mechisowin (Food from the Land).

Maywa Montenegro de Wit is a PhD candidate at the University of California at Berkeley and a former science journalist based in New York City. Her research focuses on seeds, agroecology and food sovereignty, and the politics of access to genetic resources.

Alexander Nikulin is Professor and Director of the Center for Agricultural Studies of the Russian Presidential Academy of National Economy and Public Administration, Moscow, Russia. He specializes in economic and agrarian sociology, history of the peasantry, and the current state of farming in Russia.

Antonio Roman-Alcalá is a co-founder of the San Francisco Urban Agriculture Alliance, and received his MA in 2014 from the International Institute of Social Studies in The Hague. His work focuses on the intersections of global environmental politics and local deliberative democracy, with food and farming as vehicles for political–economic critique and praxis-based interventions.

Christina M. Schiavoni is a PhD researcher at the International Institute of Social Studies (ISS) in The Hague, the Netherlands. Her current research is focused on food sovereignty and the right to food, with a particular interest in efforts to adopt food sovereignty into state policy and into global governance mechanisms.

Annie Shattuck is a PhD candidate in Geography at the University of California Berkeley, USA, and a Research Fellow at Food First/Institute for Food and Development Policy. Her work examines political ecology and agrarian change.

Max Spoor is Professor of Development Studies, International Institute of Social Studies (ISS) of Erasmus University, Visiting Professor in Barcelona (IBEI) and Guest Professor in Nanjing (NJAU). His research is on transition economies in Asia, such as Vietnam and China, and in Eastern Europe, regarding rural and environmental issues, poverty, and inequality.

Shirley Thompson is an Associate Professor at the Natural Resources Institute, University of Manitoba. Dr Thompson has a doctoral degree in Adult Education and Community Development and a Master of Environmental Engineering, both from the University of Toronto.

Zoe VanGelder is a Researcher and a Yale Fox Fellow currently based in Mexico City. Her research explores the ways gender and knowledge politics affect rural livelihoods.

Oane Visser is Assistant Professor and Senior Researcher, International Institute of Social Studies (ISS) of Erasmus University. He gained a prestigious ERC (European Research Council) Starting Grant for his research on land grabbing, financialization, poverty, and social movements in Eastern Europe and the former Soviet Union (2013–2018).

Translating the Politics of Food Sovereignty: Digging into Contradictions, Uncovering New Dimensions

ANNIE SHATTUCK*, CHRISTINA M. SCHIAVONI** &
ZOE VANGELDER***

**University of California, Berkeley, CA, USA*
***International Institute for Social Studies (ISS), The Hague, The Netherlands*
****Yale Fox Fellow, Mexico City, Mexico*

ABSTRACT *Food sovereignty, as a movement and a set of ideas, is coming of age. Rooted in resistance to free trade and the globalizing force of neoliberalism, the concept has inspired collective action across the world. We examine what has changed since food sovereignty first emerged on the international scene and reflect on insight from new terrain where the movement has expanded. We argue that to advance the theory and practice of food sovereignty, new frameworks and analytical methods are needed to move beyond binaries—between urban and rural, gender equality and the family farm, trade and localism, and autonomy and engagement with the state. A research agenda in food sovereignty must not shy away from the rising contradictions in and challenges to the movement. The places of seeming contradiction may in fact be where the greatest insights are to be found. We suggest that by taking a relational perspective, scholars can begin to draw insight into the challenges and sticking points of food sovereignty by training their lens on shifts in the global food regime, on the efforts to construct sovereignty at multiple scales, and on the points of translation where food sovereignty is articulated through historical memory, identity, and everyday life.*

Introduction

> Food sovereignty is not a fixed principle, it's a process . . . it's happening, and it's been made to happen, through the struggles of millions of people all over the world. (Paul Nicholson, La Via Campesina)[1]

In the fall of 2013, some 300 scholars and activists gathered at the Yale Program in Agrarian Studies to discuss the challenges and promise of food sovereignty. Paul Nicholson, farmer, Basque leader, and founding member of the international peasant movement La Via Campesina, addressed the gathering in his usual animated voice. 'Today', he told a packed room, 'you go to any kind of social forum and you will see that food sovereignty is the principle alternative presented against capitalism—there is no other. The others are resistance. This is a proposal' (see note 1).

In the last decade, food sovereignty—the right of people to healthy and culturally appropriate food produced through ecologically sound and sustainable methods, and their right to define their own food and agriculture systems[2]—was enshrined in the constitutions and/or national laws of Ecuador, Bolivia, Venezuela, Nepal, Nicaragua, Mali, and Senegal. The concept has inspired communities from the South Side of Chicago, to the Hawaiian Islands, to Occupied Palestine. Rooted in resistance to neoliberal globalization and free trade, movements for food sovereignty are globalizing as well; the idea now inspires collective action among tens of millions of people all over the world.

Food sovereignty is undoubtedly coming of age—as a movement and a set of ideas about how to democratize both access to resources and political power. But as the movement grows, challenges and contradictions emerge. Some scholars have remarked that food sovereignty has been only minimally successful in affecting policy or changing regulations (Edelman, 2014; Hospes, 2014). Others have noted contradictions in strategies for food sovereignty: between attempts by local activists to create food systems that are relatively autonomous from the whims of the global market and organized campaigns to change state policy and motivate institutional support for small farmers (Clark, 2013; Edelman, 2014; McKay, Nehring, & Walsh-Dilley, 2014); between proposals championing communal vs. individual rights (Agarwal, 2014; Claeys, 2014); and between a focus on making trade more fair and efforts to build autonomous local food systems (Bacon, 2015; Burnett & Murphy, 2014).

Scholars have also noted serious tensions between the interests of different participants in the food sovereignty project. For instance, the interests of small-scale farmers and different classes of rural landless workers cannot easily be reconciled (Bernstein, 2014; Patel, 2009), while the need of producers to receive fair prices seems at odds with the dependence of poor urban consumers on cheap food (Bernstein, 2014). The family farm and systems of patriarchy often go hand in hand (Agarwal, 2014). Furthermore, discourses on food sovereignty coming from the global South do not always resonate with urban communities in North America organizing around racial justice (Holt-Giménez & Wang, 2011). Questions that are at once both theoretical and practical, like 'who is the sovereign in food sovereignty?' persist as well (Edelman, 2014). These debates are not merely academic—they represent serious political challenges for a growing movement.[3]

This collection of articles builds on conversations at two events in which these contradictions loomed large. These 'critical dialogues' on food sovereignty, organized jointly by the Yale Program in Agrarian Studies, the International Institute of Social Studies (ISS), the Transnational Institute, and the Institute for Food and Development Policy (Food First) in September of 2013 at Yale University in New Haven and in January 2014 at the ISS in The Hague, were held as part of an ongoing process to advance debates on food sovereignty.[4]

Many of the contradictions outlined above have motivated scholars to question whether food sovereignty can be more than a political slogan. Noting shifting definitions and limited regulatory uptake, researchers have struggled to find a blueprint for realizing food sovereignty that can be scaled up and applied across the board (Hospes, 2014). We argue that this search is misguided and ineffectual. We offer a different approach to understanding the challenge and potential of food sovereignty—and a research agenda for critical scholars of globalization—that engages with the shifting global politics which movements now confront; that recognizes that sovereignty itself is multivalent and always contested; that contextualizes different struggles for food sovereignty as reflections of specific histories and identities; and that takes everyday life as a starting point for analysis.

Shifting Terrain, Shifting Politics of Sovereignty

Food sovereignty was born, like all ideas, as a product of its time. The concept has its roots in nationalist food politics of the 1980s (Edelman, 2014), but on the world stage, food sovereignty rose to prominence in the aftermath of structural adjustment. In the mid-1990s social movements were forced to reckon with a wave of free trade agreements. As cheap commodities flooded rural economies in the Global South, the agricultural sector consolidated dramatically.[5] These circumstances left an already weak state apparatus even weaker with respect to regulating flows of food and agricultural goods. The peasant farmers represented by La Via Campesina were, in many ways, the collateral damage of this era. Invoking sovereignty as a rallying cry framed hunger, agrarian reform, and rural economies as an issue of human rights and national control (McMichael, 2014; Patel, 2009). The call to sovereignty was a conscious effort to bring power back to the state from deregulated markets and free trade regimes—and as such, to bolster the rights and livelihoods of peasants.

Since 'food sovereignty' rose to prominence in 1996, the ground has shifted under rural social movements.[6] Peasant farmers are dealing with a confluence of events, including the growing involvement of financial actors in agricultural production and food provisioning (Isakson, 2014), increasing ecological pressures and uncertainty (Ribot, 2014), more rural–urban circular migration and multi-cited livelihoods (Hecht, 2014; Nguyen & Locke, 2014), and increasing concern with health, given the rise in diet-related disease and pesticide toxicity in both the Global North and South (De Schutter, 2011; Noyes et al., 2009).

First, as Phil McMichael explains in this issue, movements have had to confront not only a trade-centered assault on peasant economies, but also vast—and vastly complicated—financialization of agriculture (Clapp, 2014; Fairbairn et al., 2014; Isakson, 2014). Since 2007, three spikes in food prices have occurred, all partly fueled by commodities speculation. Corporations continue their patterns of vertical integration, while also turning to schemes such as contract farming to 'incorporate smallholders into global value chains': small-scale farmers may own the land, but in many cases, cede degrees of control over their economies and labor (McMichael, 2015). A new wave of investment in farmland—the oft-cited 'land grab'—is also bound up in the transformation of global agricultural politics and trade (McMichael, 2012).[7] This 'investment-led assault' (McMichael, 2015) is multifaceted and has shifted the terms of opposition to include defending '"ways of life" on the land against not only market forces ... but also organized physical and economic enclosures' (McMichael, 2015). Meanwhile, in both the global

North and South, food insecurity is becoming an increasingly urban concern, intensified by these new waves of dispossession.

Changes in geopolitics have also affected food sovereignty as the power dynamics between and within states are shifting. While the countries of the G8 remain major players in global food politics (see McMichael, 2015), they must now play alongside other powerful actors, from the BRICS countries (Brazil, Russia, India, China and South Africa) to the growing 'pink tide' of left-leaning countries in Latin America (see Schiavoni, 2015). These shifting axes of power are reflected not only in new relationships among states, but also between states and civil society, as can be seen with the newly reformed UN Committee on World Food Security (CFS) (see McMichael, 2015; Claeys, 2014). Such developments simultaneously pose new challenges and openings and raise new questions for the role of the state vis-à-vis food sovereignty—a theme that emerges throughout this issue.

These changes in geopolitics and structural transformations in the global economy come at a time of increasingly unstable climate conditions, among other challenges. Urban and rural ways of making a living are no longer as distinct as they once were: many households are stretched between spaces, with the work of childrearing and caring for the elderly in the countryside and rural youth increasingly drawn to urban life and the economic opportunities there. Migration between city and countryside is often the only way to make ends meet. Pesticide toxicity affects more farmers and farmworkers, as well as consumers, making access to healthy food a rallying cry for urban and rural communities alike; and the global movement for agroecology is rising. Now considered a twin pillar of food sovereignty, agroecology has become the practical method for building food sovereignty at the farm scale (Altieri & Nicholls, 2012).

In short, these new realities suggest that the context—socioeconomic, political, and ecological—in which food sovereignty was originally hatched has changed more than a little. The experiences, movements, and positions encompassed under the umbrella of food sovereignty have always been diverse (Desmarais & Wittman, 2014), but the shifts that we are seeing today demand a new degree of flexibility in the way that food sovereignty is imagined, researched, and put into practice.

For researchers, this shifting political terrain is a fruitful space of engagement. While there has been a flush of recent literature on financialization and the global land grab, there have been fewer investigations on other aspects of change in the global food regime, including of the effects of increasing rural–urban circular migration, the way climate change interacts with market volatility and historical inequality, new South–South trade arrangements, and corporate consolidation in the Global South, to name a few. Deeper examination of the spaces in which these changes are negotiated could help to identify where there might be opportunities for structural transformation.

Multiple and Competing Sovereignties

The circumstances of the current moment also challenge us in our understanding of *sovereignty* as such. There is no one international sphere capable of regulating booming commodities markets, financial investments in farmland, or contract farming schemes. These flows of capital and financial interests represent a real shift in power, an increase in the power of unregulated markets to distribute resources. Unlike in the heyday of the WTO, there is no single governing authority from which to regain (food) sovereignty (McMichael, 2015).

As Schiavoni explains in this issue, some of the apparent contradictions of food sovereignty may in fact be explained by contradictions inherent in the concept of sovereignty itself. She notes, as do others (Claeys, 2014; Iles & Montenegro de Wit, 2015), that political theorists describe both internal and external dimensions of sovereignty. External sovereignty, the sovereignty of nations within their own territories, is the most oft-invoked and arguably the most accepted form of sovereignty. However, sovereignty also calls upon the internal political structure of society with the belief that the absolute authority resides within the political community, or with 'the people' (Hinsley, 1986, quoted in Schiavoni, 2015). Translated to food sovereignty, this duality of sovereignty could help to explain why food sovereignty might simultaneously invoke national control over a country's food supply and productive resources, implying a more state-centric vision of sovereignty, *and* people's control internally, in a more popular vision of sovereignty. These two dimensions of (food) sovereignty need not be mutually exclusive, although how to navigate them is a major question.

Indeed, food sovereignty activists have long worked simultaneously for political change at multiple scales: for national agrarian reform; for international recognition of peasant's rights; for the creation of local markets; for the development of agroecological farming practices and for transnational farmer-to-farmer networks to disseminate and share them. Iles and Montenegro de Wit (2015) ask both scholars and activists to think about these scales from a relational perspective. In their analysis, the *relationships and processes* between levels of organizing hold the most important questions—for example, how local markets do or do not buffer farmers from the vagaries of financialized commodity markets; how transnational networks reflect and advance the politics of the grassroots; and how state agencies respond to and relate to movements. The notion of *relational scale* (Sayre, 2009, cited in Iles & Montenegro de Wit, 2015) brings into focus the channels of power through which sovereignty is exercised. 'In this view, sovereignty becomes a malleable and "negotiable" power which particular movements, peoples, or communities can seize, create, oppose, or reshape as against the state, cities, corporations, and other sovereign actors' (Iles & Montenegro de Wit, 2015). They further claim that, 'Understood in terms of relational scale, food sovereignty becomes as much a practice of creating connectivity as of creating autonomy' (Iles & Montenegro de Wit, 2015).

The relational scale approach offered by Iles and Montenegro de Wit can be helpful in research and analysis of some of the frequently cited tensions around the role of the state in food sovereignty. As many authors in this issue point out, efforts centered on the local—on building alternatives, bolstering local markets, building peasant autonomy, practicing agroecology, creating strong base organizations, and resuscitating local food cultures—are all essential and all growing. This local work is necessary, both to address immediate needs and to demonstrate tangible alternatives, but it cannot replace organized efforts to turn the power of the state toward the food sovereignty project. Few other bodies have the power to undertake reforms essential to building food sovereignty—to enact comprehensive agrarian reform, a central tenet of food sovereignty, renegotiate international trade pacts, publicly fund agroecological research and extension, or build national food reserves. Rather than regarding food sovereignty as being either 'of the state' or 'of peoples/communities', one to the exclusion of the other, understanding sovereignty as relational leaves room for different sovereign actors to coexist, with the terms of their engagement under ongoing negotiation, including which state agencies/powers are worth engaging with in any given moment.

With this view of sovereignty, it is easier to see how the food sovereignty movement challenges the foundational illusion of neoliberalism—that the state and society are separate domains. The relational view of sovereignty is akin to Gramsci's integral state—a concept in which civil society, the market, and state institutions are not hermetically sealed spheres; they are different ways of approaching power in a given conjuncture (Anderson, 1976; Hoare &

Nowell-Smith, 1971). Sovereignty, like hegemony, is built and contested within state institutions, within market conditions, within the institutions of civil society, popular culture, and the language with which people understand their daily lives. The integral state is a schema for understanding the delicate balance of coercion and consent that cements power in any given situation. This approach to power is vastly different from politics as circumscribed to struggle for the reigns of state power or narrowly defined policy change—it locates power in multiple spaces and histories, reaching deep into everyday life, identity and history, and simultaneously focusing on institutions (educational and cultural institutions especially) and civil society. Efforts to build food sovereignty must and often do engage in all these spaces, from promoting a culture of political and ecological action, in what Wittman (2009) calls 'agrarian citizenship', to social movement engagement with progressive forces within government and civil society (Borras, 2007; Holt-Giménez & Shattuck, 2011).

This effort is not without conflict or contradictions. In her study of Venezuela, where food sovereignty is enshrined in national law and is the focus of a national effort by both state and societal actors, Schiavoni found that diverse attempts to implement food sovereignty are happening both from above, by the national government, and from below, via citizen-led social institutions known as *comunas*, with dynamic interaction between the two. While this interaction is often tension filled, as a result of competing paradigms, approaches, and interests, the tension is the key to meaningful and sustained advancement of food sovereignty over the long term. Thus, building upon the work of McMichael (2009) and Patel (2009), Schiavoni finds it helpful to conceive of food sovereignty not as a singular sovereignty, but in terms of 'multiple' or 'competing sovereignties', and looks at how these multiple sovereignties are interacting with one another across different scales, jurisdictions, and geographies. As Schiavoni puts it, in resonance with the argument of Iles and Montenegro de Wit (2015), 'constructing food sovereignty is less about building silos (literally and figuratively) and more about building relationships—e.g., across scales, between the urban-rural divide, and among state and societal actors'. Far from abandoning the state, then, understanding multiple sovereignties requires a more interactive state–society approach (Fox, 1993).

In this issue, Priscilla Claeys offers an example of the kind of engaged research that might shed some light on the interplay between sovereignties at multiple scales. As La Via Campesina and other social movements are putting less of their energies toward challenging the WTO, they are pursuing new openings through which to further the food sovereignty agenda. While Claeys notes that social movements are focusing much of their efforts on regional and local scales, she points to their engagement in the newly reformed UN CFS and an international campaign urging the UN to recognize the rights of peasants as two important sites of struggle. The strategy of La Via Campesina and other actors in the food sovereignty movement involves drawing upon existing architecture, such as internationally recognized human rights language, while also pushing the boundaries of current understandings of 'rights', to include the 'right to food sovereignty' and the 'rights of peasants' (Claeys, 2014). In doing so, social movements are simultaneously calling upon the state to exert its authority toward the realization of these rights, while also recognizing and asserting 'the multiplicity of decision-making levels' inherent in food sovereignty (Claeys, 2014)—thereby challenging the state 'as the only legitimate source of law making and applying' (Falk, 1988, p. 27, cited in Claeys, 2014).

The WTO, the UN, and the CFS are certainly not the only realms in which these multiple sovereignties are negotiated or contested. We see the spaces where sovereignties begin to compete as fruitful space for both researchers and activists to engage, not a source of irreconcilable contradiction. Again, recognizing multiple and competing sovereignties reveals a research agenda that interrogates the very heart of the contradictions of food sovereignty outlined in the introduction. Asking who is the sovereign in food sovereignty is a question of power, and the multiple levels on which power is negotiated. Applying a relational approach to sovereignty reflects the different ways that power is being contested and that governance is changing, with the development of new institutions and new spaces that enable movements to contest and transform politics at multiple scales. The Venezuelan *comunas* researched by Schiavoni are one example of new institutions arising to promote and build food sovereignty at the local level and negotiate relationships with national levels of government. There are many more experiments of this kind around the world, and much innovation in institutional form that merits serious scholarly attention.

More research is needed on the institutional, cultural, and economic changes that can make food sovereignty's promises a reality. For example, food sovereignty calls for an end to violence against women, yet a better life for a farm household does not automatically translate into a better life for women and girls (Agarwal, 2014). What further shifts are needed for this promise of food sovereignty to be realized? Similarly, further research is needed on ways to reconcile the needs of urban consumers for affordable food, and the needs of farmers to receive fair prices. This research requires close collaborations with those actively working on such change.

Situating Food Sovereignty—The Role of Local History, Identity, and Memory

Given the many different scales and contexts in which food sovereignty efforts are taking place, scholars cannot simply 'beam down' an ahistorical set of theoretical principles and expect them to apply in exactly the same way in different places. A more relational approach to sovereignty moves away from an ideal, typified notion of what food sovereignty is or is not, focusing instead on how efforts to build food sovereignty change the ways in which power is structured and experienced in people's everyday lives. This allows us to see that food sovereignty does not have to—and will not—look the same everywhere. This diversity is not a product of ambiguity or confusion on 'what food sovereignty means'. Rather, these differences are the product of local history, identity, cultural memory, and political moments. Local specificities are the grounds on which strategy is negotiated, including whether, how, and in what way to engage the state.

Social movements rarely get to choose the terrain of struggle, but local identities and historical memories in this terrain can be a rich source of power. Take a central contradiction of food sovereignty—its rural origins in an urbanizing world (Bernstein, 2014). But if social relations, and not food as such, are the center of analysis (and activism), then food sovereignty principles may translate more clearly (Figueroa, 2015). How might food sovereignty principles translate in a Black community in Chicago's South Side? Meleiza Figueroa (2015) looks to histories of resistance, partly proletarianized spaces, and identity as resources with which to build the new from the skeleton of the old. In her case study of the Healthy Food Hub in Chicago, Black activists used collective buying, itself a practice brought from Jim Crow Mississippi, to carve out autonomous economic spaces, improve access to healthy food, and revive cultural memory. Whether or not the collective members in her case use the language of food sovereignty, Figueroa says, is beside the point. Figueroa asks an inverted version of Bernstein's critique of food sovereignty's relevance to an urban world (Bernstein, 2014)—not how will the opposing economic interests of the city and the countryside be resolved, 'But what does it mean to preserve "traditional" ways of life, or "peasant spaces," in a situation where people are far removed from any kind of referents for what these mean in practice?' Figueroa continues, addressing the particularities behind the long-standing question about the food sovereignty movement in urban areas, 'in a global metropolis, the diversity of experiences that exist within even a limited local context can imply very different meanings of food sovereignty for various communities'. The 'people centered approach' to food sovereignty she describes focuses first and foremost on lived experience, on the particularities and dynamism at different scales and historical contexts.

Figueroa's attention to *translation* is a key methodological challenge. Political concepts, like food sovereignty, do not just travel, they are *translated* (Ives, 2004, Kipfer & Hart, 2012). Translation is not a one-way street. As scholar Peter Ives reminds us (drawing on Gramsci), 'translation requires a change in both the original language and the one into which it is being translated' (Ives, 2004, p. 163). If the language we use to understand our world is a crucial building block of hegemony, then a key task for both scholars and activists is to translate—the deeply political practice of elaborating and transforming meaning in different contexts (Kipfer & Hart, 2012). Seen as a concept always in the process of translation, food sovereignty can take various forms. In fact, it must. Our responsibility as scholars is to examine the different particularities and permutations that food sovereignty may take.

This special issue examines the politics of food sovereignty as the idea extends its reach into new geographies and examines cases in which social movements navigate constraints and challenges on multiple scales. For example, Visser, Mamanova, and Spoor (2015) explore what food sovereignty looks like in a more authoritarian political context. The authors look at Russia's resilient peasant sector, and see a sort of 'quiet food sovereignty'. Given the current state of Russian politics, formal social movements are not strong, and in many ways, not politically possible or likely to be effective. Despite being overlooked by both the Russian state and transnational social movements, Visser and colleagues find that hidden and ad hoc strategies are preserving peasant autonomy in the Russian countryside. Drawing on the concept of 'quiet sustainability' (Smith & Jehlička, 2013), they ask scholars and activists alike not to write off peasantries that do not see themselves as part of a social movement. They argue instead that the principles of food sovereignty are widely adaptable to a variety of political contexts, including those where direct action, formal organizing, and other common tactics of the food sovereignty movement may not be politically productive.

In other spaces, explicit efforts to carve out local autonomy have become a basis for engaging and resisting a wider suite of colonial violence. Kamal, Linklater, Thompson, and Dipple (2015) found that indigenous food sovereignty in Northern Manitoba is a practical strategy for rebuilding the economic autonomy and food security lost when tribes were dispossessed of their ancestral lands for hydropower development. The O-Pipon-Na-Piwin Cree Nation (OPCN) has a staggering rate of food insecurity—100%. This is higher than any other community in Northern Manitoba, despite OPCN having rich and diverse traditional diets. The community initiated a 'food from the land' program (Ithinto Mechisowin), revitalizing cultural tradition as a basis for rebuilding sovereignty over food resources. The simple act of collecting wild foods and redistributing them in the community has become not only a helpful remedy to hunger, but also a focal point for cultural resurgence and resistance in what Kamal and colleagues see as a key step toward economic and cultural decolonization.

As Clare Gupta (2014) explains, the broad definition of food sovereignty means that it can be used as a basis for building coalitions between diverse actors. In her work with native Hawaiian food sovereignty activists on the island of Molokai, she found that food sovereignty is understood through the local concept of 'aloha āina'. Literally translated as 'love of the land', aloha āina also refers the political movement beginning in the 1970s to tackle native Hawaiian dispossession and build self-determination. Activists, both native and white, are organizing against biotechnology companies that produce genetically modified seeds on the island. This activism, for Gupta, is an interesting place to explore the tensions between indigenous political work to preserve cultural memory and autonomy, and engagement with the state over regulatory changes. She concludes

> Aloha ʻāina embodies several layers of kuleana, or responsibility ... These layers of responsibility associated with aloha ʻāina do not hold in opposition a sense of personal responsibility rooted in project-based work with state-oriented engagement and activism ... On the contrary, aloha ʻāina is about putting one's hands in the soil as well as taking the political action necessary so that Hawaiians can access that soil in the first place.

While these experiences are diverse, they all highlight the ways in which the relations of production, consumption, and cultural politics can change as a result of food sovereignty organizing. Another excellent illustration of the unexpected and diverse ways that food sovereignty is being translated on the ground is provided in this issue by Antonio Roman-Alcalá (2015). Roman-Alcalá describes an activist group in California, Occupy the Farm, who directly borrowed the language of food sovereignty and the tactic of land occupation from global peasant social movements. He uses this case to examine how the politics of food sovereignty articulate with complex histories in an urban community in the global North and examines how 'land sovereignty' specifically translates into a context vastly different from the context in which it was born.

These points of translation and articulation—between broader global understandings of food sovereignty and local, context-specific iterations—are also potentially fruitful places for collaboration between researchers and activists. How can food sovereignty be adapted to local needs without shying away from the race and class conflicts, local political limitations, and everyday desires of people on the ground? What lessons can be learned from these different translations of the food sovereignty project?

Conclusions

> Food sovereignty makes sense for people in both rural and urban areas, and poor and wealthy countries. It is as much **a space of resistance** to neoliberalism, free market capitalism, destructive trade and investment, **as a space to build** democratic food and economic systems, and just and sustainable futures. (Nyeleni Newsletter, 13 March 2013[8])

As we can see from the many examples above, food sovereignty is indeed 'happening'—or a diversity of attempts toward it are—and this multiplicity of efforts is occurring at a rate that is outstripping current academic debates. Movements on the ground are navigating multiple and competing sovereignties, and developing highly context-specific iterations of food sovereignty that vary dramatically from one space to the next. To advance the theory and practice of food sovereignty, then, we need new frameworks and new analytical methods to move beyond binaries—between urban and rural, trade and localism, and autonomy and engagement with the state. Food sovereignty, and thus these debates, exist within the movements that give them life, the concept needs to be treated as the living breathing process that it is.

The oft-cited declarations of La Via Campesina and others serve as important goalposts of this growing movement, but one cannot point to a declaration and say that it encompasses all the multiplicity of efforts across geographies equally well. The movement has simply become much more extended in reach and much more multifaceted than it was two decades ago. Scholars of agrarian politics thus require analytical frameworks that allow for an examination and engagement of the multi-scalar, multi-dimensional landscapes of power connected to food sovereignty. This special issue showcases some of these emerging frameworks. In particular, the relational approach to food sovereignty embedded throughout this special issue keeps the focus where it should be: on *power*, not simply on food (Figueroa, 2015). As food sovereignty spreads its reach, the movement offers both a practical path toward ending hunger and a proposal for a new kind of relationship between the state and society.

As researchers, these shifting political, ecological, and socio-cultural landscapes force us to seek out new methods and frames to capture, understand, and, perhaps, advance these new relationships. This volume highlights examples of research that does just this, by both zooming in and zooming out from the cutting edge of theoretical debates on food sovereignty to the front lines of current struggles and innovations on the ground. Of course, the research presented here leaves just as many, if not more, questions than we originally started with. For one, how can we continue to push the bounds of what food sovereignty research looks like, particularly engaged forms of research that challenge typical power dynamics and ways of knowledge generation, or what Brem-Wilson (2014) describes as 'active engagement'? Similarly, how can we forge new ways of research that are most effectively informed and guided by the realities on the ground, and the people behind them? And how can researchers balance transparency and accountability to communities and social movements with the need for objectivity and rigor? If this issue leaves readers with further burning questions, then this reflects the reality that food sovereignty remains an unfinished business; as long as that is the case, we will be pushed into new bounds in our pursuit to understand it. A research agenda in food sovereignty must not shy away from the rising contradictions in and challenges to the movement, nor should it obsess over consistency in movement rhetoric or the even application of policy. These places of seeming contradiction may be where the greatest insights are to be found. We suggest in this issue that by taking a relational perspective, scholars can begin to provide insight into these contradictions by training their lens on shifts in the global food regime, on the efforts to construct sovereignty at multiple scales and the places where those efforts come into conflict, and the points of translation where the food sovereignty is articulated through historical memory, identity, and everyday life.

As Raj Patel notes (2009), food sovereignty consistently means a 'right to act'. This 'right to act' can and must contest spaces of sovereignty across scales and other boundaries. In a time where global financial flows, land grabs, climate change, and urbanization have left millions with little access to food, livelihoods, or political recourse, food sovereignty requires *both* efforts to re-direct state powers and to carve autonomy from them, *both* a tactical engagement with markets and spaces of autonomy from market logics. In the widening cracks left by decades of neoliberal crisis, food sovereignty is building spaces where a new popular economy can take hold.

Acknowledgements

We are deeply grateful for the wisdom and guidance of Jun Borras in assembling and framing this special issue; for James Scott and Kalyanakrishnan (Shivi) Sivaramakrishnan at the Yale Program in Agrarian Studies for hosting Food Sovereignty: A Critical Dialog at Yale in 2014; and to Jun Borras and colleagues for hosting the dialog at ISS in January 2014. Eric

Holt-Giménez, Barry Gills, Maywa Montenegro, and Devon Sampson all gave excellent feedback. All errors are of course the authors'.

Disclosure Statement

No potential conflict of interest was reported by the authors.

Notes

1 This quote by Nicholson is from a talk given at *Food Sovereignty: A Critical Dialogue*, held 14–15 September 2013 at Yale University (for further details, see http://www.yale.edu/agrarianstudies/foodsovereignty/).
2 Food sovereignty was popularized by the international peasants' movement La Via Campesina in 1996. For a more extensive definition and framing of food sovereignty, see the Declaration and the Synthesis Report of the Nyéléni (2007) Forum for Food Sovereignty, from which the above definition of food sovereignty has been excerpted (www.nyeleni.org). While a profusion of definitions and frameworks for food sovereignty exists, the authors recognize these documents from the Nyéléni Forum as being the outcome of an important process of articulation and consensus-building among major social movements involved food sovereignty globally. For further background on food sovereignty and the context from which it was born, see Edelman (2014), Martinez-Torres and Rosset (2010), Wittman, Desmarais, and Wiebe (2010), and Patel (2009).
3 These important and persistent tensions and debates in agrarian studies are addressed in greater detail by our colleagues in the introductions to two other special issues on food sovereignty, *Critical Perspectives on Food Sovereignty* (Volume 41, Issue 6 of *The Journal of Peasant Studies*), and a forthcoming special issue of *Third World Quarterly*.
4 Along with this issue, two other special issues showcase highlights of the more than 90 papers discussed at these two meetings: a special issue of *The Journal of Peasant Studies* (41:6) released in 2014, and a special issue of *Third World Quarterly* (36:3) released in 2015.
5 Eight companies now account for over half of global sales of agricultural inputs (Fuglie et al., 2011).
6 For an excellent discussion of current issues in studies of agrarian change, see Fairbairn et al. (2014).
7 Investment funds and asset managers are increasingly interested in global agricultural markets and arable land. Though initially largely characterized as Northern sovereign states 'grabbing' land from Southern nations, evidence suggests that these large-scale land acquisitions frequently also run South–South, often involving webs of local elites, domestic and transnational corporations, state agencies, and sovereign wealth funds (Margulis, McKeon and Borras, 2013; McMichael, 2015).
8 Available at: http://www.nyeleni.org/DOWNLOADS/newsletters/Nyeleni_Newsletter_Num_13_EN.pdf

References

Agarwal, B. (2014). Food sovereignty, food security and democratic choice: Critical contradictions, difficult conciliations. *Journal of Peasant Studies*, *41*(6), 1247–1268. doi:10.1080/03066150.2013.876996
Altieri, M., & Nicholls, C. I. (2012). Agroecology scaling up for food sovereignty and resiliency. *Sustainable Agriculture Reviews*, *11*, 1–29.
Anderson, P. (1976). The antinomies of Antonio Gramsci. *New Left Review*, *100*, 5–78.
Bacon, C. M. (2015). Food sovereignty, food security and fair trade: The case of an influential Nicaraguan smallholder cooperative. *Third World Quarterly*, *36*(3), 469–488. doi:10.1080/01436597.2015.1002991
Bernstein, H. (2014). Food Sovereignty via the 'peasant way': A skeptical view. *Journal of Peasant Studies*, *41*(6), 1031–1063. doi:10.1080/03066150.2013.852082
Borras, S. M. (2007). *Pro-Poor land reform: A critique*. Ottawa, ON: University of Ottawa Press.
Brem Wilson, J. (2014). From 'here' to 'there': Social movements, the academy and solidarity research. *Socialist Studies/Études Socialistes*, *10*(1), 111–132.
Burnett, K., & Murphy, S. (2014). What place for international trade in food sovereignty? *Journal of Peasant Studies*, *41*(6), 1065–1084. doi:10.1080/03066150.2013.876995
Claeys, P. (2014). Food sovereignty and the recognition of new rights for peasants at the UN: A critical overview of La Via Campesina's rights claims over the last 20 years. *Globalizations*, *12*(4), doi:10.1080/14747731.2014.957929

Clapp, J. (2014). Financialization, distance and global food politics. *Journal of Peasant Studies*, *41*(5), 797–814.

Clark, P. (2013, September 14–15). *Food sovereignty, post-neoliberalism, campesino organizations, and the state in Ecuador*. Paper presented at Food Sovereignty: A Critical Dialogue, Yale, CT.

De Schutter, O. (2011). *The right to an adequate diet: The agriculture-food-health nexus*. Report presented at the 19th Session of the United Nations Human Rights Council.

Desmarais, A. A., & Wittman, H. (2014). Farmers, foodies and first nations: Getting to food sovereignty in Canada. *Journal of Peasant Studies*, *41*(6), 1153–1173. doi:10.1080/03066150.2013.876623

Edelman, M. (2014). Food sovereignty: Forgotten genealogies and future regulatory challenges. *Journal of Peasant Studies*, *41*(6), 959–978. doi:10.1080/03066150.2013.876998

Fairbairn, M. (2014). 'Like gold with yield': Evolving intersections between farmland and finance. *Journal of Peasant Studies*, *41*(5), 777–795.

Fairbairn, M., Fox, J., Isakson, R., Levien, M., Peluso, N., Razavi, S., ... Sivaramakrishnan, K. (2014). Introduction: New directions in agrarian political economy. *Journal of Peasant Studies*, *41*(5), 653–666. doi:10.1080/03066150.2014.953490

Figueroa, M. (2015). Food sovereignty in everyday life: Toward a people-centered approach to food systems. *Globalizations*, *12*(4), doi:10.1080/14747731.2015.1005966

Fox, J. (1993). *The politics of food in Mexico: State power and social mobilization*. New York, NY: Cornell University Press.

Fuglie, K., Heisey, P., King, J., Pray, C. E., Day-Rubenstein, K, Schimmelpfennig, D., ... Karmarkar-Deshmukh, R. (2011). *Research investments and market structure in the food processing, agricultural input, and biofuel industries worldwide* (Economic Research Report Number 130). Economic Research Service, United States Department of Agriculture.

Gupta, C. (2014). Return to freedom: Anti-GMO Aloha 'Āina activism on Molokai as an expression of place-based food sovereignty. *Globalizations*, *12*(4), doi:10.1080/14747731.2014.957586

Hecht, S. B. (2014). Forests lost and found in tropical Latin America: The woodland 'green revolution'. *Journal of Peasant Studies*, *41*(5), 877–909. doi:10.1080/03066150.2014.917371

Hoare, Q., & Nowell-Smith, G. (Eds.). (1971). *Selections from the prison notebooks of Antonio Gramsci*. New York, NY: International.

Holt-Giménez, E., & Shattuck, A. (2011). Food crises, food regimes and food movements: Rumblings of reform or tides of transformation? *Journal of Peasant Studies*, *38*(1), 109–144.

Holt-Giménez, E., & Wang, Y. (2011). Reform or transformation? The pivotal role of food justice in the U.S. Food Movement. *Race/Ethnicity: Multidisciplinary Global Contexts*, *5*(1), 83–102.

Hospes, O. (2014). Food sovereignty: The debate, the deadlock, and a suggested detour. *Agriculture and Human Values*, *31*(1), 119–1130. doi:10.1007/s10460-013-9449-3

Iles, A., & Montenegro de Wit, M. (2015). Sovereignty at what scale? An inquiry into multiple dimensions of food sovereignty. *Globalizations*, *12*(4), doi:10.1080/14747731.2014.957587

Isakson, R. (2014). Food and finance: The financial transformation of agro-food supply chains. *Journal of Peasant Studies*, *41*(5), 749–775. doi:10.1080/03066150.2013.874340

Ives, P. (2004). *Language and hegemony in Gramsci*. London: Pluto Press.

Kamal, A. G., Linklater, R., Thompson, S., & Dipple, J. (2015). A recipe for change: Reclamation of indigenous food sovereignty in *O-Pipon-Na-Piwin Cree* nation for decolonization, resource sharing, and cultural restoration. *Globalizations*, *12*(4), doi:10.1080/14747731.2015.1039761

Kipfer, S., & Hart, G. (2012) Translating Gramsci in the current conjuncture. In M. Ekers, H. Gillian, K. Stefan, & L. Alex (Eds.), *Gramsci: Space, Nature, Politics* (pp. 323–343). Oxford, UK: John Wiley & Sons.

Margulis, M. E., McKeon, N., & Borras, S. M., Jr. (2013). Land grabbing and global governance: Critical perspectives. *Globalizations*, *10*(1), 1–23.

Martinez-Torres, M., & Rosset, P. (2010). La Vía Campesina: The birth and evolution of a transnational social movement. *The Journal of Peasant Studies*, *37*(1), 149–175.

McKay, B., Nehring, R., & Walsh-Dilley, M. (2014). The 'state' of food sovereignty in Latin America: Political projects and alternative pathways in Venezuela, Ecuador and Bolivia. *Journal of Peasant Studies*, *41*(6), 1175–1200.

McMichael, P. (2009). Global citizenship and multiple sovereignties: Reconstituting modernity. In Y. Atasoy (Ed.), *Hegemonic transitions, the state and crisis in neoliberal capitalism* (pp. 23–42). New York, NY: Routledge.

McMichael, P. (2012). The land grab and corporate food regime restructuring. *Journal of Peasant Studies*, *39*(3–4), 681–701. doi:10.1080/03066150.2012.661369

McMichael, P. (2014). Historicizing food sovereignty. *Journal of Peasant Studies*, *41*(6), 933–957. doi:10.1080/03066150.2013.876999

McMichael, P. (2015). The land question in the food sovereignty project. *Globalizations*, *12*(4), doi:10.1080/14747731.2014.971615

Nguyen, M. T.N., & Locke, C. (2014). Rural-urban migration in Vietnam and China: Gendered householding, production of space and the state. *Journal of Peasant Studies*, *41*(5), 855–876. doi:10.1080/03066150.2014.925884

Noyes, P. D., McElwee, M. K., Miller, H. D., Clark, B. W., Van Tiem, L. A., Walcott, K. C., … Levin, E. D. (2009). The toxicology of climate change: Environmental contaminants in a warming world. *Environment International*, *35*(6), 971–986.

Nyéléni. (2007). *Declaration of Nyéléni*. Retrieved from http://nyeleni.org/spip.php?article290

Patel, R. (2009). Food sovereignty. *The Journal of Peasant Studies*, *36*(3), 663–706.

Ribot, J. (2014). Cause and response: Vulnerability and climate in the Anthropocene. *Journal of Peasant Studies*, *41*(5), 667–705. doi:10.1080/03066150.2014.894911

Roman-Alcalá, A. (2015). Broadening the land question in food sovereignty to northern settings: A case study of occupy the farm. *Globalizations*, *12*(4), doi:10.1080/14747731.2015.1033199

Sayre, N. F. (2009). Scale. In N. Castreeessor, D. Demerittessor, D. Livermanessor, & B. Rhoadsessor (Eds.), *A Companion to environmental geography* (pp. 95–108). Malden, MA: Wiley-Blackwell.

Schiavoni, C. (2015). Competing sovereignties, contested processes: Insights from the Venezuelan food sovereignty experiment. *Globalizations*, *12*(4), doi:10.1080/14747731.2015.1005967

Smith, J., & Jehlička, P. (2013). Quiet sustainability: Fertile lessons from Europe's productive gardeners. *Journal of Rural Studies*, *32*, 148–157. doi:10.1016/j.jrurstud.2013.05.002

Visser, O., Mamanova, N., & Spoor, M. (2015). 'Quiet food sovereignty' as food sovereignty without a movement? Insights from post-socialist Russia. *Globalizations*, *12*(4). doi:10.1080/14747731.2015.1005968

Wittman, H. (2009). Reworking the metabolic rift: La Vía Campesina, agrarian citizenship, and food sovereignty. *The Journal of Peasant Studies*, *36*(4), 805–826.

Wittman, H., Desmarais, A., & Wiebe, N. (2010). The origins & potential of food sovereignty. In H. Wittman, A. Desmarais & N. Wiebe (Eds.), *Food sovereignty: Reconnecting food, nature and community* (pp. 1–14). Winnipeg: Fernwood Publishing.

The Land Question in the Food Sovereignty Project

PHILIP McMICHAEL

Cornell University, Ithaca, USA

ABSTRACT *This essay explores the changing landscape of food sovereignty politics in the shadow of the so-called 'land grab'. While the food sovereignty movement emerged within a global agrarian crisis conjuncture triggered by northern dumping of foodstuffs, institutionalized in WTO trade rules, the twenty-first-century food, energy and financial crises intensify this crisis for the world's rural poor (inflating prices of staple foods and agri-inputs) deepening the process of dispossession. The circulation of food is compounded by global financial flows into enclosing land for industrial agriculture and/or speculation, challenging small producer rights across the world. Under these conditions, the terms of struggle for the food sovereignty movement are shifting towards a human rights politics on the ground as well as in global forums like the FAO's Committee on World Food Security. This includes in particular the need to develop a discursive politics to reframe what is at stake, namely the protection and support of a production model based on social co-operation, multi-functionality and ecologically restorative principles.*

Introduction

This essay explores the salience of 'food sovereignty' as an evolving project. While 'food sovereignty' is open to multiple interpretations, I emphasize here the relationship of 'food sovereignty' politics to food regime crisis and transformation, given the counter-movement role of food sovereignty in the food regime.[1] The current 'land grab' is a phenomenal indicator of the restructuring of the food regime,[2] forcing the food sovereignty movement to respond. Under these circumstances, the *strategic* question of sovereignty *refocuses* from asserting the right of states to food policy autonomy to asserting the right of small-scale producers to productive autonomy.

Such refocusing is by no means the whole story of food sovereignty politics, which include questions about public health, rights of consumers to local foods, food justice concerns, worker protections, urban–rural alliance building, territorial rights among land users, food sovereignty constitutionalism, opposition to genetically-modified organisms (GMOs), environmental concerns, and so on (see, e.g., Andrée, Ayres, Bosia, & Massicotte, 2014; Mann, 2014). Beyond food's materiality and nutritional qualities, food also has social, cultural, and ecological dimensions that contribute to the breadth and depth of 'food sovereignty' visioning. Nevertheless, land use and land-user rights remain foundational to the food sovereignty project—not only because it originated in peasant/farmer mobilization, but also because human/planetary survival depends on regenerative and resilient agro-ecosystems.

The refocusing of food sovereignty politics is over-determined by the 'land grab', which materially threatens small-producer livelihoods and practices at the same time as it is justified by, and justifies, a new form of strategic interventionism by political-economic elites. Fallout from the 'food crisis' renewed corporate-driven 'feeding the world' rhetoric (amplified by population projections), legitimizing a new era of large-scale investment in (industrial) agriculture (both on- and offshore), which came to be known as the 'land grab' (GRAIN, 2008). The food crisis represented a threshold in the long-simmering agrarian crisis associated with decades of neoliberal neglect of and assault on small-scale producers across the world. Accordingly, the publication of the World Bank's *2008 World Development Report* (2007) underwrote sentiment at the 2008 World Food Summit in Rome to refocus on investing in 'smallholders' in the global South, via value chains organized by agribusiness—further putting the land and land-use practices of small-scale producers in jeopardy.

In this historical moment of direct and indirect 'land grabbing', the food sovereignty project now centers on the rights of producers, and the (associated) responsibilities of states. Accordingly, 'sovereignty' is not simply about states' rights to determine food policy, but also it is increasingly about the rights of small-scale producers to their models of production and reproduction. Certainly, both forms of sovereignty have animated the peasant-driven counter-movement, which initially focused on the challenge of 'free trade' rules of the World Trade Organization (WTO).

Producer rights and state responsibilities for protecting such rights in the interests of society are food sovereignty's most substantial strategic initiatives. Realization of these related initiatives will depend on broad alliance building based in a growing recognition of the salience of food producer rights for general socio-ecological reproduction. Such alliance building (among producers and consumers, both urban and rural) has potential to reform states from within, from the bottom up (see, e.g., Claeys, 2012), and is arguably underway in different forms across the world. In the global South in particular, this means anchoring food sovereignty in land-user rights to stabilize conditions for almost a third of the world's population, but of course the struggle is broader than 'peasantism'. Thus: 'How Vía Campesina will take up the challenge to keep advancing new rights while making them relevant for the whole of society is (of) great social relevance' (Claeys, 2012, p. 855). The condition for a successful challenge is to advance a different paradigm, since the current 'development narrative' distracts citizens from recognizing the importance of low-input farming for body, soil, and atmospheric health.

Food Sovereignty Trajectory

The food sovereignty movement rose to prominence via a powerful critique by Vía Campesina of the neoliberal discourse and practice of 'food security', describing a privatized food trading system institutionalized in WTO trade rules and managed by transnational food corporations. The impact of this system was to deepen Southern food dependency on the international grain trade by undermining country-owned food and agricultural policies (already significantly weakened by structural adjustment). Sovereignty was compromised, and those who stood to lose (or had lost) their land and their ability to produce food for themselves and local markets coined the slogan 'food sovereignty' (Desmarais, 2007; Edelman, 2013; Nicholson & Delforge, 2008). Food sovereignty emerged as a grassroots-based counter-movement to a neoliberal food regime claiming to feed the world through a global system of trade provisioned from 'global granaries' such as the USA and the EU. The counter-movement was, in the first instance, protective and restorative. It politicized 'free trade' discourse by exposing the corporate illusion of 'feeding the world' by undermining farming systems (responsible for at least 50% of the world's food) and instituting a new form of colonization (Ragahavan, 1990).

In the opening decade of the new century, the WTO's architecture for 'feeding the world' unraveled through several systemic tremors: from paralysis of the Doha Round with noncompliance by large agrarian states (India, Brazil, and China), through a food price inflation shock from 2007 to 2008, to a new 'agro-security mercantilism' as prominent food-dependent states overrode WTO trade rules by investing directly in offshore land acquisition (McMichael, 2013a).[3] The institutional structure, and claims, of the corporate food regime entered into a transitional, or restructuring, process—adding a new challenge to the world's peasantry: from dumping of cheap food in local markets to threats to land and farming rights via the financialization of food and farmland.

In 2000, La Vía Campesina proclaimed: 'the massive movement of food around the world is forcing the increased movement of people'. This perceptive slogan might now be adjusted to proclaim: 'the massive movement of *money* around the world is forcing the increased movement of people'. The shift in the food regime is from a trade-centered assault on small producers with artificially cheapened agricultural commodities to an investment-centered assault on land users everywhere via land and green grabs enabled by state complicity in new forms of transnational governance that have the potential to re-order the global landscape.

Two such forms of governance are (i) the World Bank-derived Principles of Responsible Agricultural Investment (PRAI), which essentially governs the rights of capital to invest in 'underutilized' land in the global South and to expand yields;[4] and (ii) public–private partnerships (PPPs) via global value chains organized by agribusiness and sanctioned by select intergovernmental or regional alliances (such as the G8). With respect to the latter, small producers, formerly considered residual and insignificant, received a makeover in the context of the food crisis, during which the financial establishment reevaluated them as a new development vehicle via supply-chain investment. Both direct and indirect (value chain) land acquisition constitute forms of 'land grabbing' in so far as they exert control over land use, substituting industrial agriculture (McMichael, 2013b).

Contrary to the formal claim that land acquisition by or with the assistance of central states may not constitute 'grabbing', because land often belongs to the state anyway (Borras, Franco, Gómez, Kay, & Spoor, 2012, p. 858) and is acquired through legal means (Zoomers & Kaag, 2014, p. 201), there is a substantive issue. The commandeering of lands inhabited and used by small farmers, landless laborers, pastoralists, forest dwellers, or fisherfolk has two key dimensions: (i) there is a direct question of cultural and livelihood rights and (ii) there is the historic question of privileging an ultimately unsustainable 'world-scale' consumption of 'natural resources' over securing and promoting low-input land-use to provision locals (primarily) and preserve bio-diverse environments.[5]

Under these circumstances, food sovereignty movement strategies require protecting rights to, and representing the virtues of, small-scale producer systems (including pastoralism, fisheries, and forest-dwelling). This involves a growing convergence of grassroots agrarian movements focusing on land rights (Borras, Edelman, & Kay, 2008; Mann, 2014) and addressing territorial rights,[6] and farmer-to-farmer networks building local and regional knowledge, including sharing eco-farming practices, creating seed banks, managing landscapes, and training agro-ecological cadres (Da Vía, 2012; Holt-Giménez, 2010; Rosset & Martínez-Torres, 2012)—all of these practices make both cultural and practical claims to the land and its management for society. It involves embedding 'food sovereignty' platforms in national constitutions of states such as Venezuela, Ecuador, Bolivia, Mali, Senegal, and Nepal (Rose, 2012: Schiavoni, this issue).[7] And finally, it involves consolidation of years of work by movements of rural producers and progressive non-governmental organizations (NGOs) within the UN system to gain legitimacy for a 'food sovereignty' discourse and its movement protagonists (McKeon, 2009).[8] The constituents of this struggle formed the International Civil Society Organizations (CSOs) Planning Committee for Food Sovereignty (IPC), leading to inclusion in 2009 of a Civil Society Mechanism (CSM) in the Food and Agriculture Organization (FAO)'s Committee on World Food Security (CFS), representing small producers (farmers, pastoralists, fishers, and forest dwellers).

Peasant Revival?

The rise of an international peasant coalition, symbolized by its largest organization, La Vía Campesina, which unites over 200 million small producers in 160 organizations from over 80 countries (Mann, 2014, p. 3), demanding, in the 1990s, 'the right of peoples, communities, and countries to define their own agricultural, labor, fishing, and food and land policies which are ecologically, socially, economically, and culturally appropriate to their unique circumstances' (Ainger, 2003), was *unthinkable* in terms of the modern development narrative. Its basic question politicized the food regime: by what right does the global market dispossess producers, and their knowledge and culture, at the risk of increasing food *in*security? But its more fundamental question concerned why small producers, in the 'peasant way', should not be part of the solution, rather than a problem, of development?

Developmentalism was founded on the assumption of a disappearing peasantry, as it serviced urban industrialism via proletarianization (cf. Lewis, 1954). The rise of a transnational agrarian movement not only inverts this episteme, but also denaturalizes the 'global food system' by establishing (rights-based) claims of small producers to their own local food systems—which account for up to two-thirds of the world's food (Erosion, Technology and Concentration, 2009). Here, the food sovereignty frame redefines 'agrarian reform' in social justice and human ecological terms (Borras, 2008; Mann, 2014, p. 57), underscoring the global public good inherent in support for and durability of small-producer cultures:

> In the context of food sovereignty, agrarian reform benefits all of society, providing healthy, accessible and culturally appropriate food, and social justice. Agrarian reform can put an end to the massive and forced rural exodus from the countryside to the city, which has made cities grow at unsustainable rates and under inhuman conditions. (Nyeleni, 2006, http://www.nyeleni.org/spip.php?article54)

This formulation expresses a distinct ontology, re-centering farming as an environmental and social necessity for human survival, and requiring an alternative socio-political order, and model of 'development'. Here, 'sovereignty' presents as a *process* of social transformation and a reformulation of states from within (McMichael, 2006).[9] Such a vision is epochal in inverting the assumptions of modernity: of mastering nature with industrial technique, subordinating agriculture to urban industrialism, and devaluing human labor. While elimination of peasant–landlord relations has been the measure of nation-building and modernity (Moore, 1966), in the context of a 'post-national' mismatch between rural evictions and urban unemployment via a global food regime (Bernstein, 2006; Davis, 2006), the food sovereignty movement potentially performs a 'midwife' role to de-centralizing political–ecological relations.

In the meantime, the power of this movement is registered in its increased presence and legitimacy in UN forums, and particularly the FAO's CFS (Mann, 2014; McKeon, 2009). In the context of an increasing presence of producer movements and a severe food price shock, development agencies recognized a potential in 'smallholder agriculture', with the FAO 'taking the lead in urging massive investment in smallholder agriculture, acknowledging the importance of the staple food-producing capacity of peasant agriculture' (Bryceson, 2010, p. 82).

However, this switch from historical relic to historical subject is double-edged, as peasant claims for relevance and support coincide with a process of redesigning the rural world by donor and development communities, to augment flows of agricultural commodities from the peasant sector. Thus: 'In a better-late-than-never attempt to resuscitate the African agricultural advances that SAP's short-circuited in the 1980s, donors are now scrambling to think of ways of boosting smallholder agriculture' (Bryceson, 2010, p. 82). The World Bank claims that 'effective instruments in using agriculture for development' (2007, p. 4) include increasing assets of poor households, making smallholders more productive, and expanding the rural nonfarm economy. This 'new agriculture' is to be 'led by private entrepreneurs in extensive value chains linking producers to consumers and including many entrepreneurial smallholders'. For sub-Saharan Africa in particular,[10] the World Bank sidesteps the global orientation of value chains, claiming that they promise local rural development to stimulate national economic growth, even when they compromise local food security and sovereignty.

The Value-Chain Challenge

The new status of small-scale producers poses new problems for the food sovereignty movement, given the legitimizing function of 'improvement' of peasant agriculture. While development institutions, governments, and investors pay lip service to the importance of 'smallholders', this generally refers to their significance as a new extractive 'resource' as farming skills and practices are replaced with agro-inputs via forms of contract farming.[11] At the same time, it has become clear that land controversies (resource grabbing and resettlement) have propelled the investor community toward the value-chain fix (McMichael, 2013a). Thus, the most recent assessment of responsible investment practices in agriculture by the World Bank acknowledges that: 'Contract farming operations allow farmers to remain in control of their most important asset, their land, thus avoiding disputes over access to resources and community displacement. Outgrower schemes also support far more jobs than estate farms' (2014, p. 26).

As noted above, contemporary contracts represent a form of land grabbing, with value chains specializing in the business of 'control grabbing'. Thus, under the guise of smallholder support:

> for many agribusiness companies the contract farming solution is a public relations exercise designed to build alliances in the areas where they produce and source their throughput, and to

> access subsidized credit from agencies buying into the 'smallholder path' to development. In fact, access to subsidized credit seems a significant factor driving agribusiness to engage smallholders.' (Oya, 2012, p. 10)[12]

As the current object of development, peasantries[13] are redefined in entrepreneurial terms. Here, the 'new agriculture for development' is governed by market intensification, via agribusiness, with public support: 'The private sector drives the organization of value chains that bring the market to smallholders and commercial farms' (World Bank, 2007, p. 8). Thus, the Declaration following the FAO's November 2009 World Summit on Food Security stated:

> We will pursue policies and strategies that improve the functioning of domestic, regional and international markets and ensure equitable access for all, especially smallholders and women farmers from developing countries. We support WTO-consistent, non-trade distorting special measures aimed at creating incentives for smallholder farmers in developing countries, enabling them to increase their productivity and compete on a more equal footing on world markets. (FAO, 2009, p. 4)

Ignoring the existence, and value, of local markets, the value-chain project is largely geared to incorporating small producers into international markets, and to growth in agribusiness profit, turning farmers into farm labor on their own land (McKeon, 2014b; McMichael, 2013a). And the public sector is an important complement to this vision.

During the height of the food crisis, FAO director-general Jacques Diouf observed that governments, with international partners, should pursue the necessary public investment, providing favorable environments for private investments (Urquhart, 2008). PPPs tend to be organized around a business model for small producers—including bankrolling states with private funds, particularly in Africa. Thus, the Gates Foundation's financial resources 'are attracting the interest of poor African governments, making them more amenable to the suggestions of institutions from outside Africa' (Daño, 2007, p. 55). Meanwhile, Alliance for a Green Revolution in Africa (AGRA) Vice-President, Adesina, encourages public support from the G8, the International Fund for Agricultural Development (IFAD), the World Bank, and the African Development Bank for the African agricultural sector, particularly in infrastructures to facilitate private investment: 'Concentrating ODA funds on public goods will free up domestic resources to focus on providing support to smallholder farmers to take advantage of new agricultural technologies to raise agricultural productivity' (2009, p. 10).

These comments reflect AGRA's experience in leveraging from commercial banks $170 million in 'market-based and affordable loans for smallholder farmers and agricultural value chains that support them in Tanzania, Uganda, Kenya, Mozambique, and Ghana' (Adesina 2009, pp. 14–15). They also anticipated the establishment of the New Alliance for Food Security and Nutrition (NAFSN) at the G8 summit in 2012, dedicated to 'accelerating the flow of private capital' for poverty reduction via agricultural-led growth in various African countries.[14] Aligning private investment with the Comprehensive Africa Agriculture Development Program (CAADP)-driven national agricultural investment strategies defers to recipient governments, who nevertheless are obliged to sign Cooperative Framework Agreements (CFAs) with donors and companies, requiring top-down[15] policy reforms to create enabling business environments for national and global firms. Thus, Ghana's CFA includes:

> The Government of Ghana intends to improve incentives for private sector investment in agriculture, in particular, taking actions to facilitate inclusive access to and productive use of land; developing and implementing domestic seed regulations that encourage increased private sector involvement in this area; and supporting transparent inclusive, evidence-based policy formulation. (G8, 2012, p. 2)

Among the many private companies participating in the NAFSN for Ghana:

> Unilever is a global consumer products company with plans to expand its sourcing throughout Africa. It operates in more than 20 Sub-Saharan African countries . . .
>
> Africa is at the heart of its global business strategy and Unilever wants to double the size of its business there. Unilever wants to see African agricultural potential fulfilled in a way that creates sustainable business opportunities—particularly for the smallholder farmers integrated into its local and global supply chains. (G8, 2012, pp. 12–13)

Associated Growth Corridors[16] incorporate peasants into value chains as outgrowers, and target common lands alienated from small producers—millions, in the case of the Nacala Corridor in Mozambique, where common lands have been declared abandoned and leased to Brazilian and Japanese investors (Paul & Steinbrecher, 2013, p. 9). A locally incorporated firm with international financing, Rei do Agro, contracts with 50 small producers, providing agri-inputs (seeds and chemicals), extension services and mechanized field preparation for soybeans, maize, and sunflowers.

The NAFSN model, then, is to capitalize the land and labor (as contract farming) under the control of international investors, traders, and retailers (McKeon, 2014a). The reproduction of small-scale producers is organized via chains of dependence, since many of the firms involved account for 'the whole supply chain, from seeds, chemical inputs, production, processing, transport, and trade to supermarkets' (Paul & Steinbrecher, 2013, p. 2). Grow Africa,[17] a partnership platform linked to CAADP, a program of the New Partnership for Africa's Development, established by the African Union in 2003, and modeled on the World Economic Forum's New Vision for Agriculture Initiative, captures the essence of these initiatives in the slogan: 'we want to see smallholder farmers grow into businesses'.

The challenge for the food sovereignty movement is, ultimately, to disabuse state and development authorities, and private sector interests, of the assumption that all 'smallholder farmers' represent 'businesses in waiting'. In UN debates and corridors movement, activists seek to problematize the discourse in such a way as to distinguish small-scale producer practices from the industrial model and to establish distinctive terms of reference for what it takes to farm the land with saved seed as opposed to applying agro-input packages. In the process of drafting an alternative to the World Bank's Principles for Responsible Agricultural Investment (PRAI) in the CFS, CSOs strive to distinguish in particular the different meaning of 'investment' across the aisle: *financial* investment for large-scale enterprise, and *labor* investment for small-scale producers dedicated to improving soil fertility, hydrological cycles, and biodiversity (McMichael, 2014a).

This is, ostensibly, an epistemic issue, requiring recognition of the rights, practices, and benefits of small-producer communities. And it requires recognition that small-scale producers are the majority producers in the global South, and more effective at feeding themselves and their fellow citizens than the corporate regime,[18] geared as it is to commandeering land and water to produce fungible/flex commodities for only those with global purchasing power.

Human Rights Politics

As an epistemic issue, the food sovereignty principle depends significantly on rights claims. Contrary to liberal conceptions of individual (or market) rights, food sovereignty implies collective or group rights. This is expressed in grassroots resistance to 'food security' land grabbing (see, e.g., Kerssen, 2013; Klopp & Lumumba, 2014; McKeon, 2014b). The rights-based strategy builds on *extant* international rights instruments (the 1948 UN Declaration is a watershed convention), with the aim of expanding the realm of rights and concretizing them with social purpose. Thus, the current Peasants' Rights Convention campaign objective 'is not just to secure compliance with international norms, but to shift the norms themselves' (Edelman & James, 2011, p. 91). A key example is the claim by Henry Saragih (recent coordinator of Vía Campesina) that the International Convention on Economic and Social and Cultural Rights 'only mentions access to food as the fulfillment of rights to food, whereas the right to produce food is much more fundamental to fulfilling the rights to food' (quoted in Edelman & James, 2011, p. 85). That is, rather than having a market access right to food, the more fundamental right to produce food requires stabilizing the world's small-producer population, responsible for 50% of the world's food at the same time as it constitutes about 50% of the world's hungry. To reframe the question of rights in this way relates hunger to 'land grab' denial of small-producer rights to their land and livelihoods, and links 'sovereignty' to producer rights and productive capacities (including infrastructural needs).

This normative shift, which some activists term 'new generation' rights (Edelman & James, 2011, p. 93), is not simply about collective peasant rights, but also about substantiating the distinctive, multi-functional character of small-scale production. The food sovereignty movement now confronts codes of conduct that define peasants as potential 'smallholder businesses', and project a singular (commercial) mode of agricultural investment. Such misrepresentation of small-scale producers expresses the convenience of a development narrative of peasants as relics. Epistemically, it misunderstands that the 'primary raison d'être of peasant farming is livelihood and labor, not only food, and yields are closely dependent on social relationships' (Hilmi, 2012, pp. 59–60). For twenty-first century land users, land is not only an object to secure, but also is being reclaimed (through bio-reclamation and agro-ecology for restorative practices) for the purpose of resource building as 'ecological capital', and to secure territorial/cultural identity (cf. Escobar, 2008), and to re-build food self-reliance.[19] It is therefore not surprising that the concept of 'land sovereignty' has emerged to consolidate food sovereignty claims (Borras & Franco, 2012).

Here, sovereignty means not only the right to produce, but also control of production landscapes, and food sovereignty 'is a principle and an ethical lifestyle that does not correlate with an academic definition but arises from a collective, participatory process' (Stedile & de Carvalho, 2011, p. 25; see also Patel, 2009). 'New generation' rights, then, are significant in material, political, and moral terms, but they lack formal status:

> it is well known that WTO and the international investment protection regime have at their disposal strong sanction mechanisms, whereas the U.N. Human Rights System unfortunately still lacks them. Additionally, commercial and investment law regimes still do not accept the primacy of international human rights law. (Monsalve-Suárez, 2013, p. 13)

Parallel to the soft law status of human rights is the disregard for a substantive definition of the right to (produce) food in debates regarding peasants' rights underway in the UN. Such a definition is anticipated in elements of the draft Peasants' Rights Declaration:

> that demand rights to conserve and exchange or sell traditional seed varieties, to intervene in markets and set prices, to participate in economic decision-making at the international and national levels, and to 'reject interventions that can destroy local agricultural values'. (Edelman & James, 2011, pp. 96–97; final quote from La Vía Campesina)

Similarly, CFS Tenure Guidelines do not address how land should be used and managed sustainably, and circumvent the question of the salience of small farming—the effect being to leave the

G8, World the Bank, and the International Land Coalition (ILC) to advance their own interpretations (McKeon, 2014b).

Under these circumstances, the food sovereignty movement is confronted with targeting states and inter-governmental organizations that *recognize*, protect, and enhance agrarian-producing communities. Control grabbing strategies require state action, even as states have increasingly privatized in cycles of debt regime austerity—as Borras, Franco, and Wang claim: ‘mainstream economists who do not usually like the state coming into the picture are calling the state back in to facilitate the identification, quantification, acquisition, and disposition of so-called available marginal lands’ (2013, p. 169). State complicity involves both practical territorial recomposition (selling/leasing land, eviction, resettlement, and outgrower schemes)[20] and participation in or subjection to new transnational protocols (agricultural investment, certification schemes, and carbon markets). Either way, states are no longer simply subordinate to a common set of enforceable (market) rules (as under WTO protocols), but are rather more proactively involved in PPPs and in imposing and interpreting governance functions emanating from inter-governmental agreements, development agencies, and financial institutions as conditions of receipt and/or hosting investment tranches.

These are essentially individual state decisions, such that the ‘crucial role of national states in land grabbing has rendered attempts at the international governance of land grabbing a complicated undertaking. It will be a challenge for inter-governmental institutions to make these national governments responsive to international rules’ (Borras et al., 2013, p. 167). Within the CFS ‘rai process’, focused on substituting a rights-based protocol on investment in agriculture for the World Bank’s PRAI, CSM activists target member states and the CFS to uphold international human rights obligations, particularly in relation to agricultural investment. Food sovereignty politics here involve embedding a normative framework in land use protocols to be observed by states and their corporate investors, insisting on a strategic role for public investment in ensuring ‘country-owned’ food security, and distinguishing small-scale producer investment models from financial investments in ‘flex crops’.[21] Meanwhile, local movements pressure states with direct action and legal means to slow or regulate land acquisition,[22] but political elites have reason (kickbacks, debt, and brokerage) to resist such pressure, and now, under cover of ‘foreign aid’, and ‘food security’ concerns, cooperate with donors to license large-scale land grabs or value-chain enclosures (Liberti, 2013).

Meanwhile, firms and investors (and G8 states) enlist nation-states in interpreting ‘country-owned’ as governments implementing security policy frameworks with mandated agricultural technologies (including GMOs) to ensure commodity-oriented productivity on the land. The model is the Poverty Reduction Strategy Papers, whereby southern governments were enlisted in the 1990s by the international financial institutions to author their own austerity policies—rendering states accountable for poverty reduction by embedding public priorities in private relationships: in effect fashioning ‘governance states’ (Harrison, 2004). In this juncture, the task before the food sovereignty movement is to use pressure from above (in the UN) and below (grassroots mobilization) on states to recognize and *secure* the rights and capacities of their rural populations to produce food, and to regulate trade in the interests of human rights.[23]

The Strategic Importance of Sovereignty

While food sovereignty initially targeted the unfair principle of world ‘free’ trade and its impact on small producers in the name of national food policy sovereignty, the strategic meaning of sovereignty has deepened in the present conjuncture. It centers now on an ontological issue, namely, the incommensurability of small- and medium-scale family-based farming with industrial/corporate agriculture. Productivism is the operative principle for corporate and development institutions, as they concentrate on 'yield gaps' in 'smallholder' farming to justify 'improvement'. Productivism imposes a yield metric on farming comparisons that elides history, culture, and ecology. A snapshot productivity comparison between farms and agribusinesses ignores the neglect of small-scale farming, particularly in the global South, over the last three decades.[24] It also measures only plant yields (but neither efficiency of water/energy use, nor environmental externalities), rather than the ecology of farming land as wealth itself (with additional socio-cultural value). The CFS High-Level Panel of Experts Report on *Investing in smallholder agriculture for food security* defines small-scale farming in the following way:

> Smallholder agriculture is practised by families (including one or more households) using only or mostly family labour and deriving from that work a large but variable share of their income, in kind or in cash ... it includes crop raising, animal husbandry, forestry and artisanal fisheries .... Off-farm activities play an important role in providing smallholders with additional income and as a way of diversifying risk ... smallholders producing only or mainly for subsistence are not uncommon ... smallholder's families are part of social networks within which mutual assistance and reciprocity translate into collective investments (mainly through work exchanges) and into solidarity systems. (High Level Panel of Experts [HLPE], 2013, pp. 10–11)

Furthermore, 'smallholder agriculture is the foundation of food security in many countries and an important part of the social/economic/ecological landscape in all countries' (CFS 2013, p. 11), and the 'potential efficiency of smallholder farming relative to larger farms has been widely documented, focusing on the capacity of smallholders to achieve high production levels per unit of land through the use of family labor in diversified production systems' (CFS 2013, p. 12). Labor investment is the *differentia specifica* of peasant agriculture (cf. Ploeg, 2009). In short, sovereignty is about securing this mode of farming, as human-nature co-production, that is, 'agrarian citizenship' (Wittman, 2009).

Nevertheless, the vision for small-scale producers from the development establishment fixates on value chains, which, under present conditions, have exploitative contracts (McMichael, 2013a).[25] In this regard, the director of Self Help Africa, which, with PepsiCo support, works with cashew-nut farmers and processors in Benin to supply Europe, declared: 'Strengthening smallholder value chains is really about helping farmers to move from being subsistence based to enabling them to make a better profit' (Does the future of farming in Africa lie in the private sector, 2012). This is the singular solution to the under-privileged condition of small-scale producers, induced by decades of public neglect of local farming, amplified by structural adjustment policies, and of course beckoning to investors, agribusinesses, retailers, foreign-currency strapped governments, and NGOs. As an African NGO director added, the NGO role is shifting from facilitating trade between farmers and the private sector to 'watchdogging' the resulting supply chains—substituting a focus on value-chain management for looking out for farmers.

The reality of value chains of course requires the attention of the food sovereignty movement. There are two responses. The first is protective, in regulating value chains to reduce monopoly 'buyer power' and to promote more equitable outcomes for farmers and food system workers alike.[26] Such regulation is appropriately performed by states, not NGOs. Accordingly, the CSM insists that member states take responsibility for monitoring and regulating *extant* supply chains in the service of human rights.

The second response is to encourage a reorientation to domestic food production, consistent with the original food sovereignty vision, and now with CFS endorsement of the goal of the 'progressive realization of the right to adequate food in the context of national food security' in its various reports (HLPE, 2013; CFS 40 Policy Roundtable, the Voluntary Guidelines on Responsible Governance of Tenure of Land and Other Natural Resources, and the Global Strategic Framework). The recent UN Right to Food Rapporteur has recommended targeting domestic production to reduce food dependency, observing that there are 'approximately 500 million small-scale farmers in developing countries making them not only the vast majority of the world's farmers but, taking into account their families, responsible for the well-being of over two billion persons' (De Schutter, 2011, p. 13). Reclaiming this right concerns rebalancing power equations: restoring integrity to domestic farm sectors[27] and rights to producing communities, and wresting power from agribusiness, grain traders, retailers, and affluent consumers to prioritize food security as a socio-political right, rather than a market gamble.

Either way, sovereignty is critical to protection or reorientation of small-scale producers. But sovereignty also means 'epistemic autonomy': separating economic/financial and non-economic values such as sufficiency economy, reciprocity via seed networks, an ecological calculus, and so on. Even in the UN debates, in CFS 40, the persistence of the trade reflex (by which states improve their balance of payments) reproduces the notion that agriculture is a revenue operation and is best left to entrepreneurial farming.[28] One representative of the Private Sector Mechanism (PSM), from an agro-food network, made the following observations in a debate about small farmers, land, and investments:

> while there is a consensus that farmers are at the center, farming needs to be understood as a profession, and food security is about economic growth, not just growing food—thus farmers need to break the subsistence cycle and become entrepreneurs, produce more with less land, and stabilize via land ownership, inputs (agro-chemicals), knowledge, and market access.

This kind of packaged statement, with echoes in other such statements regarding smallholders being at the heart of a 'transition', including a 'new deal' for smallholders, draws on a form of economic reductionism, reproduced by PSM representatives: 'we invest in large and small'—implying scale neutrality that elides the incommensurability of small farming and industrial agriculture, and: 'agriculture investments are wonderful job creators'—suggesting either plantations or agro-industrial estates as job safety nets for displaced farmers where jobs are the currency of modernity.[29] Job provision assumes that small-scale producers are better off earning a wage (assuming that the agri-estate endures), and that small farming is no different from farm-working, which reflects considerable ontological ignorance. The emphasis on a financial calculus similarly discounts local common pool resources, managed by self-organizing land users with shared rules which 'differ from the logic of capital—they reflect, instead the interests and perspectives of the involved producers, ecological cycles and/or principles such as social justice, solidarity, or the containment of (potential) conflicts' (Ploeg, Jingzhong, & Schneider, 2012, p. 164). These principles lie at the core of food sovereignty—the term is not simply about autonomy, rather it embodies a historic, ontological alternative to the juggernaut of agro-industrialization.

Conclusion

The coordinates of the conjuncture within which 'food sovereignty' emerged as an original rural-based counter-movement have shifted as the food regime has entered a crisis phase. The terms of opposition include now a defense of 'ways of life' on the land against not only market forces (food surplus dumping) but also organized physical and economic enclosures.

At the same time, the crisis has precipitated recognition of the false claims of neoliberal 'food security', expressing a legitimacy crisis for the international institutional architecture of the food regime (McMichael, 2014b). As usual, the legitimacy crisis has, in the manner of the 'shock doctrine' (Klein, 2007), spawned a power grab to reformulate the conditions of access to farmland, labor, and product to feed and fuel the world minority with purchasing power. The conditions involve new forms of legitimation of colonization of land (including common property resources) across the world by foreign and domestic investors and governments. Land titling and capitalization, and incorporation of small-scale producers into value chains, are proclaimed as methods of improving productivity of the land and 'transitioning' farmers into agricultural entrepreneurs. The conditions also involve elaborating governance mechanisms that are geared to, among other things, 'responsibly destroying the world's peasantry' (De Schutter, 2010).

At both ground-zero level and in global (member state) forums alike, the food sovereignty movement is confronted with protecting land-users' claims (and rights) to their landscapes and territories, as well as with advancing discursive means to reframe what is really at stake. Here, the dynamics of knowledge production are critical, as it is increasingly clear that modern problems do not generate modern solutions (De Sousa Santos, 2002). As noted, corporate supporters have an interest in misrepresenting small-scale farming models as inadequate to the task of 'feeding the world', and counter-posing industrial agriculture (with 'sustainable intensification') as the solution. Value chains in particular represent a new market frontier for agro-inputs when large-scale land grabs are contentious—but they are neither necessarily permanent nor a solution, and, as such, are subject to contestation via a politics of rights and of representation (Patel, 2009).

Combining a politics of rights and representation enables construction of a counter-narrative to a mono-cultural development narrative, in a long-term crisis of unsustainability and inability to feed populations other than global consumers.[30] The food sovereignty counter-narrative concerns detailing the global array of myriad social experiments centering on low-input, ecological farming, and local food provisioning (both rural and urban). Given its origins in agrarian world-regions, for the food sovereignty project the restoration of land and territorial rights is an immediate priority, presenting an ontological alternative to communities across the world.

Acknowledgements

The author is indebted to three sturdy reviewers for critical feedback.

Funding

The author acknowledges, with thanks, the support of a Research Council of Norway grant: 'Cultures, Values, Ethics, Arguments and Justifications in the Management of Agricultural Land (FORFOOD)', Center for Rural Research, Trondheim, 2013–2016.

Notes

1 For an argument about the originary significance of the food sovereignty movement for southern agrarian societies, with which this essay is concerned, see McMichael (2013c).
2 For a fuller account of this process, see McMichael (2012).
3 At the time, the WTO was the clearly identified enemy. According to the statement prepared by the women who participated in the Vía Campesina delegation in Seattle in 1999: 'Despite all the protests in Seattle, we thank the

WTO for unifying small farmers worldwide. During the week-long work in Seattle, we have now succeeded in globalizing the struggle and globalizing our hopes' (Desmarais & Nicholson, 2013, p. 7).

4 A related form of 'governance', facilitating financial investment in large-scale operations (whether plantations or value-chain complexes) is now undergoing intensification, with the Bank's recent development of a program of *Benchmarking the Business of Agriculture*, requested by the G8 for agricultural sector benchmarking. As the Bank states, this is 'a new project that gives users information and objective measures to understand where their economies are in the process of agricultural transformation, and identify areas of improvement' (2014).

5 To the claim that small producers may choose to participate in supply/value chain production, the question must first be asked: what range of choice do they have when farming for food has been progressively devalued and starved of public support, where land has been degraded, states are hungry for foreign exchange, investors scour the world and their backyard for agricultural, mining, and water in a resource-depleting world, and offset carbon credits have become the new currency? Susanti and Budidarsono note that smallholders in Indonesia may individually 'benefit' from commercial oil palm production, but forests and rice fields suffer (2014, p. 134), not to mention environmental chemicalization at the expense of surrounding land and waterscapes (Colchester et al., 2006).

6 As Rosset (2013) underlines, the food sovereignty project has had to recognize and manage the multiple claims on territory by different minority cultures (e.g. indigenous vs. farmer vs. pastoralist communities)—the provisional concept of 'land sovereignty' (Borras & Franco, 2012) addresses this question, marking the movement's re-envisioning of 'agrarian reform' from a territorial perspective.

7 Whether and to what extent food sovereignty comes to organize state policy is quite variable, and hardly substantial yet (Clark, 2013; Giunta, 2013). Arguably this will only transpire via powerful grassroots movements.

8 In March 2006, the FAO Conference on Agrarian Reform and Rural Development acknowledged the principle of 'food sovereignty' (Mann, 2014, p. 65). In October 2013, FAO Director General Jose Graziano da Silva and Ángel Strapazzón of La Vía Campesina met to formalize an agreement of cooperation acknowledging the essential role played by smallholder food producers, focusing on key areas such as strengthening peasant based agro-ecological food production, protecting small holders' rights to access to land and water, improving farmer rights over seeds in accordance with international and national seed laws, and improving access of women and youth to land and other productive resources. Rosset (2013, p. 734) emphasizes the 'differentiated engagement' of La Via Campesina with multilateral institutions, where the WTO, International Monetary Fund and World Bank are regarded as implacable opponents.

9 This double movement of overriding the WTO food dependency regime via national sovereignty as the historic *precondition* of a simultaneous grass-roots process of democratizing domestic food systems (with urban allies) helps to resolve questions regarding a possible contradiction between state and civil society sovereignties (cf. Hospes, 2014; Schiavoni, this issue). McKay and Nehring (2013) note a discursive shift in La Vía Campesina from 'rights of nations' to 'rights of peoples' between 1996 and 2001—I would argue that this meaning was implicit in the original declaration, by *food producers* themselves (see also Claeys, 2012, p. 849). Initially, the emphasis on national sovereignty was a form of strategic essentialism (McMichael, 2013b, p. 147).

10 The African focus is telling, as, for the World Bank:

> Africa represents the 'last frontier' in global food and agricultural markets. It has more than half of the world's uncultivated but agriculturally suitable land and has scarcely utilized its extensive water resources. As Africa's population, incomes, and cities grow and spur the development of domestic markets, the prospects for agriculture and agribusiness will be better than ever (2013, p. 2).

Africa and Latin America are the world regions where about 80% of projected expansion in arable land is expected in the future (FAO, 2009, p. 40). For Sub-Saharan Africa, the Bank views growth in agricultural productivity in developmental terms: as 'vital for stimulating growth in other parts of the economy', compared with Asia, where the focus is on generating 'rural jobs by diversifying into labor-intensive, high-value agriculture linked to a dynamic rural, nonfarm sector' (2007, p. v).

11 For an extended discussion of the modalities and effects of contract farming,

> entailing relations between growers and private or state enterprises that substitute for open-market exchanges by linking nominally independent family farmers of widely variant assets with a central processing, export, or purchasing unit that regulates in advance prices, production practices, product quality, and credit (see Watts (1994, pp. 26–7), and for updates, see Gibbon and Ponte (2005) and McMichael (2013a)).

12 Nielsen and Pritchard also view 'the outsourcing of tea production in South India … as a strategic response to enhanced demands for ethical accountability along the global value chain' (2009, p. 206).

13 I use the term 'peasantries' to refer to a varied grouping of small-scale producers, including family farmers, pastoralists, forest-dwellers, and fishers (cf. Ploeg, 2009).

14 For example, Benin, Burkina Faso, Côte d'Ivoire, Ethiopia, Ghana, Malawi, Mozambique, Nigeria, Tanzania, and Senegal.

15 Oxfam reports: 'the negotiation between governments and companies has not been open to public scrutiny or the participation of small-scale producers' (2013, p. 5).

16 Tanzania's Southern Agricultural Growth Corridor (SAGCOT) of 7.5 million ha includes 2 million hectares farmed by smallholders (Paul & Steinbrecher, 2013, p. 9).

17 http://growafrica.com/

18 Not only do small producers account for 80% of the food consumed in the global South, but also there is an established scientific consensus that the relative yields of organic/agro-ecological versus non-organic farming are sufficient to provision the current daily average consumption of calories across the world (Badgley et al., 2007; Pretty & Hine, 2001; Pretty, Morison, & Hine, 2003). Pretty et al. (2006) compared 286 projects across 37 million hectares in 57 southern countries, finding agro-ecological techniques increased crop productivity by an average of 79% on over 12 million farms, with improvements in environmental services.

19 Bryceson claims pertinence here:

> Historically, peasantries have formed the demographic, cultural, and political bulwark of African nation-states, providing the ethical and social foundations upon which national stability has rested. Thus, for the sake of human welfare, agricultural productivity, and national stability, smallholder agriculture is preferable to large-scale, highly capitalized agriculture (2010, p. 81).

20 See Wolford, Borras, Hall, Scoones, and White (2013) for a summary statement of the complex relations involved in land grabbing by a variety of domestic, and foreign, actors. This essay focuses on central state responsibilities.

21 Borras, Franco, Isakson, Levidow, and Vervest (2014).

22 Resistance takes a variety of forms: including government restrictions on foreign acquisitions of land in Argentina and Brazil (Borras et al., 2012; Perrone, 2013), land governance reforms in Burkina Faso, Kenya, Tanzania, and Liberia (FOLA, 2013), and use of the Voluntary Tenure Guidelines to inform land struggles in India, Mali, Uganda, Argentina, and Italy (McKeon, 2014b), documentation of land grabbing forms and extent in Europe to encourage application of the Guidelines in the EU (Transnational Institute, 2013), land occupation by social movements in Argentina (Brent, 2013), indigenous struggles to defend territory in Guatemala (Alonso-Fradejas, 2013) and Honduras (Kerssen, 2013), and socio-political struggles in Europe (Franco & Borras, 2013).

23 Thus, De Schutter challenges the WTO's prioritizing of international trade for meeting food security needs—a challenge with enhanced credibility in the wake of the food crisis and its constitutive export bans and subsequent land grabbing. Further, he points out: 'It is precisely because the links between trade and the realization of the right to food are complex that human rights impact assessments should be conducted before free trade agreements are agreed upon' (De Schutter, 2012, p. 5).

24 For example: 'conventional agricultural research enjoyed 60 years of massive private and public sector support for crop genetic improvement, dwarfing funding for organic agriculture by 99 to 1' (Holt-Giménez, 2012, p. 1).

25 As the Global Strategic Framework has noted:

> It is recognized that the bulk of investment in agriculture is undertaken by farmers and smallholders themselves, their cooperatives and other rural enterprises, with the rest being provided by a multiplicity of private actors, large and small, along the value chain, as well as governments. Smallholder farmers, many of whom are women, play a central role in producing most of the food consumed locally in many developing regions and are the primary investors in agriculture in many developing countries (CFS, 2012, p. 13, 2nd draft).

26 'According to an IIED and Oxfam report, the value chain approach only works effectively for 2–10% of small producers, due to a number of factors which keeps them at the "mercy of larger producers"' (Henriques, 2013, p. 9).

27 In this regard, 'renationalizing and rebuilding national grain reserves and parastatal marketing boards … [including] farmer organizations' (Rosset, 2009, p. 20) is an important step. In recent WTO deliberations in Bali, India held firm to having its domestic grain reserve undefined as a restraint on trade. Kay (2014) outlines a series of public investment initiatives to strengthen 'investment from below'.

28 It also accounts for the strong, and controversial, resistance by agro-exporting states to regulation of biofuels production and circulation.

29 For an empirical critique of this assumption in World Bank claims, see Li (2011).

30 There is an emerging set of counter-narrative stories from the grassroots front, providing credibility and sharing experiences of local practices and organization (see, e.g., Franco & Borras, 2013; Holt-Giménez & Patel, 2009; Hilmi, 2012; Kerssen, 2013; Mann, 2014; McKeon, 2014b).

References

Adesina, A. A. (2009, August). *Africa's food crisis: Conditioning trends and global development policy*. Keynote speech at the International Association of Agricultural Economists conference, Beijing.

Ainger, K. (2003). The new peasants' revolt. *New Internationalist, 353*, 9–13.

Alonso-Fradejas, A. (2013). *Land and sovereignty in the Americas* (Food First/TNI Issue Brief No. 1).

Andrée, P., Ayres, J., Bosia, M. J., & Massicotte, M.-J. (Eds.). (2014). *Globalization and food sovereignty: Global and local change in the new politics of food*. Toronto: University of Toronto Press.

Badgley, C., Moghtader, J., Quintero, E., Zakem, E., Chappell, M. J., Aviles-Vazquez, K., ... Perfecto, I. (2007). Organic agriculture and the global food supply. *Renewable Agriculture and Food Systems, 22*(2), 86–108.

Bernstein, H. (2006). Is there an agrarian question in the 21st century? *Canadian Journal of Development Studies, XXVII*(4), 449–460.

Borras, S. M. (2008). La Via Campesina and its global campaign for agrarian reform. *Journal of Agrarian Change, 8*(2/3), 258–289.

Borras, S. M., Jr., Edelman, M., & Kay, C. (Eds.). (2008). *Transnational agrarian movements confronting globalization*. Oxford: Wiley-Blackwell.

Borras, S. M., Jr., Franco, J., Gómez, S., Kay, C., & Spoor, M. (2012). Land grabbing in Latin America and the Caribbean. *Journal of Peasant Studies, 39*(3–4), 845–872.

Borras, S. M., Jr., & Franco, J. C. (2012, July). *A 'land sovereignty' alternative? Towards a people's counter-enclosure*. TNI Agrarian Justice Programme discussion paper. Amsterdam: Transnational Institute.

Borras, S. M., Jr., Franco, J. C., Isakson, R., Levidow, L., & Vervest, P. (2014). *Towards understanding the politics of flex crops and commodities: Implications for research and policy advocacy*. Amsterdam: Transnational Institute.

Borras, S. M., Jr., Franco, J. C., & Wang, C. (2013). The challenge of global governance of land grabbing: Changing international agricultural context and competing political views and strategies. *Globalizations, 10*(1), 161–179.

Brent, Z. (2013). *Land conflicts in Argentina: From resistance to systemic transformation* (Issue Brief No. 4). Oakland: Food First.

Bryceson, D. F. (2010). Sub-Saharan Africa's vanishing peasantries and the specter of a global food crisis. In F. Magdoff & B. Tokar (Eds.), *Agriculture and food in crisis. Conflict, resistance and renewal* (pp. 69–84). New York, NY: Monthly Review Press.

CFS. (2012). *Global strategic framework for food security and nutrition*. Rome: FAO.

CFS. (2013). *Investing in smallholder agriculture for food security*. High Level Panel of Experts. Rome: FAO.

Claeys, P. (2012). The creation of new rights by the food sovereignty movement: The challenge of institutionalizing subversion. *Sociology, 46*(5), 844–860.

Clark, P. (2013, September 14–15). *Food sovereignty, post-neoliberalism, campesino organizations, and the state in Ecuador*. Food sovereignty: A critical dialogue. International conference, Yale University. Retrieved from http://www.yale.edu/agrarianstudies/foodsovereignty/papers.html

Colchester, M., N. Jiwan, Andiko, M. Sirait, A.Y. Ferdaus, A. Sarambo, and H. Pane. (2006). *Promised land. Palm oil and land acquisition in Indonesia: Implications for local communities and indigenous peoples*. Moreton-in-Marsh: Forest Peoples Programme and Perkumpulan Sawit Watch.

Daño, E. C. (2007). *Unmasking the new green revolution in Africa: Motives, players and dynamics*. Penang/Bonn/Richmond, South Africa: Third World Network/Church 22 Development Service/African Centre for Biosafety.

Da Vía, E. (2012). Seed diversity, farmers' rights, and the politics of repeasantization. *International Journal of Sociology of Agriculture and Food, 19*(2), 229–242.

Davis, M. (2006). *Planet of slums*. London: Verso.

Desmarais, A., & Nicholson, P. (2013). La Via Campesina: An historical and political analysis. *La Via Campesina's open book: Celebrating 20 years of struggle and hope*. Retrieved from http://viacampesina.org/downloads/pdf/openbooks/EN-10.pdf

De Schutter, O. (2010, June 4). *Responsibly destroying the world's peasantry*. Retrieved from http://farmlandgrab.org/13528

De Schutter, O. (2011, November). *The World Trade Organization and the Post-Global Food Crisis Agenda* (Briefing Note 04). Rome: FAO.

De Schutter, O. (2012, May). *Submission to the consultation on the first draft of the global strategic framework for Food Security and Nutrition of the Committee on world food security*. Rome: FAO/United Nations.

Desmarais, A. A. (2007). *La Vía Campesina. Globalization and the power of peasants*. Halifax: Fernwood Press/London: Pluto Press.

De Sousa Santos, B. (2002). *Towards a new legal common sense*. London: Butterworth.

Does the future of farming in Africa lie in the private sector? (2012, November 23). Poverty matters blog. *The Guardian*.

Edelman, M. (2013, September 14–15). *Food sovereignty: Forgotten genealogies and future regulatory challenges. Food sovereignty: A critical dialogue*. International conference, Yale University. Retrieved from http://www.yale.edu/agrarianstudies/foodsovereignty/papers.html

Edelman, M., & James, C. (2011). Peasants' rights and the UN system: Quixotic struggle? Or emancipator idea whose time has come? *Journal of Peasant Studies*, *38*(1), 81–108.

Erosion, Technology and Concentration. (2009, November). Who will feed us? *ETC Group Communiqué*, *102*, 1–34. Retrieved from www.etcgroup.org

Escobar, A. (2008). *Territories of difference: Place, movements, life, Redes*. Durham, NC: Duke University Press.

FAO. (2009). *Declaration of the world food summit on food security*. Retrieved from http://www.fao.org/fileadmin/templates/wsfs/Summit/Docs/Final_Declaration/WSFS09_Declaration.odf

FOLA. (2013). *Placing land rights at the heart of development*. Retrieved from http://www.focusonland.com/fola/en/countries/

Franco, J. C., & Borras, S. M., Jr. (2013). *Land concentration, land grabbing and people's struggles in Europe*. Amsterdam: Transnational Institute, and La Via Campesina.

G8. (2012). *The "New Alliance for Food Security and Nutrition" in Ghana*. G8 Cooperation Framework.

Gibbon, P., & Ponte, S. (2005). *Trading down. Africa, value chains and the global economy*. Philadelphia: Temple University Press.

Giunta, I. (2013, September 14–15). *Food sovereignty in Ecuador: The gap between the constitutionalization of the principles and their materialization in the official agri-food strategies*. Food sovereignty: A critical dialogue. International conference, Yale University. Retrieved from http://www.yale.edu/agrarianstudies/foodsovereignty/papers.html

GRAIN. (2008, October). *Seized: The 2008 land grab for food and financial security* (GRAIN briefings). Retrieved from http://www.grain.org/briefings/?id=212

Harrison, G. (2004). *The World Bank and Africa: The construction of governance states*. London: Routledge.

Henriques, G. (2013). *Whose alliance? The G8 and the emergence of a global corporate regime for agriculture*. Ecumenical Advocacy Alliance. Brussels: CIDSE.

Hilmi, A. (2012). *Agricultural transition. A different logic*. Oslo: The More and Better Network.

HLPE (High Level Panel of Experts). (2013). *Investing in smallholder agriculture for food security*. Rome: FAO.

Holt-Giménez, E. (2010). From food crisis to food sovereignty, the challenge of social movements. In F. Magdoff & B. Tokar (Eds.), *Agriculture and food in crisis. Conflict, resistance and renewal* (pp. 207–224). New York, NY: Monthly Review Press.

Holt-Giménez, E. (2012, May 2). We already grow enough food for 10 billion people – and still can't end hunger. *The Huffington Post*, pp. 1–2.

Holt-Giménez, E., & Patel, R. (Eds.). (2009). *Food rebellions! Crisis and the hunger for justice*. Cape Town: Pambazuka Press.

Hospes, O. (2014). Food sovereignty: The debate, the deadlock, and a suggested detour. *Agriculture and Human Values*, *31*, 119–130.

Kay, S. (2014). *Reclaiming agricultural investment: Towards public–peasant investment synergies*. Amsterdam: Transnational Institute Agrarian Justice Programme.

Kerssen, T. (2013). *Grabbing power. The new struggles for land, food and democracy in Northern Honduras*. Oakland: Food First Books.

Klein, N. (2007). *The shock doctrine. The rise of disaster capitalism*. New York, NY: Metropolitan Books.

Klopp, J. M., & Lumumba, O. (2014). Kenya and the global 'land grab': A view from below. In M. Kaag & A. Zoomers (Eds.), *The global land grab. Beyond the hype* (pp. 54–68). Halifax: Fernwood.

Lewis, W. A. (1954). Economic development with unlimited supplies of labour. *Manchester School of Economic and Social Studies*, *22*, 139–191.

Li, T. M. (2011). Centering labor in the land grab debate. *Journal of Peasant Studies*, *38*(2), 281–298.

Liberti, S. (2013). *Land grabbing. Journeys in the new colonialism*. London: Verso.

Mann, A. (2014). *Global activism in food politics. Power shift*. Houndsmill: Palgrave Macmillan.
McKay, B., & Nehring, R. (2013, September 14–15). *The 'state' of food sovereignty in Latin America: Political projects and alternative pathways in Venezuela, Ecuador and Bolivia*. International conference, Yale University. Retrieved from http://www.yale.edu/agrarianstudies/foodsovereignty/index.html
McKeon, N. (2009). *The United Nations and civil society. Legitimizing global governance – Whose voice?* London: Zed Books.
McKeon, N. (2014a). *The New Alliance for Food Security and Nutrition. A coup for corporate capital?* Amsterdam: Transnational Institute.
McKeon, N. (2014b). *Food security governance*. London: Routledge.
McMichael, P. (2006). Reframing development: Global peasant movements and the new agrarian question. *Canadian Journal of Development Studies, XXVII*(4), 471–486.
McMichael, P. (2012). The 'land grab' and corporate food regime restructuring. *Journal of Peasant Studies, 39*(3/4), 681–701.
McMichael, P. (2013a). Value-chain agriculture and debt relations: Contradictory outcomes. *Third World Quarterly, 34*(4), 671–690.
McMichael, P. (2013b). Land grabbing as security mercantilism in international relations. *Globalizations, 10*(1), 47–64.
McMichael, P. (2013c). *Food regimes and agrarian questions*. Halifax: Fernwood Press.
McMichael, P. (2014a). The CSM and the rai. Retrieved from http://www.csm4cfs.org/news/?id=163
McMichael, P. (2014b). Historicizing food sovereignty. *Journal of Peasant Studies, 41*(1), 933–957.
Monsalve-Suárez, S. (2013). The human rights framework in contemporary agrarian struggles. *Journal of Peasant Studies, 40*(1), 239–290.
Moore, B., Jr. (1966). *Social origins of dictatorship and democracy*. Boston: Beacon Press.
Nicholson, P., & Delforge, I. (2008). Vía Campesina: Responding to global systemic crisis. *Development, 51*(4), 456–459.
Nielsen, J., & Pritchard, B. (2009). *Value chain struggles: Institutions and governance in the plantation districts of South India*. Chichester: Wiley-Blackwell.
Nyeleni. (2006, March 6–9). *First manifesto/call of social movements and civil society toward the 'land, territory and dignity' forum*, Porto Alegre. Retrieved from http://www.nyeleni.org/spip.php?article54
Oxfam. (2013, September). *The new alliance: A new direction needed* (Oxfam Briefing Note). Retrieved from http://www.oxfam.org/sites/www.oxfam.org/files/bn-new-alliance-new-direction-agriculture-250913-en.pdf
Oya, C. (2012). Contract farming in Sub-Saharan Africa: A survey of approaches, debates and issues. *Journal of Agrarian Change, 12*(1), 1–33.
Patel, R. (2009). What does food sovereignty look like? *Journal of Peasant Studies, 36*(3), 663–706.
Paul, H., & Steinbrecher, R. (2013, June). African agricultural growth corridors and the New Alliance for Food Security and Nutrition. Who benefits, who loses? *EcoNexus*.
Perrone, N. M. (2013). Restrictions to foreign acquisitions of agricultural land in Argentina and Brazil. *Globalizations, 10*(1), 205–209.
Ploeg, van der J. D. (2009). *The 'new' peasantries. Struggles for autonomy and sustainability in an era of empire and globalization*. London: Earthscan.
Ploeg, van der J. D., Jingzhong, Y., & Schneider, S. (2012). Rural development through the construction of new, nested markets: Comparative perspectives from China, Brazil and the European Union. *Journal of Peasant Studies, 39*(1), 133–174.
Pretty, J., & Hine, R. E. (2001). *Reducing food poverty with sustainable agriculture: A summary of new evidence*. Final report from the "SAFE World" research project. University of Essex. Retrieved from www2.essex.ac.uk/ces/FresearchProgrammes/SAFEWexecsummfinalreport.htm
Pretty, J., Morison, J. J. L., & Hine, R. E. (2003). Reducing food poverty by increasing agricultural sustainability in developing countries. *Agriculture, Ecosystems and Environment, 95*, 217–234.
Pretty, J., Noble, A. D., Bossio, D., Dixon, J., Hine, R. E., Penning de Vries, F. W. T., & Morison, J. I. L. (2006). Resource conserving agriculture increases yields in developing countries. *Environmental Science & Technology, 40*(4), 1114–1119.
Raghavan, C. (1990). *Recolonization: GATT, the Uruguay round and the Third World*. Penang: Third World Network.
Rose, N. (2012). *Optimism of the Will. Food sovereignty as transformative counter-hegemony in the 21st century* (PhD dissertation). School of Global Studies, Royal Melbourne Institute of Technology.
Rosset, P. (2009, May–June, 16–21). *Food sovereignty in Latin America: Confronting the new crisis*. NACLA Report on the Americas.

Rosset, P. (2013). Re-thinking agrarian reform, land and territory in La Vía Campesina. *Journal of Peasant Studies, 40*(3–5), 721–775.
Rosset, P. M., & Martinez-Torres, M. E. (2012). Rural social movements and agroecology: Context, theory and process. *Ecology and Society, 17*(3), 17. Retrieved from http://www.ecologyandsociety.org/vol17/iss3/
Stedile, J., & de Carvalho. (2011). People need food sovereignty. In E. Holt-Giménez (Ed.), *Food movements unite!* (pp. 21–34). Oakland: Food First Books.
Susanti, A., & Budidarsono, S. (2014). Land governance and oil palm development: Examples from Riau Province, Indonesia. In M. Kaag & A. Zoomers (Eds.), *The global land grab. Beyond the hype* (pp. 119–134). Halifax: Fernwood.
Transnational Institute. (2013). *For a European spring*. Retrieved from http://www.tni.org/article/european-spring-2013-new-beginning
Urquhart, S. (2008, June 2). *Food crisis, which crisis? Our crisis or theirs? The battle over the world's Food supply relocates to Rome*. Guerrilla News Network. Retrieved from http://gnn.to/articles/3718/food_crisis_which_crisis
Watts, M. (1994). Life under contract: Contract farming, agrarian restructuring, and flexible accumulation. In P. D. Little & M. J. Watts (Eds.), *Living under contract: Contract farming and agrarian transformation in Sub-Saharan Africa* (pp. 1–36). Madison, WI: University of Wisconsin Press.
Wittman, H. (2009). Reworking the metabolic rift: La Vía Campesina, agrarian citizenship and food sovereignty. *Journal of Peasant Studies, 36*(4), 805–826.
Wolford, W., Borras, S. M., Jr., Hall, R., Scoones, I., & White, B. (2013). Governing global land deals: The role of the state in the rush for land. *Development and Change, 44*(2), 189–210.
World Bank. (2007). *World Development Report 2008: Agriculture for development*. Washington, DC: The World Bank.
World Bank. (2013). *Growing Africa. Unlocking the potential of agribusiness*. Retrieved from http://siteresources.worldbank.org/INTAFRICA/Resources/africa-agribusiness-report-2013.pdf
World Bank. (2014). *Benchmarking the business of agriculture*. Retrieved from: http://bba.worldbank.org/
Zoomers, A., & Kaag, M. (2014). Conclusion: Beyond the global land grab hype – ways forward in research and action. In M. Kaag & A. Zoomers (Eds.), *The global land grab. Beyond the hype* (pp. 201–216). Halifax: Fernwood.

Food Sovereignty and the Recognition of New Rights for Peasants at the UN: A Critical Overview of La Via Campesina's Rights Claims over the Last 20 Years

PRISCILLA CLAEYS

University of Louvain (UCL), Louvain-la-Neuve, Belgium

ABSTRACT *This article explores how human rights framing by the transnational agrarian movement La Via Campesina (LVC) has evolved over the last 20 years. It discusses how the movement has worked towards institutionalizing new categories of rights, such as the 'right to food sovereignty' and the 'rights of peasants', thereby contributing to the creation of new human rights standards at the United Nations (UN). It also critically addresses some of the challenges the movement has been confronted with when framing its demands in terms of rights. Its overall argument is that LVC has managed to tap the potential of the rhetoric of rights to find common ground, thanks to its innovative use of non-codified rights. This has enabled activists to 'localize' human rights and make them meaningful to their various contexts. However, it contends that further advancing the movement's goals will require serious consideration of some of the key limits of the human rights framework.*

La Via Campesina, Food Sovereignty, and Human Rights

La Via Campesina[1] (LVC) developed in the early 1990s as peasant and small-scale farmers from Central America, North and South America, Europe, and elsewhere sought to articulate a common response to the neoliberal onslaught that had devastated their lives (Desmarais, 2008a). Since then, the movement has opposed 'global depeasantization' (Araghi, 1995) and the emerging 'corporate food regime' (McMichael, 2009). It has developed a 'food sovereignty' model to counterpose the dominant 'market economy' paradigm and has managed to build a common agenda across the North–South divide (Rosset & Martínez-Torres, 2010).

To do this, LVC has deployed a powerful 'rights master frame' (Benford & Snow, 2000, p. 619). Rights occupy a central place in most LVC statements, whether in local struggles over seeds, land, territories, and resources, or in international struggles over trade and investment in food and agriculture. Rights have provided a common language to peasants' and small-scale farmers' organizations that are politically, culturally, and ideologically different. The concept of food sovereignty is often defined as 'rights-based' (Patel, 2007; Rosset & Martínez-Torres, 2010). In recent years, LVC has pursued the recognition of new human rights for peasants at the UN, such as the right to land and territory, the right to seeds, and the right to set the prices of agricultural products (Edelman & James, 2011). *Food sovereignty* itself, which has been claimed by LVC as a collective right (Claeys, 2012), could become, in the future, a new human right.

This article discusses the advantages and limitations of human rights framing, and analyses how the movement has worked towards institutionalizing new categories of rights, such as the 'right to food sovereignty' and 'the rights of peasants'. It then explores how the movement has sought to address some of the strategic challenges associated with framing demands in terms of rights. Indeed, strategic considerations are key to understanding why the two categories of rights have had distinct institutional trajectories. Its overall argument is that LVC has succeeded in using rights to find common ground, thanks to its innovative use of non-codified rights. However, it contends that further advancing the movement's goals will require serious consideration of some of the limits of the human rights framework.

The Advantages and Limitations of Human Rights Framing

Framing is one of the central activities of social movements: framing serves the purposes of diagnosing certain situations as problematic, of offering solutions, and of calling to action (Benford & Snow, 1988). The advantages of using human rights to frame claims are numerous. Human rights can be used by activists to redefine the boundaries between what is just and unjust (Agrikoliansky, 2010). Rights turn claims into universal and legitimate demands, and allow social movements to frame claims in a way that does not emphasize sectorial interests (Valocchi, 1996). Rights facilitate the integration of multiple ideologies and help export claims to movements with divergent ideological, political, or cultural references (Fillieule, Agrikoliansky, & Sommier, 2010). These advantages help explain why human rights have been mobilized in a great number of social struggles, and in particular by the civil rights movement (McAdam, 1990), by indigenous peoples (Sieder, 2011), by gay and lesbian rights groups (Plummer, 2006), and by activists defending workers' rights, welfare rights (Reese & Newcombe, 2003), and women's or migrants' rights (Elias, 2010).

Yet, to frame claims as rights may present social movements with serious challenges. First, human rights regimes continue to be dominated by a Western, liberal, and individualist conception of rights (Donnelly, 1982; Engle Merry, 1997; Rajagopal, 2003). This has forced many groups to 'define according to alien values some fundamental aspects of their identity and way of life' (GRAIN, 2007). Second, these regimes are built around the obligations of states, and fail to adequately address the responsibilities of private and transnational actors. This 'statist framework' has been challenged by numerous thinkers but continues to dominate (Stammers, 1995). This is seen as highly problematic by some in view of the agency and legitimacy it attributes to the state (Kneen, 2009). Third, human rights tend to emphasize economic liberty—understood as individual appropriation of, access to, and control over economic resources—often at the expense of equality of outcome/welfare (Charvet & Kaczynska-Nay, 2008). The discourse of human rights has even been qualified by some as 'an instrument for the pathological expansion of modern and postmodern liberalism and what accompanies it: free market capitalism' (Sardar, 1998).[2] Fourth, the replacement of responsibilities by rights may undermine social solidarity, appreciation of the public good, and communal identity (Kneen, 2009). Fifth, the absoluteness of human rights may promote unrealistic expectations, inhibit dialogue, and generate conflict, because rights are not tempered by limits or obligations (Glendon, 1991). Finally, human rights have been criticized for not helping us imagine a different future because the ideology of human rights is, in essence, 'presentist' (Gauchet, 2000, p. 272). All these factors combined can seriously hinder the subversive potential of human rights, and represent a considerable challenge for movements, such as LVC, that use rights in their struggles against capitalism and neoliberalism.

The limitations of the UN human rights framework are particularly useful to understand why LVC activists have not limited themselves to using existing rights, such as the *human right to food*, to frame their demands, but have instead claimed new human rights (Claeys, 2012). These limitations also help understand what has driven LVC activists to develop, from below, an alternative conception of human rights. Although it is still in the making, this conception emphasizes the collective dimension of claims over the individual one; targets the various decision-making levels (and actors) where food and agricultural governance issues ought to be deliberated, from the local, national, regional to the international, rather than focusing on the role of the state; and connects individual to collective autonomy, in a way that constrains economic liberty and reintroduces equality and self-determination in the food system. The following sections explore the 'right to food sovereignty' and 'peasants' rights', both as *collective action frames*—the sets of beliefs that legitimate collective action (Imig & Tarrow, 2001), and as *new human rights* (Alston, 1984; Bob, 2008).

The Right of Peoples to Food Sovereignty

The elaboration of food sovereignty as a collective action frame finds its roots in the mid-1980s in Meso-America, essentially in response to drastic structural adjustment programmes, the evaporation of state support for agriculture, and the arrival of food imports from the USA (Edelman, 2014). The development and elaboration of collective action frames are always contested processes: framing activities occur within complex and multi-organizational arenas and are affected by the cultural and political environment in which they take place. The imposition of a certain vision of reality involves dynamic framings and counter-framings to respond to events and detractors, and to attract potential movement participants (Benford & Snow, 2000). It is therefore not surprising that mentions of food sovereignty at the time occurred 'in a flow of much more commonly-used, related terms' such as food autonomy, food self-sufficiency, or food security, nor is it problematic in any way that the food sovereignty rhetoric was initially used by the Mexican government in its 1983 National Food Program (Programa Nacional de Alimentación, PRONAL) (Edelman, 2014, pp. 4–5). What the messy genealogy of food sovereignty indicates, however, is that peasant movements were successful in their strategic 'frame transformation' effort (Benford & Snow, 2000, p. 625): they managed to change the then prevailing meaning of food sovereignty to gradually impose theirs. At the core of this transformation was a double move, away from the emphasis on 'national food security' and towards a growing assertion of the 'right to continue being producers' (Edelman, 1999, pp. 102–103).

The diffusion and growing resonance of the food sovereignty frame at the beginning of the 1990s appear closely linked to its grounding in the 'rights master frame' (Benford & Snow, 2000, p. 619). As early as 1993, in its Mons Declaration, LVC demanded 'the right of every country to define its own agricultural policy according to the nation's interest and in concertación [*sic*] with the peasant and Indigenous organizations, guaranteeing their real participation', although this claim was not explicitly linked to food sovereignty (Vía Campesina, 1993). When food sovereignty made its first appearance on the international scene, in 1996, it was defined by LVC as the 'the right of each nation to maintain and develop its own capacity to produce its basic foods respecting cultural and productive diversity' (Vía Campesina, 1996). This emphasis on the right of states is attributable to the deployment of the food sovereignty frame in reaction to trade liberalization. The World Trade Organization (WTO) became one of the main targets of LVC's activities, and opposition to the WTO in those years helped federate the movement. The focus of food sovereignty (at the international level) was on bringing an end to dumping, revamping international trade rules, and ensuring tariff protection for agricultural products (Vía Campesina, 1999).

The emphasis on the nation-state as the sovereign was short-lived. More than just an alternative paradigm, LVC activists started claiming food sovereignty as a human right, to be held by communities, peoples, or regions, leaving the initial statist approach behind to insist on the sovereignty of the peoples. This is illustrated by this statement, released on the occasion of the WTO Ministerial Summit of Cancun: 'Food Sovereignty is every community's fundamental right. Every community should have the right to produce their own food, the right to food sovereignty' (Vía Campesina, 2003). The use of the emblematic term 'peoples' in many LVC statements can be interpreted as a way to embrace the multiplicity of decision-making levels where food sovereignty policies ought to be discussed, what Schiavoni (in this issue), building on Patel and McMichael, has described as localized 'multiple sovereignties'. The right of peoples to food sovereignty injects a new meaning to the very idea of 'participation', which LVC activists do not limit to what Baxi has termed 'the right to participate in development', but see as 'requiring to break the monopoly of the government in defining public interest' (Baxi, 2007, p. 132), thereby challenging the state 'as the only legitimate source of law making and applying' (Falk, 1988, p. 27).

If explicit mentions of the term 'the right to food sovereignty' are not very numerous,[3] references to food sovereignty as either a list of rights or as the 'right to' are countless. I have discussed elsewhere how the new 'right of peoples to food sovereignty' built on and reactivated 'old' collective rights recognized by the UN, such as the right to self-determination, the right to development, and the right to permanent sovereignty over natural resources. Just as these other rights, the right to food sovereignty can be analysed as having an internal dimension—the right of a people to choose their own political, economic, and social system—and an external dimension—the right of states to develop their agriculture (Claeys, 2012, p. 849). Another way of looking at the right to food sovereignty is of comprising an economic dimension—asserting the role of peasants in the economy, and their right to produce and sell on local markets—and a political dimension—emphasizing democratic control in the food system (Windfuhr & Jonsén, 2005), without omitting the important cultural, ecological, and feminist dimensions.

Since the mid-2000s, the (right to) food sovereignty frame has evolved considerably, in the face of new international events, new strategies, new member organizations, and new attacks by adversaries. Food sovereignty has integrated the movement's wide variety of struggles at the local and national levels—such as securing control over land and territory, protecting local knowledge, and creating local markets. It has also spread to new geographic regions, including more deeply in Africa.

In recent years, it has developed into a full-fledged rights-based paradigm, often described as resting on the six pillars defined at the 2007 Nyéléni Food Sovereignty Forum: (i) focuses on food for people and defends 'the right to sufficient, healthy and culturally appropriate food for all individuals, peoples and communities'; (ii) values food providers and 'respects the rights' of all those who 'cultivate, grow, harvest and process food'; (iii) localizes food systems; (iv) puts control locally; (v) builds knowledge and skills; and (vi) works with nature (Nyéléni Food Sovereignty Forum, 2007). The 'right of people to food sovereignty' is now placed at the heart of the transnational movement that 'considers the Nyéléni Declaration as its political platform' (Nyéléni Newsletter, 2013).

Institutionalizing the Right to Food Sovereignty

LVC has sought to institutionalize the *right of peoples to food sovereignty* in two ways: it has tried to translate it into alternative international trade rules for food and agriculture, and it has sought to obtain its recognition as a new human right. In the run-up to the WTO Ministerial in Doha (2001), LVC, in partnership with a large network of social movements and non-governmental organizations (NGOs), demanded that the right to food sovereignty be enshrined in an International Convention (Our World is Not for Sale, 2001). In 2004, French activist José Bové brought LVC's call for a Convention on Food Sovereignty to the then UN Secretary General Kofi Annan, whom he asked 'to support Vía Campesina organisations in their efforts to have food sovereignty recognized as a new basic human right' (Vía Campesina, 2004).

Since then, attempts to institutionalize the right to food sovereignty at the international level have been given less priority. Although the idea of an International Convention was discussed at the 2007 Nyéléni Forum, calls for such a Convention have not been reactivated by the 2007–2008 global food crisis (International Planning Committee for Food Sovereignty (IPC) and More and Better Campaign, 2009). While recognizing that 'UN recognition of food sovereignty could constitute an umbrella for all these mobilizations', LVC activist Paul Nicholson cautions that such an endeavour would require a lot of 'organizational effort' and that direct dialogue with national governments may be, strategically, more accessible. The priority today is to concentrate on 'concrete struggles like land-grabbing' (Nicholson, 2012, p. 9). Strengthening member organizations is also a critical priority.

While many LVC activists insist that the struggle for food sovereignty should be articulated at the local, national, regional, and international levels, the focus on the 'local' is increasingly striking. Activists are putting in place food sovereignty *practices* that represent concrete and feasible alternatives, here and now. Less efforts are put into elaborating on the kind of regulatory apparatus that would be needed to enable these practices to flourish (Burnett & Murphy, 2014; Clapp, 2014; Edelman, 2014), in part because of LVC's strong anti-WTO and anti-reformist position (Buisson, 2013). The long-standing demand that an end be put to the WTO was reaffirmed at the occasion of the WTO Ministerial of Bali of December 2013 (Vía Campesina, 2013b). The same month, LVC announced its withdrawal from the Our World Is Not For Sale (OWINFS) coalition, arguing that it demanded 'deeper systemic change and not a mere reform or turnaround of the WTO' (Vía Campesina, 2013c). This strategic distancing, justified by the need to avoid granting any legitimacy to the WTO, is not promising in that regard.

Efforts to institutionalize food sovereignty have not been abandoned, but have shifted to different arenas: elaborating public policies for food sovereignty at the regional, national, and municipal levels, and, to a limited extent, putting food sovereignty on the agenda of the UN Committee on World Food Security.

Food Sovereignty Policies

LVC's efforts to institutionalize food sovereignty have been particularly successful at the national and local/municipal levels (Bellinger & Fakhri, 2013). Constitutional recognition of food sovereignty has been achieved in Ecuador, Bolivia, and Venezuela, while Nicaragua, Mali, and Senegal have adopted food sovereignty policies, usually in alliance with or under the pressure of peasant movements (Beuchelt & Virchow, 2012). Similar proposals are being discussed in the Dominican Republic, Peru, and El Salvador (Godek, 2013). Overall, the various dimensions of food sovereignty have been relatively well integrated in these policies, but the endorsement of food sovereignty as a state objective/obligation has generated new contradictions (Bernstein, 2014) and challenges for peasant movements. In Bolivia, the government's food sovereignty rhetoric is compatible with conventional agricultural schemes, export-led agribusiness, and 'state-controlled' genetically modified organisms (Cockburn, 2013, p. 3). In Ecuador, the 'persistence of a logic of rural industrialization and modernization inside some strategic components of the government' is accompanied 'by a reduced protagonism of social organizations that originally sponsored the proposal of food sovereignty' (Giunta, 2013, p. 20), leaving little room for action beyond a focus on alternative practices as a way to enact 'creative new forms of policy' (Sherwood et al., 2013, p. 2). In addition, the internal dimension of food sovereignty tends to be only partially embedded in these policies, while emphasis on the external dimension has often meant increased state control over agriculture and natural resources (Clark, 2013; Cockburn, 2013). Finally, these policies have brought little structural change so far, raising new strategic considerations for the organizations that had pushed for legal change. As a result, the initial enthusiasm for food sovereignty policies within the food sovereignty movement at large has waned considerably.

Food Sovereignty at the Committee on World Food Security

Following its reform in 2009, the Committee on World Food Security (CFS) has slowly emerged as the central UN political platform dealing with food security, agriculture, and nutrition. The CFS has been celebrated for proposing an alternative governance model for decision-making on global issues, because CFS membership extends beyond states to include international institutions, foundations, the private sector, and civil society. LVC's interactions with the CFS have been ambivalent. On the one hand, LVC actively participates, through the Civil Society Mechanism, in a number of working groups, where issues such as land, agricultural investment, volatility, biofuels, and climate change are debated. On the other hand, many LVC activists (especially those who are not involved in institutional processes) regard the CFS as yet another international arena that is unlikely to bring social change. In a recent statement to announce that a collaboration agreement had been signed between LVC and the Food and Agriculture Organization, the movement cautioned that it 'remains realistic about the amount of energy that should be put into the UN, maintaining its greatest strength on the ground mobilizing farmers and building alternatives' (Vía Campesina, 2013a). The same reasoning applies to the CFS. Indeed, advances at the CFS in areas such as land rights and ways to support smallholder investments have not been matched by similar breakthroughs in discussions on biofuels or ways to tackle price volatility, and trade issues have not yet featured on the agenda of the CFS. The very concept of food sovereignty has proven difficult to mobilize at the CFS, despite the insistence of some Latin American states that it be discussed during the 39th session of the CFS of October 2012.[4] In contrast, the *right to fo*od has been used extensively by civil society, and is referred to in a number of CFS documents.

The Rights of Peasants, Women, and Men

While the *right of peoples to food sovereignty* has been mostly deployed by LVC to contest neoliberalism in agriculture, a number of other new rights are part of the movement's vocabulary. Over the last decade, the rights repertoire of LVC has flourished to include the 'right to land and territory', the 'right to means of agricultural production', the 'freedom to determine price and market for agricultural production', the 'right to the protection of agriculture values', and the 'right to biological diversity' (Vía Campesina, 2008a). These rights, listed in the movement's Declaration of the Rights of Peasants, address deeper, long-term, 'agrarian transformations' and in particular the transition of agriculture to capitalism (Bernstein, 2014; Borras, 2009).

The peasants' rights frame (and very first draft of the Declaration) was elaborated during village-level consultations with peasant communities in Indonesia, in the late 90s (Purwanto, 2013). It was further articulated in the period ranging from 2002 to 2008. What started as an essentially Indonesian process (led by the member organization Serikat Petani Indonesia) was brought to the attention of member organizations from other countries in the region, and was subsequently brought to the international level. It was put on the agenda of the work of LVC's Working Committee on Human Rights and submitted for consideration by other members of the movement during the 2008 International Conference on Peasant Rights that was organized in Jakarta (Vía Campesina, 2008b). The text was finally adopted by LVC at its Fifth International Conference in Maputo in 2008.

The biggest challenge confronting the peasants' rights frame today is one of 'frame diffusion' (Benford & Snow, 2000, p. 627). Despite the organization of internal consultations on the issue, an internal LVC document recognized in 2008 that there was a 'different level of comprehension of the declaration on the rights of the peasants in different countries and regions' and that internal debate was lacking (Vía Campesina, 2008c). The lack of appropriation of the peasants' rights frame by other regions, in particular Latin America, where references to food sovereignty dominate, and by activists who are not involved in transnational arenas remains a considerable obstacle to the diffusion of the peasants' rights frame, although there are signs that this is changing. European organizations of LVC, for example, have taken up the issue in recent months and have started to lobby their respective governments. Valeria (name changed), a long-time member and activist of the international human rights organization FIAN who has been involved in getting peasants' rights recognized at the UN, explains:

> Henry [Saragih] knows the latinos are not convinced but they have not discussed it. The Indonesians have put a lot of political capital and now they need to convince the others. In Africa, there is no aversion. In Latin America, it is different. A different colonialism? A different Marxism? I don't know.[5]

Moreover, the peasants' rights frame has not yet acquired strong mobilizing qualities: it does not constitute a uniting and mobilizing frame, although several LVC leaders have expressed their hopes that the Declaration can work as a mobilizing tool, encouraging members to refer to it and not wait for it to be recognized by the UN. In contrast with the food sovereignty frame, which has proven to be highly motivational and adaptable, the peasants' rights frame remains somewhat disconnected from grassroots activists. Valeria explains: 'Peasants' rights, it comes from the leaders and the intellectuals, we will need to see if peasants follow'.[6] At the same time, key people within LVC such as Paul Nicholson appear confident that the movement will manage to harness grassroots support for the Declaration, noting that it might be easier to achieve than the institutionalization of the right to food sovereignty:

> UN recognition of Food Sovereignty could constitute an umbrella for all these mobilizations. (. . .) But the way UN works means that representatives have to be present continuously, it is a permanent effort and a heavy task. We (. . .) must see if, within our programme, we are capable of tackling these objectives and putting organizational effort to it. Indeed, the right to Food Sovereignty represents a much larger task than mobilizing for the convention/Declaration of Peasants' Rights. (Nicholson, 2012, p. 9)

The mobilizing potential of the peasants' rights frame could indeed be considerable if it manages to reinforce the collective identity of a movement always in search of new ways to build symbolic links and confronted with an increasingly diverse membership. Now that identification with the WTO as the shared enemy no longer plays a determining role, the peasants' rights frame could become more potent, thanks to its strong focus on what Stammers has called the 'expressive' dimension—oriented toward norms, values, identities, and lifestyles (Stammers, 1999). As Alberto Gomez, a Mexican peasant leader, argues: 'The Declaration on the rights of peasants has a strong symbolic value, it gives strength to our struggle'.[7] By embracing a term traditionally used in pejorative ways, the peasants' rights frame could succeed in pursuing the task of 'frame transformation' that LVC activists have undertaken for years (Desmarais, 2008b), and thereby acquire increased resonance. Yet, it is uncertain at this stage if mobilizing in defence of the concept of peasants' rights will generate more public support, facilitate alliances, or induce rejection and criticism.

If the Declaration on the Rights of Peasants has been generally well received within the movement, it has also raised criticism for not dealing with what some activists perceive as more pressing issues. A particular source of concern, for some, is whether the work on an alternative international trade framework grounded in food sovereignty will be completely abandoned, 'now that the Indonesians are working on peasants' rights'.[8] At the same time, when asked about potential conflicts between food sovereignty and peasants' rights, most LVC activists tend to discard the possibility that conflicts might surface between the two rights frames, although they acknowledge that the movement has limited capacity to engage with international institutions and that opportunities to advance rights claims in international forums are scarce. For some, such as Jean (name changed) from the European Coordination of LVC, the issue has been little explored: 'There has been no debate between the right to food sovereignty and peasants' rights. Normally it should have been discussed in Maputo'.[9] Others argue that both frames are compatible and mutually supportive,[10] or that they simply emerged in different contexts.[11] Jean regrets: 'But peasants' rights are not an agricultural policy issue'.[12] These critiques are well received by Henry Saragih, the former Secretary General of LVC, who has been leading the peasants' rights initiative: 'We don't pressure other regions. We know it is difficult for national organizations to add new issues. Latin America is about land and indigenous peoples. (. . .) Different regions have different issues.'[13]

Institutionalizing the Rights of Peasants

Despite these challenges and uncertainties, LVC has worked actively over recent years to bring the Declaration on the Rights of Peasants to the UN Human Rights Council (HRC), with the support of trusted human rights experts. These efforts have recently brought results. On 24 September 2012, the HRC adopted a resolution (A/HRC/21/L.23) leading to the creation of an open-ended intergovernmental working group with the mandate of negotiating a draft UN Declaration on the Rights of Peasants and Other People Working in Rural Areas (Human Rights Council, 2012b). Negotiations started in July 2013 and are expected to extend over the next few years, following the adoption in June 2014 of a new resolution renewing the mandate of the working group.

The assertion of new rights to resources—such as the right to land—is likely to constitute a stumbling block in the negotiations, either because of the collective nature of the rights claimed, or because of their lack of consistency with existing standards, and because of the challenges that their implementation would represent (Golay, 2013). The definition of the peasantry as a (socio-economic or cultural?) group to be granted new specific rights also promises to be controversial. The ambiguous relationship between peasants' rights and the right to food sovereignty will also need to be clarified. The 2008 Declaration adopted by LVC recognized the 'right to food sovereignty'(art. 5.9), but provided no definition of it and oddly placed it under article 5 which dealt with the right to seeds. In the latest version of the Declaration on the Rights of Peasants presented by the Advisory Committee of the HRC in 2012, the 'right to food sovereignty' is recognized under article 2.5, which states that peasants have 'the right to healthy and culturally appropriate food produced through ecological sound and sustainable methods, and the right to define their own food and agriculture systems' (Human Rights Council, 2012a). Interestingly, this formulation was taken from the Nyéléni Declaration, but leaves out the reference to food sovereignty as a 'right of peoples'. Needless to say, it is uncertain what will happen to this article in the course of the negotiations process.

From a strategic perspective, the use of human rights presents three interrelated challenges for social movements. First, the human rights framework is heavily associated with strong and responsible (national) institutional and legal frameworks (Kolben, 2008). Human rights praxis tends to be reduced to a praxis that is organized through and oriented towards institutionalized structures of power. This may seriously endanger the 'emancipatory thrust' of human rights (Stammers, 2009, p. 106, p. 225). Second, the level of expertise required to deploy human rights arguments is such that human rights have more often than not been defended by human rights lawyers (Riles, 2006) and not by average citizens. As a result, conflicts framed in human rights terms tend to be solved in specialized arenas and run the risk of undermining social movements' efforts to organize and mobilize. Third, human rights claims tend to be constructed in ways that demand their codification in law, but the institutionalization of human rights claims may hinder the subversive potential of human rights (Stammers, 2009).

How has LVC dealt with these challenges? Can the movement pursue the recognition of new rights for peasants at the UN without undercutting the subversive potential of its rights-based claims? Will food sovereignty—not only as a right, but also as a vision, as a platform for action—and peasants' rights reinforce or undermine each other?

Contrary to the UN Declaration of the Rights of Indigenous Peoples, which relies on self-identification, the Declaration on the Rights of Peasants gives a definition of peasants as rights-holders. This definition is broad and inclusive in the sense that it includes agricultural workers and the landless, but it omits certain categories and risks to overlook the complex and evolving identity of the contemporary rural family (Edelman, 2013; Golay, 2009). Moreover, the Declaration highlights the importance of maintaining 'traditional food cultures' (art. 3.5) and emphasizes the existence of values and of a way of life that are based on household and community (art. 10.4; art. 10.5), thereby attributing social and cultural characteristics to the peasantry. It celebrates harmony with nature and defines peasants as those who have 'a direct and special relationship with the land and nature' (art. 1). This emphasis on what all the 'people of the land' have in common has certainly helped activists from distinct sociopolitical and economic environments find common ground. However, there is a risk that 'peasant essentialism' (Bernstein & Byres, 2001, p. 6) might lead to exclusions once identities become fixed in law.

Looking at the way human rights have been institutionalized historically, Stammers concludes that the codification of new human rights often leads to the 'institutionalization of particularity' (Stammers, 2009, p. 102). The essentialization of culture and social categories has been denounced as inherent to the making of claims for cultural rights (Cowan, Dembour, & Wilson, 2001, p. 3). It has also been noted as a common feature of many indigenous peoples' rights campaigns, with potentially serious political consequences, such as a 'drift to racism' when the so-called cultural identity becomes the basis for 'privileged' or 'exclusive' rights, for example to resources (Kuper, 2003, pp. 390–392).

Will LVC manage to build alliances and gain the support of other rural and urban constituencies while advancing new rights for peasants as a group? Experience with other UN processes aiming at creating new human rights standards shows that to be successful in the longer term, those involved in standard setting need to build a broad and inclusive base and reach out to governments, civil society organizations, experts, victims and beneficiaries, and UN agencies (International Council on Human Rights Policy, 2006). If food sovereignty proved to be a relatively good vehicle for alliance building, the struggle for peasants' rights may make things more complicated, although the movement is well aware of the importance of building alliances across sectors. In the framework of the peasants' rights process, efforts have been made to reach out to other rural constituencies whose concerns are so far not adequately reflected in the draft Declaration. A first meeting was held in Geneva in April 2014 to start a dialogue with pastoralist organizations, nomadic people, fisherfolk, and agricultural workers, which was promising. Yet, there are dangers that, in order to convince reluctant states, LVC activists will need to emphasize issues of discrimination, identity, and recognition, more than issues of redistribution, such as access to the means of production, alternative trade rules, and fair prices. This is a key challenge if this new legal instrument is to contribute to the movement's struggle against capitalism and neoliberalism in agriculture.

Conclusion

By defending a conceptualization of peasants' rights as group rights, of individual autonomy as connected to collective autonomy, and of self-determination as resting both on the individual and the collective,[14] LVC activists have succeeded in 'localizing' human rights, and making them meaningful to their various contexts (Feyter, Parmentier, Timmerman, & Ulrich, 2011). They have revitalized the human rights project with subversive dimensions, because they have managed to frame new rights in a way that combines what Santos has called the *global validity* and *local legitimacy* of human rights (Santos, 1997). LVC's experience with human rights also points to the importance of political mobilization for the success of rights-based strategies, and of finding an adequate balance between *institutional* and *non-institutional* movement activity. It remains to be seen if LVC will manage, in the future, to move beyond making 'reactive claims for rights'[15] to build on *both* food sovereignty and human rights, to elaborate, together with other social groups, an alternative vision of the common good.

Notes

1 Various names circulate for the 'La Via Campesina' network. I use the term 'La Via Campesina' in accordance with a decision taken by the network in 2013. However, many statements issued in earlier years are listed as 'Vía Campesina'.
2 Cited in (Kneen, 2009, p. 16).
3 A web search conducted on LVC's website on 10 January 2013 provided 17 occurrences of the 'right to food sovereignty' and 18 occurrences of 'el derecho a la soberania alimentaria'. The 'right to food sovereignty' frame was reactivated on the occasion of the WTO Ministerial of Bali in December 2013 (Vía Campesina, Gerak Lawan, and Social Movements for an Alternative Asia (SMAA), 2013).
4 These observations are based on participant observation at the 38th, 39th, and 40th sessions of the Committee on World Food Security in 2011, 2012, and 2013, as well as on participation in the negotiations of Voluntary Guidelines on the responsible governance of the tenure of land, fisheries, and forests, and of new principles for responsible agroinvesment.
5 Interview with the author, 23 June 2009.
6 Interview with the author, 23 June 2009.
7 Interview with the author, 14 August 2009.
8 Interview with the author, 2 June 2009.
9 Interview with the author, 2 June 2009.
10 Interview with CETIM representative, 3 July 2009.
11 Email exchange with representative of FIAN International, March 2009.
12 Interview with the author, 2 June 2009.
13 Interview, 22 March 2010.
14 I owe the idea of articulating individual and collective self-determination to Camilo Perez-Bustillo who describes it as 'Sen+' (Pérez-Bustillo, 2011).
15 Taken from Kneen in an interview with Devlin Kuyek: 'Food politics and the tyranny of rights: A profile of Brewster Kneen', January 5, 2010 in *Briarpatch* Magazine.

References

Agrikoliansky, E. (2010). Les usages protestataires du droit. In La Découverte (Ed.), *Penser les mouvements sociaux. Conflits sociaux et contestations dans les sociétés contemporaines* (pp. 225–243). Paris: La Découverte.

Alston, P. (1984). Conjuring up new human rights: A proposal for quality control. *The American Journal of International Law*, *78*(3), 607–621.

Araghi, F. A. (1995). Global depeasantization, 1945–1990. *The Sociological Quarterly*, *36*(2), 337–368.

Baxi, U. (2007). *Human rights in a posthuman world. Critical essays.* New Delhi, India: Oxford University Press.

Bellinger, N., & Fakhri, M. (2013). The intersection between food sovereignty and law. *Natural Resources & Environment*, *28*(2), 1–4.

Benford, R., & Snow, D. (1988). Ideology, frame resonance, and participant mobilization. *International Social Movements Research*, *1*, 197–217.

Benford, R. D., & Snow, D. A. (2000). Framing processes and social movements: An overview and assessment. *Annual Review of Sociology*, *26*, 611–639.

Bernstein, H. (2014). Food sovereignty via the 'peasant way': A sceptical view. *Journal of Peasant Studies*, 1–33. doi:10.1080/03066150.2013.852082

Bernstein, H., & Byres, T. J. (2001). From peasant studies to agrarian change. *Journal of Agrarian Change*, *1*(1), 1–56.

Beuchelt, T. D., & Virchow, D. (2012). Food sovereignty or the human right to adequate food: Which concept serves better as international development policy for global hunger and poverty reduction? *Agriculture and Human Values*, *29*(2), 259–273.

Bob, C. (2008). Introduction: Fighting for new rights. In Clifford Bob (Ed.), *The international struggle for new human rights* (pp. 1–13). Philadelphia: University of Pennsylvania Press.

Borras, S. (2009). Agrarian change and peasant studies: Changes, continuities and challenges. *Journal of Peasant Studies*, *36*(1), 5–31.

Buisson, M. (2013). *Conquérir la souveraineté alimentaire.* Paris: L'Harmattan.

Burnett, K., & Murphy, S. (2014). What place for international trade in food sovereignty? *Journal of Peasant Studies.* Advance online publication. doi:10.1080/03066150.2013.876995

Charvet, J., & Kaczynska-Nay, E. (2008). *The liberal project and human rights. The theory and practice of a new world order*. Cambridge: Cambridge University Press.
Claeys, P. (2012). The creation of new rights by the food sovereignty movement: The challenge of institutionalizing subversion. *Sociology, 46*(5), 844–860.
Clapp, J. (2014). Financialization, distance and global food politics. *Journal of Peasant Studies*. Advance online publication. doi:10.1080/03066150.2013.875536
Clark, P. (2013). *Food sovereignty, post-neoliberalism, campesino organizations and the state in ecuador. In food sovereignty: A critical dialogue*. Paper presented at the conference held on 14–15 September, Yale University, Yale.
Cockburn, J. (2013). *Bolivia's food sovereignty & Agrobiodiversity: Undermining the local to strengthen the state? In food sovereignty: A critical dialogue*. Paper presented at the conference held on 14–15 September, Yale University, Yale.
Cowan, J. K., Dembour, M.-B., & Wilson, R. A. (2001). *Culture and rights: Anthropological perspectives*. Cambridge: Cambridge University Press.
Desmarais, A. A. (2008a). *La Vía Campesina, une réponse paysanne à la crise alimentaire*. Montréal: Ecosociété.
Desmarais, A. A. (2008b). The power of peasants: Reflections on the meanings of La Vía Campesina. *Journal of Rural Studies, 24*, 138–149.
Donnelly, J. (1982). Human rights and human dignity: An analytic critique of non-western conceptions of human rights. *The American Political Science Review, 76*(2), 303–316.
Edelman, M. (1999). *Peasants against globalization. Rural social movements in Costa Rica*. Stanford, CA: Stanford University Press.
Edelman, M. (2013). *What is a peasant? What are peasantries? A briefing paper on issues of definition*. Prepared for the first session of the Intergovernmental Working Group on a United Nations Declaration on the Rights of Peasants and Other People Working in Rural Areas, Geneva, 15–19 July 2013.
Edelman, M. (2014). Food sovereignty: Forgotten genealogies and future regulatory challenges. *Journal of Peasant Studies*. Advance online publication. doi:10.1080/03066150.2013.876998
Edelman, M., & James, C. (2011). Peasants' rights and the UN system: Quixotic struggle? Or emancipatory idea whose time has come? *Journal of Peasant Studies, 38*(1), 81–108.
Elias, J. (2010). Transnational migration, gender, and rights: Advocacy and activism in the Malaysian context. *International Migration, 48*(6), 44–71.
Engle Merry, S. (1997). Changing rights, changing culture. In J. K. Cowan, M.-B. Dembour & R. A. Wilson (Eds.), *Culture and rights: Anthropological perspectives* (Chapter 2). New York: Cambridge University Press.
Falk, R. (1988). The rights of peoples (in particular indigenous people). In J. Crawford, (Ed.), *The rights of people* (pp. 17–38). Oxford: Clarendon.
Feyter, K. De., Parmentier, S., Timmerman, C., & Ulrich, G. (2011). *The local relevance of human rights*. Cambridge: Cambridge University Press.
Fillieule, O., Agrikoliansky, E., Sommier, I. (2010). *Penser les mouvements sociaux?: Conflits sociaux et contestations dans les sociétés contemporaines* (La Découverte, Ed.). Paris: Editions La Découverte.
Gauchet, M. (2000). Quand les droits de l'homme deviennent une politique. *Le Débat, 110*(août), 258–288.
Giunta, I. (2013). *Food sovereignty in Ecuador: The gap between the constitutionalization of the principles and their materialization in the official agri-food strategies*. Paper presented at the conference entitled 'Food Sovereignty: a Critical Dialogue' that was held on September 14–15 at Yale University, Yale.
Glendon, M. A. (1991). *Rights talk. The impoverishment of political discourse*. New York: The Free Press, Macmillan.
Godek, W. (2013). *The complexity of food sovereignty policymaking: The case of Nicaragua's law 693. In Food sovereignty: A critical dialogue*. Paper presented at the conference held on 14–15 September, Yale University, Yale.
Golay, C. (2009). *Les droits des paysans. Cahier critique n°5*. Geneva: Centre Europe Tiers-Monde (CETIM).
Golay, C. (2013). *Legal reflections on the rights of peasants and other people working in rural areas*. Briefing paper prepared for the first session of the working group on the rights of peasants and other people working in rural areas, Geneva, 15–19 July 2013.
GRAIN. (2007, October 28). What's wrong with 'rights'? *Seedling*, GRAIN.
Human Rights Council. (2012a). *Final study of the human rights council advisory committee on the advancement of the rights of peasants and other people working in rural areas (A/HR/19/75)*. Geneva: United Nations.
Human Rights Council. (2012b). *Resolution on the promotion of the human rights of peasants and other people working in rural areas (A/HRC/21/L.23)*. Geneva: United Nations.
Imig, D. R., & Tarrow, S. G. (2001). *Contentious Europeans: Protest and politics in an emerging polity*. Lanham, MD: Rowman & Littlefield.

International Council on Human Rights Policy. (2006). *Human rights standards: Learning from experience. International council on human rights policy*. Versoix, Switzerland. http://www.ichrp.org/en/projects/120

International Planning Committee for Food Sovereignty (IPC), and More and Better Campaign. (2009). *Peoples' comprehensive framework for action to eradicate hunger*. Retrieved from http://www.foodsovereignty.org/

Kneen, B. (2009). *The Tyranny of rights*. Ottawa, Canada: The Ram's Horn.

Kolben, K. (2008). Labor rights as human rights? *Virginia Journal of International Law*, *50*(2), 450–484.

Kuper, A. (2003). The return of the native. *Current Anthropology*, *44*(3), 389–402.

McAdam, D. (1990). *Freedom summer*. Oxford: Oxford University Press.

McMichael, P. (2009). A food regime genealogy. *Journal of Peasant Studies*, *36*(1), 139–169.

Nicholson, P. (2012). *Terre et liberté! A la conquête de la souveraineté alimentaire. Paul Nicholson, La Via Campesina. avec les contributions de Xavier Montagut et Javiera Rulli. Sous la direction de Julie Duchatel*. PubliCetim n°36 (English version). Geneva: Centre Europe Tiers-Monde (CETIM).

Nyéléni Food Sovereignty Forum. (2007). *Synthesis Report*. Nyéléni, Mali: Nyéléni Forum for Food Sovereignty (2007).

Nyéléni Newsletter N°16. (2013). Retrieved from www.nyeleni.org

Our World is Not for Sale. (2001). *Priority to peoples' food sovereignty. WTO out of Food and Agriculture*. Retrieved from http://www.ourworldisnotforsale.org/

Patel, R. (2007). Transgressing rights: La via campesina's call for food sovereignty. *Feminist Economics*, *13*(1), 87–116.

Pérez-Bustillo, C. (2011). *The Making and remaking of human rights: Latin American origins and development, from below*. Unpublished manuscript shared by the author.

Plummer, K. (2006). Rights Work. Constructing lesbian, gay and sexual rights in late modern times. In L. Morris (Ed.) *Rights: Sociological Perspectives* (pp. 152–167). Abingdon: Routledge.

Purwanto, H. (2013). Local to global?; How Serikat Petani Indonesia has accelerated the movement for Agrarian Reform. In *La Via Campesina's open book: Celebrating 20 years of struggle and hope*. Vía Campesina. Retrieved from www.viacampesina.org

Rajagopal, B. (2003). *International law from below: Development, social movements, and third world resistance*. Cambridge: Cambridge University Press.

Reese, E., & Newcombe, G. (2003). Income rights, mothers' rights, or workers' rights? Collective action frames, organizational ideologies, and the American welfare rights movement. *Social Problems*, *50*(2), 294–318.

Riles, A. (2006). Anthropology, human rights, and legal knowledge: Culture in the iron cage. *American Anthropologist*, *108*(1), 52–65.

Rosset, P., & Martínez-Torres, M. E. (2010). La Vía Campesina: The birth and evolution of a transnational social movement. *Journal of Peasant Studies*, *37*(1), 149–175.

Santos, B. de S. (1997). Vers Une Conception Multiculturelle Des Droits de L'homme. *Droit et Société*, *35*, 79–96.

Sardar, Z. (1998). *Postmodernism and the other the new imperialism of Western culture*. London: Pluto Press.

Sherwood, S., Arce, A., Berti, P., Borja, R., Oyarzun, P., & Bekkering, E. (2013). Tackling the new materialities: Modern food and counter-movements in Ecuador. *Food Policy*, *41*(C), 1–10.

Sieder, R. (2011). Emancipation' or 'regulation'? Law, globalization and indigenous peoples' rights in post-war Guatemala. *Economy and Society*, *40*(2), 239–265.

Stammers, N. (1995). A critique of social approaches to human rights. *Human Rights Quarterly*, *17*(3), 488–508.

Stammers, N. (1999). Social movements and the social construction of human rights. *Human Rights Quarterly*, *21*(4), 980–1008.

Stammers, N. (2009). *Human rights and social movements*. London: Pluto Press.

Valocchi, S. (1996). The emergence of the integrationist ideology in the civil rights movement. *Social Problems*, *43*(1), 116–130.

Vía Campesina. (1993). *Mons declaration of La Vía Campesina*. Retrieved from www.viacampesina.org

Vía Campesina. (1996). *Tlaxcala declaration of the Via Campesina* (Declaration of the Second International Conference of Via Campesina, Tlaxcala, Mexico). Retrieved from www.viacampesina.org

Vía Campesina. (1999, December 3). *Seattle declaration: Take WTO out of agriculture*. Retrieved from www.viacampesina.org

Vía Campesina. (2003, September 2). *Position Via Campesina Cancun*. Retrieved from www.viacampesina.org

Vía Campesina. (2004). José Bové meets Kofi Annan: Civil society raises food sovereignty issue (at the occasion of the UNCTAD meeting of 14–18 June 2004, in São Paulo). Retrieved from www.viacampesina.org

Vía Campesina. (2008a). *Declaration of rights of peasants, women and men*. Retrieved from www.viacampesina.org

Vía Campesina. (2008b). *In the 60th anniversary of the Universal declaration of human rights, we peasants demand our own convention*. Final declaration of International Conference on Peasants' Rights (Jakarta). June 25. Retrieved from www.viacampesina.org

Vía Campesina. (2008c). The global campaign on the international convention on the rights of the peasants [internal document]. Retrieved from www.viacampesina.org

Vía Campesina. (2013a, October 11). *Gaining support for the peasant's way—La Via Campesina at UN's leading food security institutions*. Retrieved from www.viacampesina.org

Vía Campesina. (2013b, November 29). *La Via Campesina will be in Bali to call for an end to the WTO and the free trade Regime*. Retrieved from www.viacampesina.org

Vía Campesina. (2013c, December 4). *Letter announcing the withdrawal of La Via Campesina from the OWINFS network*. Retrieved from www.viacampesina.org

Vía Campesina, Gerak Lawan, and Social Movements for an Alternative Asia (SMAA). (2013, December 8). *The WTO pushes through bad deal in the final hours; Developed countries and TNCs are the big winners*. Retrieved from www.viacampesina.org

Windfuhr, M., & Jonsén, J. (2005). *Food sovereignty. Towards democracy in localized Food Systems*. London: FIAN International, ITDG Publishing.

Competing Sovereignties, Contested Processes: Insights from the Venezuelan Food Sovereignty Experiment

CHRISTINA M. SCHIAVONI

International Institute of Social Studies (ISS), The Hague, The Netherlands

ABSTRACT *This article explores how 'competing sovereignties' are shaping the political construction of food sovereignty—broadly defined as 'the right of peoples to healthy and culturally appropriate food produced through ecologically sound and sustainable methods, and their right to define their own food and agriculture systems'. This study was motivated by a lack of clarity on the 'sovereignty' of food sovereignty, as noted by numerous scholars—sovereignty for whom, and how? As there is a growing consensus that there are in fact 'multiple sovereignties' of food sovereignty that cut across jurisdictions and scales, there is the question of how these sovereignties are competing with each other in the attempted construction of food sovereignty. This question is becoming ever more relevant as food sovereignty is increasingly adopted into state policy at various levels, calling for state and societal actors to redefine their terms of engagement. This article explores questions of 'competing sovereignties' by developing an analytical framework, using the lenses of scale, geography, and institutions, and applying it to Venezuela, where for the past 15 years a food sovereignty experiment has been underway in the context of a dynamic shift in state–society relations.*

Food Sovereignty at a Crossroads

A source of inspiration, perplexity, fascination, and frustration, nothing has shaken agrarian studies and related fields in recent decades quite like the concept of food sovereignty—broadly defined as 'the right of peoples to healthy and culturally appropriate food produced through ecologically sound and sustainable methods, and their right to define their own food and agriculture systems' (Nyéléni, 2007a). Nearly two decades since its emergence on the international stage through the efforts of the transnational peasant movement La Via Campesina, food sovereignty is now at a crossroads. Some of the very same movement leaders who fought for years in the streets outside of the UN Food and Agriculture Organization now find themselves on the inside through the recent reform of the UN Committee on World Food Security (Claeys, 2014; McMichael, 2014). At the national level, food sovereignty is part of the constitution and/or national legislation of at least seven countries and counting (Beauregard, 2009; Godek, 2013). At the local level, food sovereignty-inspired initiatives are increasingly making their way into local policy, such as the 'local food sovereignty ordinance' of the town of Sedgwick, Maine in the USA (Kurtz, Retberg, & Preston, 2013).

The gradual warming of state actors to food sovereignty as a policy framework is both an advance and a challenge for the food sovereignty movement, raising questions that are at once political, philosophical, and practical. Most fundamentally, it brings to the surface unresolved tensions around the 'sovereignty' of food sovereignty—sovereignty for whom, and how? This article seeks to address these tensions through exploring the question of 'competing sovereignties' in the political construction of food sovereignty, looking in particular at the dimensions of scale, geography, and institutions.

Multiple and Competing Sovereignties

Who is the sovereign of food sovereignty? Scholars have been raising this question, and movements have been grappling with it, as they seek to put food sovereignty into practice, particularly once adopted into state policy. On the one hand, food sovereignty was born out of a perceived weakening of state control over domestic food systems and a need to reclaim some of that control in the face of neoliberal policies (McMichael, 2014). On the other hand, inspired and informed by radical agrarian populism, food sovereignty has also been associated with the idea of a 'local community-led' political project independent from the state (Borras, 2010). The adoption of food sovereignty into state policy, then, calls for a redefining of the terms of engagement between state and society.

Adding to the complexity of state–society interaction in the construction of food sovereignty is the fact that the concept upon which it is built, *sovereignty*, is deemed 'a perennial source of theoretical confusion' (Bartelson, 1995, p. 12). Among the reasons behind this confusion, according to Bartelson (1995), is that sovereignty is associated with both internal and external dimensions. Externally, sovereignty can be seen as 'a reciprocal agreement among national governments giving independent states the right to pursue policy within their own territory free from external interference' (Lupel, 2009, p. 3). Conversely, 'in the context of the internal structure of a political society, the concept of sovereignty has involved the belief that there is final and absolute authority in the political community' (Hinsley, 1986, p. 158). Bartelson (1995, pp. 16–17) claims that this duality of sovereignty, in which 'the concept seems to connote two contradictory ideas simultaneously', has gone largely overlooked and helps to explain why sovereignty has been so difficult to grasp analytically.

Could the dual nature of sovereignty help to explain some of the confusion around food sovereignty, particularly the oft-cited lack of clarity around food sovereignty vis-à-vis the state (e.g. Bernstein, 2014; Edelman, 2014; Hospes, 2013)? It would seem that the external dimensions of sovereignty are far easier to grapple with conceptually than the internal dimensions when applied to food sovereignty. For instance, the idea of external sovereignty readily translates over to food sovereignty in the assertion that a country's domestic food production and distribution capacities should not be undermined by the WTO, World Bank, multinational corporations, etc. The internal dimension of sovereignty, on the other hand, is much murkier when applied to food sovereignty, at least following the traditional definition of Hinsley above. By its very definition, food sovereignty runs contrary to the idea of there being any singular, absolute authority with respect to the food system. Food sovereignty, then, entails a reconceptualizing of internal sovereignty and of sovereignty more broadly.

Some important insights on this matter have been shared by Patel (2009, p. 668):

> ... one of the most radical moments in the definition of food sovereignty is the layering of different jurisdictions over which rights can be exercised. When the call is for, variously, nations, peoples, regions, and states to craft their own agrarian policy, there is a concomitant call for spaces of sovereignty. Food sovereignty has its own geographies, one determined by specific histories and contours of resistance ... In blowing apart the notion that the state has a paramount authority, by pointing to the multivalent hierarchies of power and control that exist within the world food system, food sovereignty paradoxically displaces one sovereign, but remains silent about the others ...

In Patel's articulation, the state still figures into food sovereignty, but in a departure from traditional notions of sovereignty, the state is 'de-centered' (Litfin, 1998), making way for other actors across a variety of scales and jurisdictions. In other words, there is no singular sovereignty of food sovereignty, but 'multiple and competing sovereignties' (Patel, 2009, p. 668). McMichael notes a similar phenomenon across many of the movements countering corporate globalization:

> Instead of the single-point perspective associated with the modern state, these movements practice a multi-perspectival politics asserting the right to alternative forms of democratic organization and the securing of material well-being through *multiple sovereignties* based in cultural, environmental, and economic sustainability. (2009, p. 39, emphasis added)

As Patel (2009) points out, however, while food sovereignty makes room for other sovereign actors beyond the state, it is unclear how this can/will actually play out in practice. What is clear is that in opening up a claim to sovereignty to multiple actors with overlapping and contested jurisdictions, tensions are bound to arise. The existing definitions and frameworks for food sovereignty only complicate the matter (Patel, 2009), leaving significant gaps in current understandings of food sovereignty. There is much room for interpretation and much to be worked out in practice. For instance, how is the desire for states to assert their sovereignty over domestic food systems in the face of neoliberal policies to be reconciled with the desire for communities to assert their own sovereignty over local food systems? Can both the state and units lying within it be sovereign with respect to food at the same time? Are all communities to be equally sovereign with respect to food, rural and urban alike? What does this mean when some communities have greater food production capacities than others? These questions speak to a complex array of 'competing sovereignties' at play in the construction of food sovereignty, particularly once adopted into state policy.

The following pages will explore the question of *how 'competing sovereignties' are shaping the political construction of food sovereignty* through the three interconnected analytical lenses of scale, geography, and institutions:

- ***Scale*** can be understood as the 'spatial, temporal, quantitative, or analytical dimensions used to measure and study any phenomenon' (Cash et al., 2006, p. 8). 'Competing sovereignties' around scale can be seen, for instance, in debates over models of production (e.g. 'large-scale' vs. 'small-scale' agriculture) and in questions over the level(s) upon which food sovereignty is to be exercised, particularly when these levels may intersect and overlap (Patel, 2009).
- ***Geography*** essentially deals with questions of spatiality and 'social relations stretched over space' (Massey, 1994, p. 23), and is concerned with the processes and relationships by

which places and spaces come into being. Here it is used to look at the spatial divisions constituting 'urban' and 'rural' and the associated social, economic, political, and cultural divisions that have been constructed around this dichotomy.

- ***Institutions*** can be understood as 'both formal organizations and informal rules and procedures that structure conduct' (Thelen & Steinmo, 1992, p. 2). 'Competing sovereignties' can be seen both in interactions among different actors within institutions (Fox, 1993) and in tensions between different types of institutions as they compete for power, particularly community-based social institutions vs. institutions of the state.

Underlying each of these areas of tension are questions around the role of the state, the role of society, and the interactions between the two. To explore this issue in a way that connects theory to practice, lessons will be drawn from the case of Venezuela, where for the past 15 years a food sovereignty experiment has been underway in the context of a dynamic shift in state–society relations in the country and surrounding region.

Insights from the Venezuelan Food Sovereignty Experiment

In considering questions of 'competing sovereignties' and state–society interaction in the political construction of food sovereignty, it is instructive to look at Latin America, where the adoption of food sovereignty into state policy is among the trends associated with the region's 'left turn' that has brought a new wave of progressive governments into power in a number of countries, in response to widespread poverty and social and economic inequalities (Clark, 2013; Enriquez, 2013; Giunta, 2014; Godek, 2013; McKay, Nehring, & Walsh-Dilley, 2014; Menser, 2013; Schiavoni & Camacaro, 2009). Among these is Venezuela, which, in 1999, at the start of its process of social transformation known as the Bolivarian Revolution, became among the world's first countries—by some accounts, *the* first country (Beauregard, 2009)—to adopt a national policy of food sovereignty. Its newly reformed constitution guaranteed its citizens the right to food through a secure national food supply based on sustainable agriculture as a strategic framework for rural development (Ministerio de Comunicación e Información, 1999), to be carried out through a series of laws, institutes, and programs under the banner of 'food sovereignty'. This move could be seen as a leap of faith for a country that had largely abandoned agriculture as it built its economy around its petroleum industry from the 1930s onward (Wilpert, 2006). Indeed, successfully implementing such a policy would essentially entail a 180° turn for what was the first Latin American country to be a net importer of food and home to the one of the most urbanized populations in Latin America (Wilpert, 2006).

Efforts toward food sovereignty in Venezuela are framed here as 'the Venezuelan Food Sovereignty Experiment' for several reasons. First is the largely unprecedented and truly experimental nature of what is transpiring. As food sovereignty was in its earliest stages of articulation and development in 1999, efforts in Venezuela have evolved alongside the global movement that originally inspired them. This framing also allows for an examination of a diverse set of actors and dynamics, since there is currently a patchwork of different, at times divergent, efforts happening at various scales, some led primarily by the government, some by civil society, and most by some combination of the two. This complex package is encompassed in 'the Venezuelan Food Sovereignty Experiment'.

With this in mind, it is important to consider two main dynamics that come together to shape food sovereignty efforts in Venezuela. First is a national effort, guided by the constitution and a subsequent series of laws, to shift Venezuela from a situation of food *dependency* to one of food *sovereignty*. This involves moving away from a domestic food system characterized by historically high levels of imports and significant disparities in land and food access to one in which all citizens are guaranteed the right to food through a secure national food supply based on sustainable domestic production. The other dynamic, which has received less attention, is an attempted shift from *representative* to *participatory* democracy, in which ordinary citizens take a more active role in politics and governance. One of the main vehicles for doing so has been communal councils: local, self-organized governing bodies through which communities determine their own priorities, manage their own budgets, and interface with the government. Supported by the Communal Council Law of 2006, there are upwards of 43,000 communal councils in Venezuela today.[1]

Most recently, coming from both above and below is a major push toward the construction of *comunas*, or communes, through the joining of multiple communal councils across a shared territory. The stated goal is for power to gradually be transferred from the state to the *comunas* as they become increasingly organized. As of October 2013, there were 220 *comunas* officially registered with the government and, according to a recent national census, over 1000 more under construction (González, 2013; Rojas, 2013). By September 2014, the number of registered comunas had reached 803 (Gobierno Bolivariano de Venezuela, n.d.). The construction of the *comunas* is seen as the cornerstone of the latest stage of the Bolivarian Revolution.

In trying to make sense of the complex dynamics at play in these ambitious visions, it is helpful to draw from the influential study of Fox (1993) on food politics in Mexico in the 1980s. In assessing the factors contributing to the unexpected relatively successful outcomes of a state-supported food program, he found that they could best be explained through an *interactive approach* focused on the 'interaction between state and society, the institutions that mediate such interaction, and the factors that account for how those institutions are in turn transformed' (Fox, 1993, p. 39). Through this approach, Fox was able to uncover how certain openings from above facilitated by reformist actors within the state were met with mobilization by societal actors from below that 'shifted the boundaries of what was politically possible' (Fox, 1993). Similarly, the most interesting developments related to food sovereignty in Venezuela—and those most relevant to the question of competing sovereignties—are to be found at the intersection of state and society.

For the study informing this article, insights on the question of 'competing sovereignties' in the process of building food sovereignty in Venezuela were drawn from critical analysis of existing literature and field research conducted in the summer of 2013, building upon seven years of prior research (see Schiavoni & Camacaro, 2009). The study was carried out as an exploratory case study, as it focused on an emerging topic for which little prior empirical data existed. Individual and collective semi-structured interviews with 20 key informants were complemented by participant observation in four different states and in both urban and rural settings. The key informants were selected for their involvement in food sovereignty efforts and were thus not representative of society at large. The majority were grassroots actors involved in the construction of *comunas*, and five held government positions. Similarly, the projects examined were not intended to reflect the full breadth of food- and agriculture-related efforts in Venezuela, nor was the intent to assess the overall progress of such efforts. The aim was to gain insights into how those working toward food sovereignty are both perceiving and navigating the 'competing sovereignties' that emerge. In particular, the research sought to uncover tensions existing between state and societal actors and how those tensions were being addressed. An area of focus was the construction of *comunas* as dynamic spaces of citizen organization and main vehicles for state–society interaction in Venezuela today.[2]

Beyond Boundaries: Competing Sovereignties Across Scale

When social movement leaders from across the globe came together in Sélingué, Mali, for the Nyéléni 2007 Forum for Food Sovereignty to articulate a collective vision for a growing global movement, among the outputs were the following six pillars of food sovereignty (Nyéléni, 2007b):

I. Focuses on Food for People
II. Values Food Providers
III. Localises Food Systems
IV. Puts Food Locally
V. Builds Knowledge and Skills
VI. Works with Nature

Given the explicitly local emphasis of two out of the six pillars of this globally recognized framework, what are the implications for efforts to implement food sovereignty on a national scale? This question brings us to 'competing sovereignties' around scale.

In *Building relational food sovereignty across scales: An example from the Peruvian Andes*, Iles and Montenegro (2013) note a lack of consistency in the use of the term 'scale' in reference to food sovereignty.[3] Invoking the work of Sayre, they suggest looking at the three following dimensions of scale as related to food sovereignty: *scale as size*, *scale as level*, and *scale as relation*, with an emphasis on the last. This framework will be employed to examine tensions around scale in the Venezuelan Food Sovereignty Experiment.

Scale as Size

Iles and Montenegro (2013, p. 14) argue that 'the tendency in food sovereignty discourse has been to align scale with size (or a proxy such as capital intensity). Yet size is only one dimension of scale, and arguably the least interesting from the standpoint of food sovereignty'. Robbins (in press), on the other hand, makes the case that the size dimension of scale, when associated with capital intensity, is one of several defining features determining the extent to which a food system is oriented toward food sovereignty. That is, on one end of the spectrum, oriented away from food sovereignty, is larger scale, capital-intensive, industrial production, while on the other end, oriented toward food sovereignty, is smaller scale, less capital-intensive production.

This is quite relevant to Venezuela, where these competing ends of the spectrum are a source of great tension. Indeed, as a process of agrarian reform is making it possible to re-envision and reshape what agriculture looks like for the country (Enríquez, 2013; Schiavoni & Camacaro, 2009), there is an internal battle over the model and scale of agriculture upon which Venezuela's food sovereignty should be based. For some, there is no question that the *conuco*, a traditional form of small-scale agriculture with indigenous origins, should serve as the foundation for food sovereignty, with '*Viva el conuco!*' becoming a rallying cry for the agroecology and anti-GMO (genetically modified organisms) movements. For others, given the radical shift that Venezuela is attempting to make from heavy dependence upon imported foods to self-sufficiency through domestic production, the only path to reach this goal in the foreseeable future is via large-scale industrial agriculture. In an apparent contradiction, these competing visions are currently being supported by different state policies and programs, from credits for agroecology projects and support for biological control laboratories to the provision of large-scale agricultural machinery and chemical inputs. The general sentiment, however, is that state support is currently skewed to the latter, particularly given the central role that petroleum continues to play for the country's economy.

Scale as Level

The scale of agricultural production has implications for how the broader food system is organized, which brings us to *scale as level*. In Venezuela, those favoring larger scale agriculture similarly tend to favor larger scale, more centralized distribution systems, while those who support peasant-based agriculture advocate for more decentralized local and regional food systems. In the earlier stages of the agrarian reform process starting in 2001, an initial push for the formation of cooperatives was met with limited success. Priority was given to the granting of collective titles to newly recovered land holdings, coupled with government support for the formation of cooperatives. But while some of these cooperatives succeeded and flourished, many of them failed, for reasons including economic unviability; lack of alignment between the goals and values connected to cooperative promotion program and those of the participants; and lack of experience on the part of participants (Clark, 2010; Page, 2010). In response, the government shifted its approach to promoting Social Production Enterprises, which, as described by Clark (2010, pp. 148–150), generally 'entail more state oversight and regulation than cooperatives, though they are worker/community-controlled at the local level'. These new enterprises involve a shift in scale in that they tend to be larger and more industrial in nature than the average cooperative, and, for the most part, are geared to feed into national supply channels via the state-run Venezuelan Food Corporation (CVAL).

As *comunas* are increasingly taking on food sovereignty efforts, some are encountering tensions with the more centralized mechanisms of the state. This can be seen, for example, in the rural *comuna* El Maizal, which sells its corn to CVAL as a condition for receiving credit from the state. Some *comuna* members say they would prefer to process, distribute, and consume their own local corn. Moreover, there is the irony of periodic shortages of cornmeal in El Maizal due to ongoing issues with national distribution channels, a major challenge currently confronting the state. Angel Prado of El Maizal (23 August 2013) emphasizes that El Maizal members are committed to contribute to national food sovereignty. They simply feel that national-level, state-run efforts toward food sovereignty should support and not hinder more localized, grassroots efforts. This will involve a shift on the part of state actors:

> I think that the functionaries, more than anything, want to show numbers—numbers and results from their work. But they do not have it clear that we are headed toward a communal state with a very clear orientation in which the people organize themselves ...

A goal of El Maizal, he explains, is to shift away from supplying raw goods to CVAL by developing the internal capacity of the *comuna* to process and distribute its own locally produced food, first, among the 7000 inhabitants of the *comuna*, and then, to help supply food to other *comunas*, 'especially to urban *comunas* that do not have the same food producing capacities'. Prado adds that he does not envision the dissolution of state-run distribution networks, but a scenario in which state-run and community-run networks complement one another.

Scale as Relation

The vision described by Prado, in which food sovereignty efforts start locally and build outward, was a common theme over the course of the field research and gets to the third dimension of scale, that is, *scale as relation*. According to Iles and Montenegro (2013, p. 14), this dimension

> is much more difficult to grasp, as it requires a sharp break from conceiving organizational tiers consisting of bounded, static units. Relational scale is defined as the spatial and temporal relations among processes at different levels, as well as the processes connecting elements within levels.

This shift from conceiving of scale in terms of boundaries to conceiving of it in terms of relationships seems to describe a dynamic already underway in Venezuela, particularly in the construction of the *comunas*. For instance, none of the respondents expressed autonomous local food systems as the end goal. A recurring theme was that the local is seen as a starting point in the construction of food sovereignty, which must then extend to the regional and national scales. Among those doing locally grounded work, there was a strong sense of being connected to a broader national effort. Laura Lorenzo of the Jirajara Peasant Movement (1 August 2013) adds that the construction of food sovereignty also extends past state borders, as part of a vision of regional integration and solidarity. Ana Felicien of GMO-Free Venezuela (6 August 2013) adds yet another perspective, explaining that it is not simply about building food sovereignty outward from the local scale, but the fact that other scales, such as the national and international, condition what is possible locally.

The Geography of Competing Sovereignties: Addressing the 'Urban–Rural Divide'

A common concern among both critics and proponents of food sovereignty is how it translates over to non-agrarian contexts. That is, how relevant is food sovereignty to the broader non-farming population, particularly the more than 50% of the global population (and growing) that lives in cities? In his critique of food sovereignty from a Marxist agrarian political economy perspective, Bernstein (2014, p. 22) expresses skepticism over the capacity to feed cities through a vision of food sovereignty favoring peasant-based production and adds, 'Even supposing that an adequate surplus was possible, the second question that follows is the downstream one: how will that surplus reach non-farmers and on what terms?' While certain headway has been made in bridging the needs of urban and rural populations in efforts toward food sovereignty, much work remains to be done (Clendenning & Dressler, 2013; Robbins, in press; Schiavoni, 2009). This section will explore 'competing sovereignties' across urban and rural divides and how they are being addressed in Venezuela.

Feeding the City

With over 90% of its population living in urban areas (World Bank, n.d.), Venezuela's food sovereignty is arguably no more of a rural question than an urban one. Among the immediate challenges at the outset of the Bolivarian Revolution was to ensure the food needs of the country's predominantly urban population. Initially, this was largely carried out through a series of government 'missions' created to bypass bureaucratic infrastructure and connect directly with communities. Among the results of these early efforts are 6000 *casas de alimentación* or 'feeding houses' run through a community–government partnership that reach 900,000 of the most vulnerable Venezuelans (Mastronardi, 2013) and a national network of subsidized supermarkets to make affordable food more universally accessible. These programs and others have enabled Venezuela to surpass the first Millennium Development Goal of halving hunger in advance of 2015, as recently recognized by the FAO (2013a). According to a national census, 96.2% Venezuelans now eat 3–4 meals per day, and the government has pledged to reach the remaining 3.8%, with the goal of achieving 'Zero Hunger' by 2019 (AVN, 2013).

It should be mentioned that these developments came at a time when the media was focused on reported food shortages, presenting quite a different scenario from that recognized by the FAO. It is true that shortages of particular food (and some non-food) items are still a regular occurrence in retail outlets across Venezuela (Mallett-Outtrim, 2013). Some attribute this to government-set price regulations creating disincentives for companies to sell food products in the country. Others point to politically motivated hoarding and withholding of products intended to destabilize the government. They see it as no coincidence that the two main items most frequently missing from supermarket shelves in 2013 were corn flour and toilet paper, two household essentials, and consider this part of an 'economic war' by the members of the political opposition who own the country's largest private food companies (Robertson, 2013). The government has taken a series of measures to combat these shortages, including dialogue with the private sector, cracking down on illegal practices, and increasing imports of certain goods from neighboring countries such as Brazil.

According to many of those interviewed, the government's ability to ensure that the population's nutritional needs are met despite the shortages indicates that Venezuela has reached a certain level of food *security*, but is still far from food *sovereignty*. Gabriel Pool (6 August 2013), member of the Jirajara Peasant Movement and employee of the state-run 'Legumes of ALBA' Mixed Socialist Enterprise, explains that at the moment, levels of food imports in the country do not correspond to levels of production and that continued importation—which has decreased since the 1990s but still remains high at 50% (Mallett-Outtrim, 2013)—is above all a matter of business interests. According to Pool,

> Now that a lot of food is being produced in the countryside, we're trying to structure a proposed alliance between popular movements in the city and in the countryside, in order to cut the 'destructive distance' that lies between us.

Lorenzo shares similar sentiments: 'We know that food security is achieved through resources, but food sovereignty has to be a process coming from the bottom up—from the peasant, from the communities.'

Rethinking Territory

Lorenzo and Pool point to a new way forward—not only moving beyond what Pool calls a 'logic of importation', but also beyond a one-way flow of goods from the countryside to the city. Felicien adds that this will involve breaking down barriers that have traditionally stood between urban and rural populations, or what she calls the 'territorial division of labor'.

Felicien's point gets to a key challenge confronting not only Venezuela, but the food sovereignty movement as a whole. Just as sovereignty has traditionally been understood as authority over a given territory (dell'Agnese, 2013; Litfin, 1998), food sovereignty is often associated with collective control over the land, water, and other productive resources within a territory. While this idea might seem straightforward enough to envision, if challenging to implement, within a rural context, what does it mean for urban populations? This question connects to related discussions around shifting notions of sovereignty and territory in the face of global environmental issues that transcend geopolitical boundaries. Litfin (1998, p. 12) argues: 'If territory provides the container for state sovereignty, then transnational environmental problems and efforts to address them seem to be reshaping that container.' This reshaping of the 'container' of territory bears relevance to the global food system, through which much of the population is distanced from both food production and those who produce it (Robbins, in press). One goal of the food sovereignty movement is to lessen this distancing, but given a context such as Venezuela, in which the vast majority of the population is physically separated from the territory where most food production takes place, how is this to be done?

Building upon Litfin's point, it is helpful to examine how understandings of territory are evolving. Bryan (2012) notes that the trend by states to recognize territorial rights as part of a neoliberal agenda is leading social movements to rethink how they relate to territory. One way that they are doing so is by moving from notions of territory as 'cartographic space' to more culturally based understandings of space and territory that take on a more relational approach. These shifting understandings of territory eschew traditional exclusionary approaches in which sovereignty for one group can mean displacement of another. The focus then becomes 'less about the defense of place as a physical location per se than about maintaining a set of relationships' (Bryan, 2012, p. 222). Bryan's points are strikingly similar to those of Iles and Montenegro (2013), particularly their assertion that there are instances in which sovereignty 'needs to extend beyond spatial and temporal frame[s]' (p. 16), which would seem to apply to the food sovereignty of urban populations. Relatedly, Bryan points to urban-based movements of Indigenous people in Bolivia 'shifting attention from control over land and resources to questions of collective well-being in order to survive territorial displacement' (Mamani Ramirez 2011, cited in Bryan, 2012, p. 223). This example resonates with the Venezuelan experience, since the majority of the urban poor are those who were displaced from the countryside or their offspring.

Transforming Relationships and Identities

The fact that most urban communities in Venezuela are no more than a generation or two removed from their rural counterparts points to what are often artificial or arbitrary binaries erected between 'urban' and 'rural' and 'producers' and 'consumers' (de Haan & Zoomers, 2003; Kay, 2009; Robbins, in press). One of the ways that this is being addressed is through building and strengthening relationships across traditional urban and rural divides. This is happening not only through the creation of direct marketing channels, but through the co-construction of food sovereignty as a common political project shared by rural and urban Venezuelans. That is, people are increasingly seeing themselves as connected via the *process* of constructing food sovereignty. In this process, they are not only changing their relationships to one another, but also their *relationship to food* and to the processes of food production, distribution, and consumption. Relatedly, a term gaining in popularity is *prosumidor(a)*, a combination of the words for producer (*productor(a)*) and consumer (*consumidor(a)*), in an attempt to blur the lines between the two.

A particularly interesting urban–rural partnership involves an urban *comuna*, El Panal 2021 of Caracas, and the Jirajara Peasant Movement. El Panal already has an established sugar packing local enterprise that the Jirajara movement will begin to supply with sugar. They are also working on joint farmers markets and other distribution projects, but most interestingly, the Jirajara movement has helped El Panal acquire land in the countryside, which they will work together in partnership. According to Robert Lanza of El Panal (25 August 2013): 'We're building national points of connection between the urban and the rural that allow us to break capitalist chains of distribution and production.' The *comuna* has several other projects underway in the countryside, which include training and educational components that enable *comuna* members to (re)connect to processes of production. These efforts are complemented by a fairly extensive urban agriculture effort within El Panal, supported by government programs. Lanza explains that it is a process of ongoing learning that combines life in the city with life in the countryside.

New Institutional Frameworks for Navigating Competing Sovereignties

The question of institutions sometimes sits uncomfortably among advocates of food sovereignty, given the above-mentioned tensions between the food sovereignty movement and the state, and the perception of institutions as being static, bureaucratic, and intended to maintain the status quo. Yet as food sovereignty continues to be adopted into policy, the question of what type of institutional framework might best support it becomes increasingly relevant (Godek, 2013).

In an overview of institutionalism in comparative politics, Thelen and Steinmo (1992, pp. 16–17) describe four types of institutional dynamism. First is when new socioeconomic or political circumstances give a new sense of relevance to an existing institution. Second is when existing institutions are put to the service of different ends, as 'new actors come into play who pursue their (new) goals through existing institutions'. Third is when external changes lead to new goals being pursued by old actors within existing institutions. Fourth, in 'moments of dramatic change', is when circumstances give rise to entirely new institutions. A combination of each of these forms of institutional change is currently underway in Venezuela. The construction of *comunas* is giving rise to a new form of social institution, while existing state institutions are being mandated both to facilitate the construction of *comunas* and to support them once they exist, which, for many, would entail a radically different way of functioning. Added to these dynamics is a gradual blurring of the lines between state and societal actors, as societal actors are engaging in governance not only through the *comunas*, but increasingly through existing state institutions as well—a process not without its tensions.

Rather than having clearly delineated roles and responsibilities between the state and society, most respondents emphasized the need for ongoing, open dialogue between the two—and many looked toward the *comunas* as spaces to facilitate such dialogue and interaction. Furthermore, because they view food sovereignty as an evolving process, they recognize that what is true one week/month/year may very well not be the case the next, and therefore, it is important for institutional relationships to be flexible and dynamic. This echoes Thelen and Steinmo's (1992, p. 6) point that 'More important than the formal characteristics of either state or societal institutions per se is how a given institutional configuration shapes political interactions.' It also exemplifies Iles and Montenegro's (2013, p. 17) point about sovereignty being a relational concept: 'sovereign units are always defined in relation to something else and are always a process rather than "a state"'.

In many ways, the construction of *comunas* is a real-life example of 'multi-scalar social institutions' described by Iles and Montenegro (2013) as being key for facilitating relational food sovereignty. First, (recalling Bartelson's, 1995, point about the duality of sovereignty), it is important that those working toward food sovereignty have both internal and external recognition of their sovereignty. The very formation of a *comuna* is a demonstration of internal sovereignty in that, through joining together and organizing themselves into a *comuna*, the communal councils and communities that run them are demonstrating their intent to function as a sovereign unit. In doing so, they also lay the groundwork for external recognition of their sovereignty because *comunas* are recognized by law and state institutions have been mandated to work with and support them. A third key factor in addition to creating a base of sovereignty and building recognition of sovereignty is the creation of 'multiple, interdependent bases of sovereignty'

(Bartelson, 1995, p. 27). The *comunas* are doing this by building a national network of semi-autonomous communal bodies that interface not only with the state, but with one another.

Fourth, as Iles and Montenegro (1995, p. 19) have pointed out, sovereignty need not imply complete autonomy: 'Power sharing is implicit in this concept of relational sovereignty ... some forms of sovereignty grow out of sharing, not pure self-reliance alone.' This is highly relevant to the *comunas*, not only for the relationships that they are building with one another, but also for their relationship to the state, which is framed in terms of *corresponsabilidad*, or 'co-responsibility' (interview with Ulises Daal, 5 August 2013). First, *corresponsabilidad* is seen as necessary in the construction of the *comunas* through a massive push both from above and below. Second, once a *comuna* exists, *corresponsabilidad* describes the process through which institutions of the state must actively work to transfer power over to the *comuna*, while members of the *comuna* organize themselves to be able to assume new responsibilities. In this sense, *corresponsabilidad* is seen as a means of bridging the formation of popular power and the existence (and gradual redistribution) of established state power.

Of course, tensions abound. According to Felicien, although certain transformations have been made, the underlying structures of the state remain bourgeois in character, and as long as that remains the case, 'We have to be clear that constituted power (of the state) and constituent power (of the people) are going to be in permanent conflict with one another.' This connects to what Enríquez (2013) has described as a situation of 'dual power' characterized by competing tendencies within the Venezuelan state, some newer and more revolutionary, and others connected to the power structures of the past. This dual power often manifests itself in contradictory and clashing approaches toward food and agriculture coming from state institutions, as with the simultaneous support for agroecology and industrial agriculture.

Still to be addressed are the other types of institutional dynamism described above, involving changes to existing institutions. As mentioned earlier, parallel to the construction of the *comunas* is a reform of state institutions, which are being mandated to work directly in partnership with *comunas*. On the one hand, this is an example of old actors taking on new roles. At the same time, through this reform, new actors are also coming into existing institutions, including social movement leaders like Laura Lorenzo, who works for a state enterprise that lends machinery to farmers.

The transformation of institutions through the incorporation of new actors, however, is not simply a matter of 'grassroots engagement' or 'bringing everyone to the table', but instead about a fundamental transformation of the institutions from within. According to Ulises Daal, former member of and current advisor to the Venezuelan National Assembly, this is reflected in a new institutional framework of the state referred to as *nueva institucionalidad*. Daal emphasizes, however, that as long as the Bolivarian Revolution continues, there will be a permanent confrontation between traditional power structures and new emerging structures, and this confrontation will produce both contradictions and polarization. This connects back to the points of Felicien and Enríquez (2013) above, as well as to a statement by Fray Silvera of the Tres Rs Cooperative in the state of Yaracuy (16 August 2013), in an apparent paraphrasing of Gramsci, that 'the old has not yet finished dying and the new has not yet finished being born'.

'Competing Sovereignties' and Beyond

The case of Venezuela demonstrates that some of the same theoretical stumbling blocks of food sovereignty in academia also pose practical challenges for those attempting to implement it. At the same time, these challenges are indeed being navigated on the ground, to various degrees of success, and there is much to be learned from this process. Perhaps among the key takeaways is that, as food sovereignty is a dynamic process, the institutions facilitating it must be equally dynamic, and in Venezuela, this is being attempted through approaches such as *corresponsabilidad* and *nueva institucionalidad.* Similarly, constructing food sovereignty is less about building silos (literally and figuratively) and more about building relationships—for example, across scales, between the urban–rural divide, and among state and societal actors.

A burning question that remains, looking at Venezuela, is the extent to which newly emerging grassroots-led food sovereignty efforts and already existing food security efforts will coexist, clash, or complement one another. It is important to recall that Venezuela's hunger rates were drastically reduced through a major effort on the part of the state (in partnership with communities), through an approach that arguably fits most within the paradigm of food security, particularly for its reliance on imports and centralized mechanisms of the state. At the same time, some of the most cutting-edge efforts at this moment, including those being piloted by the *comunas*, are squarely within the paradigm of food sovereignty. A question moving forward, recalling the experience of the *comuna* El Maizal, is what possibilities there are for these two paradigms to come together. This question extends beyond Venezuela, particularly given the recent commitment of heads of state to work for 'Zero Hunger' for all of Latin America and the Caribbean (FAO, 2013b), while social movements in the region are also getting increasingly organized and forging new alliances in pursuit of food sovereignty.

Acknowledgements

Many thanks to Jun Borras, Annie Shattuck, Zoe VanGelder, and three anonymous reviewers for their feedback; Mary McGee for her editing; William Camacaro for his research support and collaboration; and the many others who made this project possible.

Disclosure Statement

No potential conflict of interest was reported by the author.

Notes

1 Ulises Daal (personal communication, August 5, 2013).
2 Further details on the methodology of this study are available in Schiavoni (2014).
3 See also Iles and Montenegro de Wit (2014).

References

AVN. (2013). Gobierno Nacional Mantiene Meta de Desnutrición Cero Para 2019. Retrieved October 17, 2013, from http://www.avn.info.ve/contenido/presidente-maduro-aspira-lograr-meta-desnutrici%C3%B3n-cero-2019

Bartelson, J. (1995). *A genealogy of sovereignty*. Cambridge: Cambridge University Press.

Beauregard, S. (2009). *Food policy for people: Incorporating food sovereignty principles into state governance* (Senior comprehensive report). Los Angeles, CA: Urban and Environmental Policy Institute, Occidental College.

Bernstein, H. (2014). Food sovereignty via the 'peasant way': A skeptical view. *Journal of Peasant Studies*, *41*(6), 1031–1063.

Borras, S. (2010). The politics of transnational agrarian movements. *Development and Change*, *41*(5), 771–803.

Bryan, J. (2012). Rethinking territory: Social justice and neoliberalism in Latin America's territorial turn. *Geography Compass*, *6*(4), 215–226.

Cash, D., Adger, W., Berkes, F., Garden, P., Lebel, L., Olsson, P., ... Young, O. (2006). Scale and cross-scale dynamics: Governance and information in multilevel world. *Ecology and Society, 11*(2), 8–19.
Claeys, P. (2014). Food sovereignty and the recognition of new rights for peasants at the UN: A critical overview of La Via Campesina's rights claims over the last 20 years. *Globalizations*. Advanced online publication. doi:10.1080/14747731.2014.957929
Clark, P. (2010). Sowing the oil: The Chavez government's policy framework for an alternative food system. *Humboldt Journal of Social Relations, 33*(1), 135–165.
Clark, P. (2013, September 14–15). *Food sovereignty, post-neoliberalism, Campesino Organizations, and the state in Ecuador*. Paper presented at Food Sovereignty: A Critical Dialogue, Yale, CT.
Clendenning, J., & Dressler, W. (2013, September 14–15). *Between empty lots and open pots: Understanding the rise of urban food movements in USA*. Paper presented at Food sovereignty: A critical dialogue, Yale, CT.
dell'Agnese, E. (2013). The political challenge of relational territory. In D. Featherstone & J. Painter (Eds.), *Spatial politics: Essays for Doreen Massey* (pp. 115–124). Oxford, UK: Wiley-Blackwell.
Edelman, M. (2014). Food sovereignty: Forgotten genealogies and future regulatory challenges. *Journal of Peasant Studies, 41*(6), 959–978.
Enríquez, L. (2013). The paradoxes of Latin America's 'Pink Tide': Venezuela and the project of agrarian reform. *Journal of Peasant Studies, 40*(4), 611–638.
FAO. (2013a). 38 countries meet anti-hunger target for 2015. Retrieved October 17, 2013, from http://www.fao.org/news/story/en/item/177728/
FAO. (2013b). FAO en CELAC: ¿podemos ser la primera generación de latinoamericanos y caribeños en vivir sin hambre? Retrieved September 7, 2014, from http://www.fao.org/americas/noticias/ver/en/c/230191/
Fox, J. (1993). *The Politics of food in Mexico: State power and social mobilization*. New York, NY: Cornell University Press.
Giunta, I. (2014). Food sovereignty in Ecuador: Peasant struggles and the challenge of institutionalization. *Journal of Peasant Studies, 41*(6), 1201–1224.
Gobierno Bolivariano de Venezuela. (n.d.). Ultimas Comunas Registradas. Retrieved September 2, 2014, from http://www.mpcomunas.gob.ve/
Godek, W. (2013, September 14–15). *The complexity of food sovereignty policymaking: The case of Nicaragua's Law 693*. Paper presented at Food sovereignty: A critical dialogue, Yale, CT.
González, N. (2013). Comunas Registradas Ascienden a 220 en Todo el País. Retrieved October 31, 2013, from http://www.mpcomunas.gob.ve/comunas-registradas-ascienden-a-220-en-todo-el-pais/
de Haan, L., & Zoomers, A. (2003). Development geography at the crossroads of livelihood and globalisation. *The Royal Dutch Geographical Society KNAG, 94*(3), 350–362.
Hinsley, F. (1986). *Sovereignty*. Cambridge: Cambridge University Press.
Hospes, O. (2013). *Food sovereignty: The debate, the deadlock, and a suggested detour*. Wageningen: Wageningen University. Retrieved September 24, 2013, from http://link.springer.com/article/10.1007/s10460-013-9449-3/fulltext.html
Iles, A., & Montenegro, M. (2013, September 14–15). *Building relational food sovereignty across scales: An example from the Peruvian Andes*. Paper presented at Food sovereignty: A critical dialogue, Yale, CT.
Iles, A., & Montenegro de Wit, M. (2014). Sovereignty at what scale? An inquiry into multiple dimensions of food sovereignty. *Globalizations*. Advanced online publication. doi:10.1080/14747731.2014.957587
Kay, C. (2009). Development strategies and rural development: Exploring synergies, eradicating poverties. *Journal of Peasant Studies, 36*(1), 103–137.
Kurtz, H., Retberg, H., & Preston, B. (2013, September 14–15). *Scaling biopolitics: Enacting food sovereignty in Maine (USA)*. Paper presented at Food sovereignty: A critical dialogue, Yale, CT.
Litfin, K. (1998). The greening of sovereignty: An introduction. In K. Litfin (Ed.), *The greening of sovereignty in world politics* (pp. 1–27). Cambridge, MA: MIT Press.
Lupel, A. (2009). *Globalization and popular sovereignty: Democracy's transnational dilemma*. London: Routledge.
Mallett-Outtrim, R. (2013). Scarcity and starvation? Venezuelan food FAQs. Retrieved October 4, 2013, from http://venezuelanalysis.com/analysis/10071
Massey, D. (1994). *Space, place and gender*. Minneapolis: University of Minnesota Press.
Mastronardi, N. (2013). Gobierno Nacional refaccionará 111 Casas de Alimentación en Caracas. Retrieved October 31, 2013, from http://www.correodelorinoco.gob.ve/nacionales/gobierno-nacional-refaccionara-111-casas-alimentacion-caracas/
McKay, B., Nehring, R., & Walsh-Dilley, M. (2014). The 'state' of food sovereignty in Latin America: Political projects and alternative pathways in Venezuela, Ecuador and Bolivia. *Journal of Peasant Studies, 41*(6), 1175–1200.

McMichael, P. (2009). Global citizenship and multiple sovereignties: Reconstituting modernity. In Y. Atasoy (Ed.), *Hegemonic transitions, the state and crisis in neoliberal capitalism* (pp. 23–42). New York, NY: Routledge.
McMichael, P. (2014). Historicizing food sovereignty. *Journal of Peasant Studies, 41*(6), 933–957.
McMichael, P. (2014). The land question in the food sovereignty project. *Globalizations*. Advanced online publication. doi:10.1080/14747731.2014.971615
Menser, M. (2013). The territory of self-determination: Social reproduction, agroecology, and the role of the state. In M. J. Massicotte, P. Andrée, J. Ayres, & M. Bosnia (Eds.), *Globalization and food sovereignty: Global and local change in the new politics of food* (pp. 53–83). Toronto: University of Toronto Press.
Ministerio de Comunicación e Información. (1999). Constitution of the Bolivarian Republic of Venezuela. Retrieved March 13, 2013, from http://venezuela-us.org/live/wp-content/uploads/2009/08/constitucioningles.pdf
Nyéléni. (2007a). Declaration of Nyéléni. Retrieved March 16, 2013, from http://www.nyeleni.org/spip.php?article290
Nyéléni. (2007b). Synthesis report of Nyéléni 2007 forum for food sovereignty. Retrieved March 13, 2013, from http://www.nyeleni.org/IMG/pdf/31Mar2007NyeleniSynthesisReport-en.pdf
Page, T. (2010). Can state create *Campesinos*? A comparative analysis of the Venezuelan and Cuban repeasantization programmes. *Journal of Agrarian Change, 10*(2), 251–272.
Patel, R. (2009). Food sovereignty. *Journal of Peasant Studies, 36*(3), 663–706.
Robbins, M. (in press). Food sovereignty: Understanding the 'localization' dimension. *Third World Quarterly*.
Robertson, E. (2013). Venezuelan government announces 'massive' food imports to combat shortages. Retrieved July 29, 2013, from http://venezuelanalysis.com/news/10122
Rojas, M. (2013). Ya se Pueden Conocer los Resultados del Censo Comunal 2013 por Estados. Retrieved September 22, 2013, from http://www.mpcomunas.gob.ve/conoce-los-resultados-del-censo-comunal-2013-desglosados-por-estados/
Schiavoni, C. (2009). The global struggle for food sovereignty: From Nyéléni to New York. *Journal of Peasant Studies, 36*(3), 682–689.
Schiavoni, C. (2014). *Competing sovereignties, contested processes: The politics of food sovereignty construction* (ISS Working Paper No.583). The Hague: International Institute of Social Studies.
Schiavoni, C., & Camacaro, W. (2009). The Venezuelan effort to build a new food and agriculture system. *The Monthly Review, 1*(3), 129–141.
Thelen, K., & Steinmo, S. (1992). Historical institutionalism in comparative politics. In S. Steinmo, K. Thelen, & F. Longstreth (Eds.), *Structuring politics: Historical institutionalism in comparative analysis* (pp. 1–32). New York, NY: Cambridge University Press.
Wilpert, G. (2006). Land for people not for profit in Venezuela. In P. Rosset, R. Patel, & M. Courville (Eds.), *Promised land* (pp. 249–264). New York, NY: Food First Books.
World Bank. (n.d.). *Rural population (% of total population)*. Retrieved November 8, 2013, from http://databank.worldbank.org/data/views/reports/tableview.aspx#

Sovereignty at What Scale? An Inquiry into Multiple Dimensions of Food Sovereignty

ALASTAIR ILES & MAYWA MONTENEGRO DE WIT

University of California at Berkeley, Berkeley, CA, USA

ABSTRACT *Food sovereignty has struggled to make inroads into changing the structures and processes underlying the corporate food regime. One reason is that scale is still underspecified in the politics, strategies, and theories of food sovereignty. We suggest that much can be learned from examining the multiple dimensions of scale inherent in ongoing food sovereignty struggles. A gap exists between these* in vivo *experiments and the maturing academic theory of scale. The concept of 'sovereignty' can be opened up to reveal that movements, peoples, and communities, for example, are creating multiple sovereignties and are exercising sovereignty in more relational ways. Relational scale can aid movements and scholars to map and evaluate how spatial and temporal processes at and among various levels work to reinforce dominant agri-food systems but could also be reconfigured to support progressive alternatives. Finally, we apply relational scale to suggest practical strategies for realizing food sovereignty, using examples from the Potato Park in the Peruvian Andes.*

1. Introduction

Food sovereignty has emerged as an idea and practice that could transform current agri-food systems to far more democratic, decentralized, and ecologically sustainable forms. Many movements worldwide are creating or reviving alternatives, from food policy councils in the USA to *campesino-a-campesino* networks in Central America, to seed sharing coalitions in India. Nonetheless, food sovereignty[1] has struggled to make deep inroads into changing the structures and processes underlying the corporate food regime (CFR).[2]

Scholars and activists have offered various explanations. For example, Hospes (2014) argues that international institutions such as FAO and the WTO remain impervious to the principles of food sovereignty. Though several countries such as Ecuador and Bolivia have adopted food sovereignty policies and constitutional provisions, their implementation remains fragmentary. Analysts such as Patel (2009) and McMichael (2009b) find entrenched capitalist power structures favoring the CFR frequently thwart official state level recognition. In contrast, others attribute the weakness of food sovereignty to the conceptually vague nature of 'sovereignty' (e.g. Agarwal, 2014; Claeys, 2012; Edelman, 2014; Hospes, 2014). These critics commonly use La Via Campesina's evolving definition of sovereignty—changing markedly from 1996 to the present—to argue inherent inconsistency even though this can also reflect diverse approaches depending on context (Patel, 2009). Moreover, they suggest, there appear to be fundamental contradictions between food sovereignty's solidarity vision and individual farmer rights. How to respond to these challenges has incited a similarly polarized conversation: some want to re-formulate food sovereignty in terms that are more palatable to powerful elites, while others call for oppositional strategies against dominant institutions. Still others seek greater juridical definitional rigor.

A thread running throughout these debates, though seldom explicitly interrogated, is that of scale. Both academics and activists, we suggest, use, invoke, and depend upon scale in conceptualizing food sovereignty and agri-food systems more broadly. Yet they are still wrestling with a precise conceptualization of scale (both physically and metaphorically) in their politics, strategies, and theorizing. For example, localized food systems are often opposed to the CFR but the scale in question may be ambiguous. What does 'local' mean, how is it bounded, and by whom?[3] Should the small be the primary scale at which production occurs? Does the grassroots contain or connect to other levels as well?

What appears to have gone awry is a two-part dilemma: first is scant appreciation of the multiple dimensions of scale inherent in many food sovereignty experiments already underway around the world. Some movements, peoples, and communities employ a more malleable, 'relational' ontology of food sovereignty in their work to unseat dominant institutions. Second is a gap between developments on the ground and maturing academic theory on scale. Particularly amongst human geographers and political ecologists, relational scale has emerged as a more dialectical way of thinking about space, time, measurement, and process for any given phenomenon.

We suggest that exploring the concept of relational scale could pluck food sovereignty efforts off the horns of this dilemma. By reminding us all that sovereignty is not an extraneously existing object but is a *living process*, it foregrounds the conscientious building and maintaining of relationships between people, institutions, technologies, ecosystems, and landscapes across multiple scales. It provokes more attention to the how of systemic change than to the what. To date, food sovereignty scholars and movements have tended to assume that scale is a matter of size or level, which organize and bind familiar parts of agri-food systems: level often refers to the institutional levels of government and markets (e.g. local and national), while size means spatial or organizational reach (e.g. small farms and multi-national corporations). In contrast, relational scale encompasses the spatial, temporal, epistemic, and social infrastructure connections among processes within and across different levels. Relational scale can be conceptualized as networks of elements and processes in a complex adaptive system. Such systems exhibit the hallmark features of complexity, including threshold effects, emergent properties, and network-dependent cascades across the system that put it into a different state, potentially undermining dominant power structures.

This process of contingent sovereignty is illustrated in the Parque de la Papa (or Potato Park). This alliance of indigenous farmer communities in the Peruvian Andes aspires to protect its seed sovereignty and agrobiodiversity through maintaining its traditional farming landscape—but has discovered that it needs to make strategic alliances with scientific research centers, government agencies, and global treaty negotiations at levels ranging from the municipality of Cusco to the United Nations. It has also articulated a concept of biocultural heritage that is at once congruent with Quechua cosmovisions and readily suited to use in political debates, institutional procedures, and across these levels. As a result, the Potato Park has begun exercising sovereignty over its local agricultural terrain but reinforces this power by enlisting the sovereign powers of various other actors and institutions; the latter help legitimate the park through 'recognition' and can provide critical resources such as support for traditional markets and livelihoods. As its networks expand, the Park is being recognized more and more readily as a sovereign actor.

Considering relational scale, however, leads to a questioning of the ontology of sovereignty itself. Relational scale, we suggest, resonates with the concept of multiple sovereignties that are now emerging in contemporary societies around the world (McMichael, 2009a; Patel, 2009; Schiavoni, this issue). According to McMichael (2014), La Via Campesina initially invoked 'sovereignty' as a trope; it was a cognitive and political maneuver to reclaim state-centered, national sovereignty from the WTO and the global markets in the face of increasing free trade and deregulation. But food sovereignty is now metamorphosing into something more ontologically fertile than nationalist choreography. For example, some movements are recreating sovereignty as non-state-based and grounded in new instantiations of territorial and communal relationships, such as the Brazilian MST movement's efforts to foster agrarian citizenship through empowering peasant farmers to practice agroecology (Wittman, 2009). The concept of multiple sovereignties sees the growth of many actors, communities, and institutions wielding or seeking sovereign power over things such as seeds, knowledge, and farming practices; parts of food systems; and their cultural and territorial worlds. Equally important, in this view, sovereignty becomes a malleable and 'negotiable' power[4] which particular movements, peoples, or communities can seize, create, oppose, or reshape as against the state, cities, corporations, and other sovereign actors.

We propose that food sovereignty involves (1) creating and sustaining these multiple sovereignties and (2) turning sovereignty itself into a relational form and a process. In this paper, we explore how these developments are intertwined, beginning with a review of how sovereignty has developed over the past few centuries. We then define relational scale and discuss how this can provide analytical optics that analysts can use to understand and act on the multiple dimensions of scale. Finally, we apply relational scale to suggest some practical strategies for realizing food sovereignty, using examples from the Potato Park.

2. The Legacy of Sovereignty

It is critical to interrogate what precisely movements and scholars are doing when they call on one of the most hallowed artifacts of political theory and practice: sovereignty. We begin by revisiting the concept of sovereignty. Sovereignty appears to naturally occur as an immutable part of the political system. Yet, sovereignty is remarkably ambiguous for the conceptual weight it is asked to support. The modern concept of sovereignty is still only 350 years old, having coalesced during the Westphalia era as nations began to demarcate their borders more clearly, and solidifying as national governments acquired new political and economic functions during the industrial revolution period. Sovereignty is now closely identified with the modern state as a form of political organization. According to Hinsley (1986), the state is sovereign because it monopolizes the use of coercive power, controls fixed territory, and can make and enforce laws governing the behavior and lives of the peoples that live within its territory.

Sovereignty therefore has a heavily spatial and juridical character: in principle, nation-states have undivided, supreme legal authority within their territory (Bartelson, 1995).

In most conventional accounts of the emergence of sovereignty, there is a linear progression toward a 'stripped down' sovereignty concentrated in a nation-state that is increasingly bureaucratic, dependent on legal and taxation mechanisms, and supported by military forces. Over three centuries from the 1600s onwards, states 'consolidated control over their territories and then defined social, cultural, economic, and security structures to be coincidental with territorial boundaries' (Ilgen, 2003a). Alternative forms of political organization became much less plausible. Several bases for state-centered sovereignty have developed, ranging from the notion that peoples are making a social contract to form a state, to the argument that states are sovereign in representing the political community of their peoples. Nonetheless, a difficult tension exists between sovereign power and individual freedom, which the framework of participatory democracy is meant to help resolve in some countries (Bartelson, 1995). The assumption underlying these bases is that enabling sovereignty calls for the surrender of power and autonomy to whatever entity is regarded as sovereign. The sovereign itself is then autonomous, largely free from the demands of others, and able to exclude others from participating in its affairs.

This composition of sovereignty contrasts with what has been described as 'medieval sovereignty'. Ilgen (2003a) explains that prior to the 1600s, sovereignty took a far more multi-layered, overlapping, and multi-directional form in the many city-states, republics, regions, and confederations of West Europe. Crucially, sovereigns existed *in relation to each other*: even though a hierarchy existed, each level was obliged to perform its responsibilities toward lower and higher levels while also having power to rule over lower levels. Sovereigns thus often needed to negotiate with one other, while following customary and religious conventions, and relying on shared social institutions to help manage conflicts. This Euro-centric account, of course, ignores the great variety of political systems across the planet, such as pre-Incan societies in the Andes, the Native American confederations, or the clan-based societies of West Africa. These systems reveal that sovereignty can manifest more diverse and interdependent forms than its modern conception.

Taking this historical perspective, we can appreciate that sovereignty is a social construction that can be challenged and remade, especially during moments of political turbulence. Sovereignty is filled with tensions that need to be negotiated repeatedly over time and space. Even in existing government systems that are ostensibly stable, whether federal or unitary, negotiations abound as a condition of workability. Camilleri (1990) notes usefully that 'sovereignty is not a fact but rather an expression of a claim about the way that political power is or should be exercised'. Over the past 40 years, a conjunction of developments has made national boundaries increasingly permeable. A familiar roll-call includes the historically unprecedented magnitude and pace of economic and technological exchanges, emboldened multi-national corporations trading with each other, the growing realization that environmental problems transgress borders, and the rise of unconventional wars that challenge centralized military forces (Camilleri, 1990; Ilgen, 2003a). Nation-states have been forced not only to acknowledge that they must share sovereignty with other states, international institutions, global civil society movements, and the workings of a capitalist global economy—but that multiple sovereignties are present within their territories and societies.

Two developments within this larger context are of particular relevance to food sovereignty movements. First, sovereignty is no longer simply juridical and territorial. Sovereignty is also being expressed in forms that political scientists have long described as 'soft power'. Second, as nation-states have become more porous, experimentation with institutional arrangements has increased, particularly in Europe, Latin America, and Asia.

In reviving non-territorial definitions, economic sovereignty or power has led the way, as sub-national regions and cities around the planet seek to integrate themselves into a global economy. Conversely, national governments, whether industrial or developing, are struggling to defend their ability to regulate their economies as banks and companies swiftly move their capital and manufacturing from place to place, creating their own sovereign power. Indeed, corporations arguably have pioneered the practices of multiple sovereignties through their accelerating intra-firm trade, influence over many national legislatures, and supply networks.[5] In many cases, it has been businesses that have invented key components of agri-food systems, such as industrial-scale abattoirs or standardized grain exchanges.

Ilgen (2003a) defines sovereignty as the capacity to make binding decisions and to oversee their implementation. We would add that sovereignty includes the capacity to act authoritatively (or asserting agency); the ability to influence political and economic processes; and the rights to participate and to be consulted. That is, sovereignty may not be felt in the 'bindingness' of decisions, but be exerted through the active reshaping of cognitive, political, and economic arrangements. Taking broader courses of action and the creation of new interpretative conventions may be as important as making specific decisions. Moreover, we argue that sovereignty can take the form of influence or control over a wide variety of social and ecological goods. These may encompass cultural heritage, scientific and traditional knowledge, technologies, environmental resources such as water, biomass, minerals, and energy, and genetic resources such as seeds. While economic sovereignty is more familiar, especially in the dominant economistic frames prevailing in current political systems, these sovereignties also matter and are being asserted by many social movements, indigenous peoples, and localities. It is clear that sovereignty does not have to follow territorial boundaries but can follow flows of energy, genes, knowledge, materials, and peoples.

In turn, regarding the emergence of institutional experimentation, Fosler (2006) notes that, over the past 25 years, there have been many attempts to adapt existing institutions to new flows of capital and political power. Some national governments and the European Union have devolved some authority to lower institutional levels, adopting the principle of subsidiarity (or the idea that decision-making should be matched more carefully to the appropriate scale). Sullivan (2003) argues that in the area of water sovereignty, local and regional governance regimes are taking on greater significance compared to national governments. In turn, Ilgen (2003b) investigates the emergence of some smaller cities in the USA as sites of development as city governments pursue financial investments and technology transfers from the global level. These authorities are often much more cognizant of their local features than more remote government units, which may also be ponderous and ineffectual in their capability to govern. In Europe, Asia, and Latin America, there is a nascent turn toward regional networks that can cross national borders, following geographical, ecological, and cultural commonalities. Even though institutional arrangements and jurisdictions in general remain durable and entrenched, there are many efforts underway to loosen these.

Sovereignty, then, has a highly spatial-*temporal* character. It is not static or immutable but is historically contingent and dependent on the practices of humans and their institutions. Far from being a linear progression toward a specific state-centric form, sovereignty is better understood as co-evolving with changing societal actors, political processes, and ecological and economic conditions. The scope and characteristics of sovereignty will vary over time and space: sometimes it will be centralized and sometimes decentralized; it can be more or less durable.

Importantly, if sovereignty is socially constructed, there is a politics of making sovereignty. Sovereignty is something that is 'negotiable'—capable of being built, re-shaped, and fought over—rather than prescribed by institutional writ or frozen in a political community ideal. What sovereignty means and what it empowers actors to do are not fully known in advance or reducible to constitutions. As a result, sovereignty is growing more multi-dimensional again, extending far beyond the traditional state-centric model.

3. Integrating Scale into Sovereignty

Patel (2009) argues:

> In blowing apart the notion that the state has a paramount authority, by pointing to the multivalent hierarchies of power and control that exist within the world agri-food system, food sovereignty paradoxically displaces one sovereign but remains silent about the others. (p. 668)

That is, while movements seek to depose the traditional sense of sovereignty, they have not yet figured out how to share, combine, or connect the array of sovereignties that exist at multiple scales within and beyond the umbrella of current food sovereignty movements. Relational scale may offer guidance in this regard, enabling advocates to follow the flows, locations, and processes of sovereign power.

Of utmost importance to fields ranging from ecology to human geography, mathematics to agronomy, scale has recently been defined as 'the spatial, temporal, quantitative, or analytical dimensions used to measure and study any phenomenon' (Cash et al., 2006). Cash et al. (2006) suggest that multiple types of scales co-exist—including temporal, spatial, jurisdictional, and knowledge scales—and that it is possible to trace 'cross-scale interactions' within nested systems. However, this definition of scale focuses solely on the *epistemology* of scale measurement and observation; it does not consider the ontological aspect of scale, insofar as levels of organization and scalar processes exist in the material world. It therefore leaves aside the notion that epistemological and ontological 'moments' of scale (cf. Sayre) can influence one another. It also assumes a fixed hierarchy of levels—a rigidity that may not actually exist, or may not be necessary for organizing a system. Despite the fact that conceptions of scale range across a spectrum of 'intimidating diversity' (Sheppard & McMaster, 2008, p. 256), we believe that food sovereignty demands a more careful interrogation of the meaning of scale—both in and for sovereignty. A good place to begin, we suggest, is Sayre's (2005, 2009) delineation of scale's three components: size, level, and relation.

Scale as size is the most familiar: it is the carving up of space and time into standardized units of measure—length, volume, velocity, and size, to take common examples. Scale as level refers to organizational groupings such as organism, population, species, and community (in biological systems) or household, village, nation-state, and world (in social systems). Sayre considers both the ways in which elements in nature and society are themselves organized (an ontological view) and how humans group elements together for the purposes of observation (an epistemological view). Scientists tend to classify phenomena into levels based on the scales at which they can be observed and measured. Scale-as-relation is more difficult to grasp, as it requires a sharp break from conceiving organizational tiers consisting of bounded, static units. Relational scale is the spatial and temporal relationship among processes at different levels, as well as the processes connecting elements between levels.

The idea of process is central to relational scale, namely tracing processes at and across levels, and understanding how they are helping configure and constrain food production. Relational scale also suggests that 'the whole is greater than the sum of its parts'. Complexity theory has shown that behaviors that exist among units at one level, when combined at the next level up, may display patterns of self-organization and properties that cannot be observed in the behavior at the original level (Sayre, 2009). Similarly, for three decades, political ecologists have explored how economic, ecological, biological, climate, and political processes can work at local levels but are mediated or caused by institutions, markets, and policies found at other levels and at some spatial and temporal distance (Robbins, 2012). Blaikie and Brookfield (1987), for example, originated the practice of following 'chains of explanation' from immediate local phenomena to national and global level developments.

Thus, relational scale can support valuable analytical optics that scholars and movements can apply to better engage with the multiple dimensions of scale. These optics, moreover, suggest how thinking relationally, in both diagnostic and interventionist modes, enables advocates to better tackle the CFR.

In diagnostic mode, relational scale helps us in the following ways:

3.1. *Understand Why Capitalist Agriculture Processes Are Difficult to Target*

A fundamental question that academics and activists aligned with the food sovereignty movement is wrestling with how to counter the substantial power of capitalist agriculture in shaping agri-food systems. Some analysts have developed a cogent analysis of power and political economy in the food system; this structural critique is among their greatest strengths (e.g. Holt Giménez & Shattuck, 2011; Wittman, Desmarais, & Wiebe, 2010). Others call for localized, decentralized, and smaller-sized food processes in opposition to anomic 'globalized' capitalism and to centralized state authority. Nonetheless, many analysts may not have recognized enough that the CFR is also territorial and local, or that capital is both thing and process (Harvey, 2014). The regime is embedded in countless local places, from supermarkets, contract farms, and processing factories, to trading floors and hedge fund offices. It may depend on flows of abstract and fictitious things (e.g. money, futures, debt obligations) but it also contains material flows such as farmworkers, vegetables, fertilizer, and water. Moreover, the regime contains many friction-generating points of transitions between capital as thing (like physical infrastructure or trucks) and capital as process (like money or work). It takes substantial labor to make such transitions and to turn production into capital: farms and factories must be built and run, workers found, minerals or biomass extracted, and products sold. Many barriers must be surmounted; yet, Harvey (2014) suggests, 'The continuity of the flow is a primary condition of capital's existence. Capital must circulate continuously or die' (p. 73). Capital seeks to accelerate biological, material, and economic processes as a result.

In this light, the CFR is constituted through local/global dynamics, may be located at or across various sectors and levels of the political economy, and has certain needs. Movements need therefore to be ready to collaborate with—and as importantly, to resist—actors and processes at compatible scales. One cannot adopt a fixed, small-scale approach to confront such a flexible, 'many-headed beast' as capitalist agriculture. Indeed, capitalism is potent in part because agri-food companies and investors now function as self-anointed sovereigns, freely re-configuring their production and capital worldwide to seize lower cost and labor advantages, or engaging in accumulation by dispossession. Over the past 35 years, agri-food capital has worked to re-frame what 'the state' can legitimately do and to define private enterprise as more efficient providers of societal goods. Nonetheless, movements can move beyond dividing between local and global, find ways to disrupt the transitions of capital between thing and process, target the CFR's roots, and find local crises to amplify to slow down capital's velocity.

3.2. *Appreciate How Path Dependency Can Work to Inhibit Systemic Change*

Path dependency is a fundamental but ill-understood feature of the CFR. In seeking alternative production systems, movements often encounter what appear to be immutable and entrenched pathways that food systems must follow. For example, many CFR actors claim that the only feasible way to feed the planet is to further industrialize production, use GM crops, and rely on pro-poor strategies to integrate smallholders into global markets. We have already seen that capital creates a larger context for agriculture. Within this, various technological, economic, institutional, and behavioral 'lock-ins' may exist (De Schutter, 2014), encouraging farmers, traders, eaters, legislators, and companies to believe that more diverse pathways are not possible. Change may appear implausible because so many processes need adjusting, or are thought too fundamental to a system's functioning to be tampered with. Such lock-ins include technological and infrastructure systems that favor industrial producers; government policies subsidizing commodity crops and cheap processed foods; and consumer preferences for year-round availability of perfect foods.

What is often not appreciated is that path dependency is constituted relationally: a 'feasible' path is the result of multiple processes working together at and across levels. This is less perceptible if we focus on a specific level or size. Looking relationally, how processes reinforce each other becomes more obvious. GM crops are an example: scientific research and corporate plans develop the technology, regulators approve it, food companies require its use through contract farming, and it becomes difficult to segregate GM from non-GM crops. As more farmers are forced to adopt GM crops, a critical mass emerges, where farming norms are reset to a GM baseline, processing technologies are adapted, pesticides are used even more intensely, and consumers are conditioned to expect GMOs in their food supply. In effect, a GM crop culture emerges. These processes of creating path dependency are often creeping but suddenly solidify into a structural constraint. Crops bred for agroecology now initially require much more effort to contemplate, develop, and introduce compared to GM crops. It is this shifting balance of 'activating energy' that is central to whether or not path dependency materializes. Scholars and movements, then, need to think critically about linking processes together in ways that can create alternative pathways by decreasing this activating energy, or by by-passing or loosening existing lock-ins.

3.3. *Map Relationships Across Time, Space, Epistemic Communities, etc. in Terms of Multiple Sovereignties*

Movements and scholars can map where and how multiple sovereignties are developing in their arenas, as well as at other levels that may affect their work. What relationships can they build with those who influence the ecological, political, and economic processes that they are interested in? Where does their sovereignty come from, and does it depend on conventional or other bases of sovereignty? Is their sovereignty likely to be interdependent with those of other actors? Are there, in fact, multiple sovereignties already existing, or do they need to be nurtured?

For example, movements may not realize that their power depends on being recognized as authoritative sovereign units both *internally*—by the peoples of their intended local territory—and *externally*, by institutions and publics at higher (or lower) levels. They may presume it is self-evident that they should have sovereign status because they represent a people or a territory or an alternative food system. Yet, food sovereignty movements—in common with other social movements—may struggle to gain external acknowledgement, precisely because they do not fit easily into dominant institutional and constitutional structures. For example, there are few or no institutional procedures that food sovereignty movements can call on to broker settlements of conflicts. Indeed, movements may run into entrenched conflicts, where the institutional architecture forces them into not only struggles against government agencies but also into complying with standardized analytics such as cost–benefit analysis just to participate in government processes.

These struggles for recognition notwithstanding, social movements that lack legal status are increasingly acknowledged as exerting practical power through organizing their own programs. This 'practical sovereignty' offers a potential inroad, as over time, movements may win legitimacy from powerful institutional actors and publics, thus legitimating their existence and work. Sovereignty is not something that simply exists: it has to be built up, recognized, and maintained over time and space. Thus how the authority of a sovereign unit is created is central to its emergence and success.

Relational scale also allows us to evaluate the differences that exist within and between 'alternative' food systems, rather than presuming that solutions are homogenous. Far from acting as benign agents to democratize a concentrated and centralized system, multiple sovereignties can create many inequalities in their own right. Localism, for example, has received much constructive criticism from authors who point to the potential for 'the local' to play into neoliberal governance strategies (Guthman, 2007) and to reinforce racism, sexism, xenophobia, and other forms of inequality historically embedded in locales (e.g. DuPuis & Goodman, 2005; Hinrichs, 2000). Yet if there is no guarantee of justice or equity in the local, movements must develop ways to provide the higher level oversight and monitoring (e.g. anti-discrimination rules) needed to diminish local power abuses. The state remains central to the governance of agri-food systems and economies more broadly, and movements can work with and through its authority.

In the interventionist mode, relational scale can help us.

3.4. *Mobilize Power, Resources, and Knowledge Across Scales, as Expressions of Sovereignty*

Relational scale can aid analysts in thinking more creatively about how sovereignty is being exercised at and across levels. What does sovereignty mean, and what forms does it take? How can sovereignty exert an effect on actors and levels that are seemingly 'distant' geographically, culturally, or politically? What conditions are needed for making sovereignty more 'negotiable' (rather than fixed and immutable)? Instead of limiting sovereignty to conventional power resources (such as institutional, military, and juridical) and to specific territories or arenas, movements can appraise how they might wield new kinds of power reaching across levels into processes that can support their efforts.

A particularly intriguing form of sovereignty is epistemic. Often, food sovereignty movements desire to affirm knowledge that Scott (1998) calls *metis*—that is, grounded in local and lay knowledge, experiential data, indigenous or farmer practice, and other forms of situated knowing. These movements draw boundaries against the Western positivist knowledge that has already gained power and traction within existing institutions (e.g. Jasanoff, 1999)—such knowledge is commonly seen as technical, juridical, and scientific in character, and as exclusionary of metis. Because of this epistemic rift, sovereignty movements may struggle to influence powerful institutions, which either do not recognize, or do not validate alternative knowledge. Yet knowledge politics—if understood in relational terms—are more multivalent and scalar. Local knowledge does not need to be geographically bounded: any knowledge can be 'local' to wherever it is produced and used. Similarly, technical knowledge does not need to be generated and imposed from the top-down: it can also be produced in 'grassroots' and local settings, to the advantage of food sovereignty movements. The ways in which different forms of knowledge shuttle between local and global ambitions deserve far more scrutiny. Movements can extend the parameters of knowledge to include other forms of data and reasoning, and can develop concepts, norms, and practices that are taken up into discourses and institutions at other levels, influencing their cognitive processes and knowledge. Yet explicit discussion of the politics of making and using knowledge is frequently absent from movements and academic work.

3.5. *Create and Work Through Rooted Networks as Influential Actors in Agri-Food Systems*

Relational scale is especially relevant to explaining why networks are influential in changing parts of agri-food systems. In recent years, much research in network theory has grappled with multi-scalar dynamics (e.g. Barabasi, 2002). A network can comprise a set of peoples, institutions, technologies, geographical locations, or ecological functions being interconnected through nodes and ties of varying strengths.[6] Networks can be effective because they are 'a specific flexible, dynamic, and self-organized manifestation of much deeper and wider webs of relations', both cultural and natural (Rocheleau, 2011). Rocheleau speaks of 'rooting strategies', in which actors in a network can create connections to places and territories, but also of network-building strategies in which these actors reach out to new nodes. She shows that in the Dominican Republic, a rural development federation consciously 'link[ed] with myriad other actors in the organizational landscape (as allies, in solidarity, as clients, or in bargaining mode)'. The federation was, then, able to persuade government agencies to provide public services and missing infrastructure in its rooted locations. Its power came from its roots but was reinforced by sovereign power from elsewhere.

These networks are potentially capable of by-passing institutions, points of lock-ins, and re-distributing power, knowledge, and resources through much 'faster', non-hierarchical processes across many levels than established political and epistemic institutions may allow. They can enable plucking off actors from inside dominant institutions to become collaborators and allies. They can also operate as processes of rescaling, from particular sizes or levels to larger or smaller ones. Sayre notes: 'It is precisely by rescaling processes that networks have the potential to bypass or subvert conventional hierarchies of power' (2009, p. 105). We have already witnessed this in the CFR: firms and governments have increasingly understood how to build networks that differ markedly from traditional Fordist production and political structures. As a consequence, they have helped rapidly diffuse a neoliberal economic ideology and undermined previously powerful welfare or nationalist states.

Sovereignty is often seen in terms of 'how to grow food', 'who we will obtain food from', or 'what foods we will eat'. Yet sovereignty also pertains to the ability to *connect together* technologies, knowledge, peoples, and institutions into networks that can leverage sovereign power much more. That is, networks do not just comprise people but material things/flows and shared cognition. In the case of social learning, as Holt-Giménez (2006) has shown, the *Campesino-a-Campesino* movement comprises many networks of farmers and small-scale farms that are linked together in larger scale networks of sharing agro-ecological learning and practice. Each unit is small in size and scale of food production, but the broader network effectively rescales the production of knowledge and technological innovations across farms and territories, thus creating new sovereignty over farming methods and crops. Such rescaling can help create social infrastructure, new commons, and collective actions that are authentic alternatives to the CFR.

3.6. *Work Toward Nonlinear Change Rather than Simply Gradual or Incremental Change*

Relational scale emphasizes that agri-food systems are complex adaptive systems, in which changes may take nonlinear and non-hierarchical forms. The creation of feedback loops, for example, means that changes at one level can re-configure processes and elements at other levels, in turn driving further changes at the initial level. Further, such feedbacks may not be limited to levels 'above' and 'below'. Of particular importance for food sovereignty, we suggest, is the implications of nonlinear behaviors for theories—and strategies—of transition and change. A key feature of complex adaptive systems is their ability to self-organize along a number of different pathways with possible sudden shifts between relatively stable states. A freshwater lake, for example, may be stable in a state full of oxygen and diverse life, or in an algae-dominated, de-oxygenated one. Conventionally, we have tended to view the transition between such states as gradual. But there is increasing evidence that systems seldom respond to perturbations in a smooth way: The clear lake seems hardly affected by fertilizer runoff until nutrient loading reaches a critical threshold at which the water goes turbid. Driven by biofuel production and financial speculation, booms and busts in food prices often exhibit similar nonlinear effects, creating dire material consequences for farmers and eaters worldwide (e.g. Lagi, Bar-Yam, Bertrand, & Bar-Yam, 2011).

Finally, like economies and ecologies, social movements can themselves be seen as complex adaptive systems. Movements may be working and working, and not 'seeing' observable change because they are focused on only their part of the food system (whereas the broader system, seen relationally, may be in flux). It may take a certain buildup of pressures, influences, and resources over time until there is a sudden shift to a different stable state. The same could hold true for a buildup of smaller movements coming together across space to reach a critical threshold. Described by Simon Levin as 'made up of lots of individual agents that act together in smaller scales' (Phelan, 2009), such systems can settle into a number of stable equilibria (opening up potential for regime shifts), and can also propagate ideas and information virally depending upon how actors are linked together. As Levin puts it, contagion behavior depends on the topology of network interactions.

Using these optics, scholars and movements can develop practical strategies to foster food sovereignty.

4. Developing Multi-Scalar Sovereignty in Practice

Scholars and movements can work to integrate relational scale into food sovereignty and engage more effectively with the multiple dimensions of scale, rather than idealizing a particular sense, such as the local, the small farm, or the peasant collective. We have suggested that food sovereignty entails (1) creating and sustaining these multiple sovereignties and (2) turning sovereignty itself into a relational form and a process. Finding institutional, epistemic, economic, and ecological processes to bridge across multiple scales can enable movements to gain greater traction in changing food systems. These processes work, in part, by turning sovereignty into something that is 'negotiable' and whose terms can be challenged and remade; allowing the growth of multiple sovereignties within and beyond established institutional structures; and building new networks and relationships to foster greater interdependence rather than stressing autonomy. We examine two brief examples; further work is needed to identify and explicate more such processes.

The first process is the creation of *multiple bases of sovereignty* that exist alongside state-centric sovereignty. The conventional ontology of sovereignty is founded on the state's exclusive control over territory, ability to govern its people, and monopoly over coercive force. This authority is grounded in the state's political representation of its people or in the people's consent to the state having power over them. Yet this basis reflects a 'stripped down' understanding of what (or whom) sovereignty comes from. It is the result of mass acquiescence over 300 years to the processes of solidifying modern states around more rigid hierarchies of levels and sizes compared to the heterogeneous, complex, and irreducible cultures they govern (Scott, 1998). In addition to state simplifications, it is also the production of scale through the definitions and measures through which states have come to define their relations with their peoples. Sovereignty, then, appears non-negotiable beyond the limited room that institutional arrangements may permit to manage inevitable frictions. To expose sovereignty as ontology—not natural phenomenon—movements can create more diverse bases of sovereignty.

We suggest that the ontology of sovereignty can expand to reflect a greater 'medieval' character adapted to contemporary conditions (Camelleri, 1990). That is, sovereignty is more interdependent than autonomous, more emergent through how peoples and communities decide to collaborate than prescribed in advance. Power sharing (not appropriation) is implicit in this concept of sovereignty. Importantly, movements may find that they can only become sovereigns by networking with others to support their respective sovereignties. This move is already seen in countless sovereignty-seeking movements, from La Via Campesina's global network, to Native American tribes, to worker cooperatives in Spain. Going a significant step further, sovereignty could also be grounded, for instance, in ecological relationships and the stewardship of socio-ecological processes (e.g. Wittman, 2009). Socio-ecological systems emerge from the processes through which humans and natural systems co-evolve. Movements can claim biocultural sovereignty through managing and sustaining these interdependent relations. Efforts to support biocultural sovereignty are currently isolated; yet as more and more such efforts gain support, they may also connect to one another and achieve synergies, and suddenly change the norms of sovereignty. Though difficult to predict, there may be emergent properties, in which these movements become more than the sum of their parts. The very meaning of sovereignty may tip toward more fluid, interconnected forms, and create new space for alternative social arrangements.

Both kinds of broadening sovereignty can be seen in what a consortium of potato farmers in the Potato Park is accomplishing near Cusco in the Peruvian Andes. In 1998, six indigenous communities began creating a community-based conservation area called Parque de la Papa, or Potato Park. Over 4000 villagers jointly manage their agrobiodiversity and traditional knowledge according to indigenous philosophies of equilibrium, dualism, and reciprocity (Argumedo & The Potato Park Communities, 2011). Instead of adopting a hierarchical sovereignty, the Potato Park villages have revived their traditional pre-Incan *ayllu* system, which they understand as a socio-ecological cosmovision that integrates biological and cultural spheres of three types: domesticated plants and animals; wild animals, plants, and crop relatives; and the community of the sacred. The biocultural *ayllu*, moreover, provides customary norms for sharing land and labor 'ownership'. Based on a model that combines this customary law and Peruvian state law, the villages in 2010 negotiated an intercommunity agreement for Park governance and sharing the benefits of their agrobiodiversity resources (including potatoes, medicinal herbs, and other knowledge based-resources). As such, the Potato Park is not simply struggling against established institutional architecture; it is also insisting that its traditional sovereignty prevail alongside government authority as part of a longer term process of negotiating sovereignty. In turn, the Potato Park has helped develop the concept of indigenous biocultural heritage areas that legally acknowledge the role and power of indigenous communities as managers of complex biocultural systems (Argumedo & The Potato Park Communities, 2011; Argumedo & Wong, 2010). Invoking their knowledge and ability to manage Andean vertical farming processes, the villagers and their NGO supporters have worked to promote 'biocultural heritage' as part of ongoing biodiversity negotiations at the global level (such as the Convention on Biological Diversity) and vis-à-vis Peruvian authorities.

The second process supporting rescaling is seeking *recognition as a sovereign*. Traditionally, a state's sovereignty comes in part from having its authority recognized by its own population and by other states. Yet, a people, community, collective, or organization can also be recognized by both their constituents and outsiders as having and exerting sovereignty. Here, recognition does not simply have its juridical meaning: something is recognized as sovereign because of its practical authority over territory, a supply chain, a pool of germplasm, and so on. Recognition also includes political and existential affirmation that the sovereign is worthy of acceptance as such. Schlosberg (2004) argues that the importance of recognition in helping create or perpetuate environmental injustices is largely overlooked. The lack of recognition of a people's identity (e.g. as an indigenous community entitled to control its own culture and land) in governmental policies or public discourse can result in weakening their status in a society. Conversely, providing recognition can enable people not only to resist this marginalization but to strengthen their sense of identity. As Schlosberg says, 'The call for justice, in this instance, is a call for recognition and preservation of diverse cultures, identities, economies, and ways of knowing' (Schlosberg, 2004). In Brazil, for example, agricultural laborers insist that they be recognized as legitimate farmers and holders of land they have seized, rather than as landless peoples without rights (Wittman, 2009).

In most situations where actors are claiming food sovereignty, they are not recognized as being sovereign by governments, corporations, or societies. Individual farmers, a rural landless movement, a farmer peer-to-peer learning network, or a cooperative business are not seen as 'sovereign' in terms of state-centric sovereignty. Lack of recognition may hamper greatly their efforts to create and propagate alternatives in agri-food systems. It may limit the ongoing emergence of multiple sovereignties across these systems, and can demoralize people over time as they realize that they are not taken seriously by powerful institutions.

Yet movements can seek recognition from their own peoples, and from powerful government and corporate actors as well as publics at other scales. Recognition can happen though many mechanisms and processes, as seen in the Potato Park's experience. Remarkably, the Potato Park appears to be navigating the hostile Peruvian state with an assemblage of mechanisms that effectively 'bypass' the national level for now (Argumedo & The Potato Park Communities, 2011; Argumedo & Wong, 2010). Since 2004, the villagers have forged partnerships with organizations such as the London-based International Institute for Environment and Development and with the United Nations University headquartered in Japan. The park is also accepted as a participant in the Nagoya biodiversity protocol negotiations to define how benefits from genetic resources may be shared more fairly. At the sub-national level, the park has successfully built a relationship with the Cusco government, resulting in a ban on transgenic crops and an anti-piracy law at regional level. Indeed, the park is enhancing Cusco Province's authority within an increasingly restive Peruvian nation-state by bringing new global prestige to the area. Many of these acts of recognition stemmed from a dramatic development in 2004, when the park made an unprecedented agreement with the Lima-based International Center for the Potato to repatriate hundreds of potato varieties back to the villagers (Indians in Peru Regain Potato Rights, 2005). By entering the authority hub of the CGIAR's global agricultural science research network, the park gained new legitimacy for regional and national policymakers as well as potential donors and collaborators. These developments illustrate that the most socially robust forms of recognition are relational: recognition of a movement does not simply occur at a particular level but emerges through how multiple acts cumulatively take place at multiple levels. Moreover, increasing recognition can mean that a certain threshold is reached, or a particularly important node in the network recognizes the movement, thus suddenly creating much greater legitimacy in a nonlinear way.

5. Conclusions

For multiple sovereignties to flourish and help create far more egalitarian agri-food systems, movements and academics can take a relational scale view of the processes and objectives/goals for which they are striving. Thus far, they have had an oddly impoverished vocabulary for making institutional changes. Yet, as seen in Schiavoni's (this issue) discussion of the emergence of *comunas* in Venezuela, some movements are developing a number of 'mediating' multi-scalar institutions/networks. These often urban-based communal councils are 'local, self-organized governing bodies through which communities determine their own priorities, manage their own budgets, and interface with the government'. While *comunas* have diverse goals and projects, many are beginning to organize their local food production and distribution, and to collaborate with other *comunas*, and crucially, to link to rural producers. Understood in terms of relational scale, food sovereignty becomes as much a practice of creating connectivity as of creating autonomy.

Relational scale can also help movements and the many people struggling for substantive change in agri-food systems to better understand the dynamics they confront. At the heart of capitalist agriculture is a potent scalar force: ideologies and practices geared toward ever larger scales of economy. These mono-dimensional scales of production and consumption economy demand compound growth and deny the value of rootedness in places, communities, and socio-ecological realities. The example of GM crops suggests just how quickly and relentlessly capitalist pressures can 'tilt' human practices and technological systems toward particular pathways, creating apparent lock-ins that deter experimentation with alternatives. Instead of scales of economy, we can pursue multi-dimensional scales of sufficiency (cf. Princen, 2005) that are far more matched to rooted places and communities. Movements can work toward lowering the activating energy needed to engender more egalitarian and diverse agri-food alternatives to emerge—with this work depending fundamentally on many levels, sizes and relationships. Progress toward achieving sovereignty, in the end, must bind the epistemic and the ontological in order to both create and perceive how 'another world is possible'.

Notes

1 Many definitions exist. A commonly cited one is the 2007 Nyleni Declaration definition crafted by diverse social movements, including the transnational peasant movement La Via Campesina (LVC), as 'the right of peoples to

healthy and culturally appropriate food produced through ecologically sound and sustainable methods, and their right to define their own food and agriculture systems' (Nyleni, 2007 cited in Wittman et al., 2010).

2 The contours of the corporate food regime are sprawling and complex. Summarizing McMichael's extensive work, Fairbairn (2010) explains that the CFR aims at 'removal of social and political barriers to free flows of capital in food and agriculture and is institutionalized through international agreements such as the WTO's Agreement on Agriculture.' For Southern agricultural production, she offers, this regime portends 'increasing focus on export-driven agriculture, increasing dependence of farmers on transnational agrifood corporations for their means of production, and the ongoing dispossession and displacement of peasant populations and their cultures of provision'.

3 As Robbins (in press) points out, localization as an approach needs to be critically interrogated. Local food systems are not a uniform category and need to be differentiated from each other. They contain tremendous diversity in their com position, cultures, production and consumption practices, justice, and sustainability.

4 By 'negotiable', we do not mean that movements and communities are undertaking negotiations or compromising with powerful agri-food actors such as Cargill or FAO to make agreements. We mean that the concept of sovereignty is 'up for grabs'.

5 It is important to realize that multiple sovereignties are not limited to civil society, government, or community actors: they may feature businesses and financial networks. The nature of multiple sovereignties may neither be benign nor malevolent in itself: much depends on the power relations and politics of specific sovereign actors. Fostering multiple sovereignties alone is not necessarily conducive to greater democracy. Indeed, neoliberal economics and policies have encouraged the selective devolution of state functions to private authority over the past 30 years. The broader philosophical and political context of multiple sovereignties matters greatly.

6 As many activists and scholars have emphasized, food sovereignty movements frequently take a network form, building relations between diverse actors at and between local, regional, and national levels (e.g., Desmarais & Wittman, 2014). This work, however, may not adequately integrate sovereignty over technology, resources, knowledge, distribution, or infrastructure.

References

Agarwal, B. (2014). Food sovereignty, food security and democratic choice: Critical contradictions, difficult conciliations. *Journal of Peasant Studies* (ahead-of-print), 1–22. doi:10.1080/03066150.2013.876996

Argumedo, A., & The Potato Park Communities. (2011). *Community biocultural protocols: Building mechanisms for access and benefit-sharing among the communities of the Potato Park based on Quechua norms.* London: International Institute for Environment and Development.

Argumedo, A., & Wong, B. (2010). Satoyama inititive: The Ayllu System of the Potato Park, Cusco, Peru. United Nations University Institute of Advance Studies. Retrieved from http://satoyama-initiative.org/en/case-studies/americas/agriculture/ayllu-system

Barabasi, A. L. (2002). *Linked: How everything is connected to everything else and what it means.* New York: Plume Editors.

Bartelson, J. (1995). *A genealogy of sovereignty.* Cambridge: Cambridge University Press.

Blaikie, P., & Brookfield, H. (1987). *Land degradation and society.* Methuen: London.

Camilleri, J. A. (1990). Rethinking sovereignty in a shrinking, fragmented world. In R. B. J. Walker & S. H. Mendlovitz (Eds.), *Contending sovereignties: Redefining political community* (pp. 13–44). Boulder, CO: L. Rienner.

Cash, D. W., Adger, W. N., Berkes, F., Garden, P., Lebel, L., Olsson, P., . . . Young, O. (2006). Scale and cross-scale dynamics: Governance and information in a multilevel world. *Ecology and Society, 11*(2), 8–19.

Claeys, P. (2012). The creation of new rights by the food sovereignty movement: The challenge of institutionalizing subversion. *Sociology, 46*(5), 844–860.

De Schutter, O. (2014). *Report of the special Rapporteur on the right to food. Final report: The transformative potential of the right to food.* Retrieved March 19, 2014, from http://www.srfood.org/en/final-report-to-un-human-rights-council

Desmarais, A. A., & Wittman, H. (2014). Farmers, foodies and First Nations: Getting to food sovereignty in Canada. *Journal of Peasant Studies* (ahead-of-print), 1–21. doi:10.1080/03066150.2013.876623

DuPuis, E. M., & Goodman, D. (2005). Should we go 'home' to eat?: Toward a reflexive politics of localism. *Journal of Rural Studies, 21*(3), 359–371.

Edelman, M. (2014). Food sovereignty: Forgotten genealogies and future regulatory challenges. *Journal of Peasant Studies*, 1–20. doi:10.1080/03066150.2013.876998

Fairbairn, M. (2010). Framing resistance: international food regimes and the roots of food sovereignty. In H. Wittman, A. Desmarais, & N. Wiebe (Eds.), *Food sovereignty: Reconnecting food, nature & community* (pp. 15–32). Fernwood: Halifax.
Fosler, R. S. (2006). Human governance and the state: The global challenge to sovereignty. In D. J. Eaton (Ed.), *The end of sovereignty? A transatlantic perspective* (pp. 13–96). Münster: Verlag.
Guthman, J. (2007). The Polanyian way? Voluntary food labels as neoliberal governance. *Antipode*, *39*(3), 456–478.
Harvey, D. (2014). *Seventeen contradictions and the end of capitalism*. Oxford: Oxford University Press.
Hinrichs, C. C. (2000). Embeddedness and local food systems: Notes on two types of direct agricultural market. *Journal of Rural Studies*, *16*(3), 295–303.
Hinsley, F. (1986). *Sovereignty*. Cambridge: Cambridge University Press.
Holt-Giménez, E. (2006). *Campesino a campesino: Voices from Latin America's farmer to farmer movement for sustainable agriculture*. Oakland, CA: Food First Books.
Holt Giménez, E., & Shattuck, A. (2011). Food crises, food regimes and food movements: Rumblings of reform or tides of transformation? *The Journal of Peasant Studies*, *38*(1), 109–144.
Hospes, O. (2014). Food sovereignty: the debate, the deadlock, and a suggested detour. *Agriculture and Human Values*, *31*(1), 119–130.
Ilgen, T. L. (2003a). Recognfigured sovereignty in the age of globalization. In T. L. Ilgen (Ed.), *Reconfigured sovereignty: Multi-layered governance in the global age* (pp. 6–35). Aldershot: Ashgate.
Ilgen, T. L. (2003b). Ontario: Tiger of the Inland empire. In T. L. Ilgen (Ed.), *Reconfigured sovereignty: Multi-layered governance in the global age* (pp. 168–184). Aldershot: Ashgate.
Indians in Peru Regain Potato Rights. (2005). *NewScientist*, January 22. Retrieved from http://www.newscientist.com/article/mg18524833.500-indians-in-peru-regain-potato-rights.html
Jasanoff, S. (1999). The songlines of risk. *Environmental Values*, *8*, 135–152.
Lagi, M., Bar-Yam, Y., Bertrand, K. Z., & Bar-Yam, Y. (2011). The food crises: A quantitative model of food prices including speculators and ethanol conversion. Retrieved March 19, 2014, from http://arxiv.org/pdf/1109.4859.pdf&embedded=true
McMichael, P. (2009a). Global citizenship and multiple sovereignties: Reconstituting modernity. In Y. Atasoy (Ed.), *Hegemonic transitions, the state and crisis in neoliberal capitalism* (pp. 23–42). New York, NY: Routledge.
McMichael, P. (2009b). A food regime genealogy. *Journal of Peasant Studies*, *36*(1), 139–169.
McMichael, P. (2014). Historicizing food sovereignty. *Journal of Peasant Studies* (ahead-of-print), 1–25. doi:10.1080/03066150.2013.876999
Nyéléni. (2007). *Declaration of Nyéléni*. Retrieved March 19, 2014, from http://www.nyeleni.org/spip.php?article290
Patel, R. (2009). Food sovereignty. *Journal of Peasant Studies*, *36*, 663–706.
Phelan, B. (2009). The ecology of finance. *Seed Magazine*. Retrieved March 19, 2014, from http://seedmagazine.com/content/article/ecology_of_finance/
Princen, T. (2005). *The logic of sufficiency* (Vol. 30). Cambridge, MA: MIT Press.
Robbins, M. (in press). Food sovereignty: Understanding the 'localization' dimension. *Third World Quarterly*.
Robbins, P. (2012). *Political ecology: A critical introduction*. Malden, MA: John Wiley & Sons.
Rocheleau, D. (2011). Rooted networks, webs of relation and the power of situated science: Bringing the models back down to earth in Zambrana. In M. Goldman, M. Nadasdy, & M. Turner (Eds.), *Knowing nature: Conversations at the intersection of political ecology and science studies* (pp. 209–226). Chicago: University of Chicago Press.
Sayre, N. F. (2005). Ecological and geographical scale: Parallels and potential for integration. *Progress in Human Geography*, *29*(3), 276–290.
Sayre, N. F. (2009). Scale. In N. Castree, D. Demeritt, D. Liverman, & B. Rhoads (Eds.), *A companion to environmental geography* (pp. 95–108). London: John Wiley & Sons.
Schlosberg, D. (2004). Reconceiving environmental justice: Global movements and political theories. *Environmental Politics*, *13*(3), 517–540.
Scott, J. C. (1998). *Seeing like a state: How certain schemes to improve the human condition have failed*. New Haven: Yale University Press.
Sheppard, E., & McMaster, R. B. (Eds.). (2008). *Scale and geographic inquiry: Nature, society, and method*. Malden, MA: Wiley.
Sullivan, J. (2003). Water and sovereignty: Wales and Southern California. In T. L. Ilgen (Ed.), *Reconfigured sovereignty: Multi-layered governance in the global age* (pp. 185–207). Aldershot: Ashgate.
Wittman, H. (2009). Reworking the metabolic rift: La Via Campesina, agrarian citizenship, and food sovereignty. *The Journal of Peasant Studies*, *36*(4), 805–826.
Wittman, H., Desmarais, A., & Wiebe, N. (Ed.). (2010). *Food sovereignty: Reconnecting food, nature & community*. Halifax: Fernwood.

Food Sovereignty in Everyday Life: Toward a People-centered Approach to Food Systems

MELEIZA FIGUEROA

University of California, Berkeley, Berkeley, CA, USA

ABSTRACT *This paper proposes a theoretical approach that de-centers 'food' in food-related research, placing social life as the point of departure for a critical analysis of food systems and the search for alternatives. Using a relational conception of food as a nexus of multiple, intersecting social-historical processes, a 'people-centered' approach illuminates the social elements that can inform resonant and locally inflected strategies for food sovereignty, particularly for urban communities in the USA. Building on theoretical concepts of primitive accumulation, articulation, and everyday life, as well as empirical work with the Chicago-based Healthy Food Hub, this paper explores the relationship between everyday food practices and historical processes of proletarianization as they are produced, reproduced, and contested at multiple conjunctures. In these spaces of contestation, the capacity for diverse communities to re-articulate social relations through everyday food practices could provide a potentially powerful pathway not just to food sovereignty, but an alternative to life under capitalism.*

Introduction: The Social Lives of Food Systems

> The sons and daughters of what used to be here in Pembroke—the largest black farming community north of the Mason Dixon line—came here and did not want to know how to farm. They did not want to know anything to do with dealing with the land ... we kept meeting this experience of people being in a lot of pain with the earth. And so we literally buried the pain here ... not only did we put the pain back into the earth, we also picked up our power, of our relationship with the earth. We have strawberries for love and forgiveness, and calendula for wound healing ... fellows came from Uganda and Kenya, and they shared in it ... maybe we can begin to do a global process

> where we'll release our colonialization and our suffering, and regain our power again. (Dr. Jifunza Wright, co-founder, Healthy Food Hub)

In recent years, the terms 'sustainable food', 'food justice', and 'food sovereignty' have entered common parlance in the academic and popular political discourse. The 'perfect storm' of converging economic, ecological, and agrarian crises has affected communities the world over, from peasants in the Global South to poor families in the decaying urban cores of the post-industrial United States. Protests against various aspects of the global capitalist 'food regime' (McMichael, 2005) have animated some of the most high-profile social movements in recent memory.

Many of these movements, as well as the bodies of critical scholarship that inform them, have eloquently demonstrated the failings of the prevailing food system and their relationship to broader socio-economic injustices. Articulating practical alternatives to the system, especially ones that can encompass the varied and seemingly disparate struggles of affected communities, has been less clear. In other words, we know quite well what food justice, food sovereignty, and sustainable food systems are not; what they are, and what transitions to more just and sustainable systems could look like is far more complex and difficult to define in practice.

This paper attempts to look with a fresh perspective at the multifaceted nature of crises in the global food system, aiming to formulate new strategies to address the environmental, social, and political aspects of the broader crisis of which problems in the food system are an integral part. While critical food scholarship and discourses within food movements have mostly concentrated on the 'food' in food systems—the technical, political economic, and social developments that surround food, as the saying goes, from the field to the dining table—this paper proposes a theoretical approach that de-centers 'food' as the focus of study. Instead, it emphasizes everyday practice and social life as the central point of departure for a critical analysis of the industrial capitalist food system and the search for alternatives. Centrally, this article is concerned with ways of addressing the challenges and prospects for food sovereignty in a US-based context (and a Global North context more generally), and how a 'people-centered' approach can speak to the particular concerns surrounding food sovereignty in the USA, especially in urban-based communities.

Underlying the many difficulties in adapting food sovereignty to a North American and urban context is the fact that this concept emerged from peasant-based struggles and rural movements in the Global South. The central demands of food sovereignty—autonomy, access to land and means of production, and preservation of 'traditional' agrarian foodways and farming systems—are easily understood and expressed in arenas where there are clear referents for comparison: spaces of peasant production, traditional social formations, and moral economies that warrant defense against the encroachment of capitalist social relations and the industrialization of agriculture. But what does it mean to preserve 'traditional' ways of life, or 'peasant spaces', in a situation where people are far removed from any kind of referents for what these mean in practice, and where they may not have any immediate knowledge, experience, or even desire to engage with them? In a global metropolis, the diversity of experiences that exist within even a limited local context can imply very different meanings of food sovereignty for various communities.

The seeming incongruity of the US experience vis-à-vis that of the Global South also brings up the question of how US-based movements for food sovereignty can build international connections and solidarity across disparate cultures, as well as with social justice movements within the US concerned with labor, racial and gender inequities, housing, and other pressing socio-economic issues. In the absence of the kinds of concrete referents that inform peasant movements, imaginaries associated with sustainable food systems are often presented as abstract and utopian 'visions', based on an affective connection with land and nature. The assumed universality of these imaginaries—especially as commodified in the ethics and esthetics of food consumption—could help to explain some of the failures of US food movements to connect and resonate with communities that are struggling with more immanent social problems.

In shifting the theoretical lens from 'food' to the social formations and historical trajectories that produce particular experiences of food, a relational, historically and culturally grounded, 'people-centered' approach can highlight the social elements that create and/or strengthen resonant, locally inflected political strategies for food sovereignty in urban communities. Seeing food as an essential means of reproduction also entails questions of the production and reproduction of human beings as labor, and labor-power. Thus, the theoretical approach outlined in this paper explores the ways in which proletarianization must continually be reproduced, is increasingly partial or incomplete, and is contested at multiple conjunctures—in which food, as an essential means of subsistence, becomes a key arena for struggle.

This 'people-centered approach' to food sovereignty rests on two main theoretical premises. First, a relational conception of food, building on Stuart Hall's notion of articulation (Hall, 1996), helps to re-situate the deep connections among diverse experiences in varied local contexts. Instead of an iterative 'impact' framework, in which global processes simply impose themselves on local communities, this approach highlights the interconnected roles various communities and localities play in constituting the global process as a whole, revealing conditions of possibility for uniting spatially and culturally disparate forms of struggle.

Second, a focus on everyday life—as a structuring principle of food relations and a potential source for contestation and alternatives—helps make explicit the connections between food and other social phenomena, such as class exploitation and racism, that shape particular experiences and struggles. Drawing upon Henri Lefebvre's dialectical view of the contradictions and possibilities posed by everyday life (2002) this approach also calls attention to the production of space and meaning through social practice, and how these manifest in and through a community's foodways.

I explore these themes empirically through my ethnographic work with the Healthy Food Hub, a community-based cooperative market on the South Side of Chicago. The Healthy Food Hub utilizes collective purchasing of food items, mainly grown in Black farming communities, as a means of not only getting good food for less money, but also building cultural ties and creating economic opportunities for community members. In the face of deindustrialization, soaring levels of poverty and unemployment, and an urban food crisis, the predominantly African-American families that comprise the Healthy Food Hub are developing innovative forms of food praxis whose effectiveness stems directly from revival of household practices carried over from rural origins, a 'culture of collective working',[1] contemporary connections to rural Black farming communities, and a fundamental commitment to self-determination. For the dispossessed former industrial workers of Black South Chicago, access to fresh and healthy food through the Healthy Food Hub is not about 'chasing our piece of pie in the new green economy'.[2] It is, rather, a point of entry into a larger project: to build forms of 'community wealth' that can provide them with much-needed autonomy and resilience against the forces that continue to lay waste to their communities.

Forks over Justice: Limits and Contradictions in 'Food-centric' Discourse

Stemming from a common critique of the industrial food system, critical food scholarship and food movement discourses have elaborated the interconnected historical processes that have transformed the global food system from one end to the other. Many critiques have focused on the technical and spatial aspects of food production, documenting the environmental and health impacts of industrial agriculture, while calling attention to the ecological and nutritional benefits of alternative farming systems such as agroecology (Altieri, 2009). Others concentrate on the political economy of food production—economic impacts of Green Revolution technologies, the 'pesticide treadmill' and high input costs on small farmers (Perfecto, Vandermeer, & Wright, 2009), labor conditions for farm workers (Brown & Getz, 2011), and the ways in which the dynamics of global 'food regimes' adversely affect multiple aspects of smallholder production, while yielding the lion's share of economic benefits to large agribusiness corporations (McMichael, 2005).

On the other end of the supply chain, other domains of critical food scholarship focus on various issues relating to food consumption and the rise of alternative food networks (AFNs). Much of urban-based food scholarship falls within this area, addressing issues of fair trade, relocalization, urban agriculture, and access to healthy and adequate food, particularly in communities of color (Alkon & Agyeman, 2011). Studies (and critiques) of popular food movements abound, examining multiple facets of AFNs from farmers' markets and school-based food initiatives to community garden projects and municipal/regional food policy reform efforts (Goodman, Goodman, & Dupuis, 2011).

Food movements and the perspectives informing them, particularly in the USA, tend to share a common orientation toward the ethics and esthetics of food consumption, a 'narrative linking the production and consumption of local organic food to positive economic, environmental, and social changes' (Alkon & Agyeman, 2011). This often leaves the concerned reader or activist with an impression that the best way to resist the industrial food system is to 'vote with your fork'—a market-based solution based on ethical consumption (Pollan, 2006). Policy-oriented efforts in the institutional domain of governments and NGOs advocate for technocratic solutions that can be applied generally over a wide variety of local contexts (Pelletier, Kraak, Mccullum, & Uusitalo, 2000).

While a critique of the global capitalist economy is often implicit, and sometimes even explicit, in some of these analyses, many of the solutions promoted by mainstream food movements have proved compatible with, and have even been adopted by, large food and agribusiness corporations whose practices contribute to the very problems the food movement purports to address. In this way, various currents of food movement scholarship and discourse 'seem to produce and reproduce neo-liberal forms, spaces of governance, and mentalities' (Guthman, 2008b). In addition, questions of difference—race, class, gender, and the legacies of slavery and colonialism—are often elided in discourses around food. As a result, popular approaches to solving food-related problems often reflect and reproduce the cultural sensibilities and economic privileges associated with a white, middle-class subjectivity (Alkon & Agyeman, 2011).

Where mainstream food movements have addressed communities of color and the ways in which food issues intersect with other historical oppressions such as racism and poverty—for example, in the 'food desert' discourse (Gallagher, 2006)—those communities are often perceived through a 'deficit' lens, requiring top-down educational, technocratic, and aid-based solutions that rely on a high level of intervention on the part of outside actors. Even where grassroots approaches to food issues within urban communities proliferate, the utopian universalism as well as the 'deficit thinking' (Valencia, 1997) that pervades much of mainstream food movement discourse often ignores the specific histories and differential ways that structural inequalities affect minority and low-income communities in urban centers. In doing so, these efforts not only fail to engage the very communities they are trying to reach (Guthman, 2008a), but also fail to recognize potentially useful forms of knowledge and social practice that already exist within those communities.

In contrast to these approaches, the discourse of food sovereignty—which asserts the 'right of nations and peoples to control their own food systems—markets, production modes, food cultures and environments' (Wittman, Desmarais, & Wiebe, 2010), places questions of power, difference, and democracy at the forefront of its critical perspective. The Nyeleni Declaration on Food Sovereignty:

> suggests that there are a range of conditions that are necessary for food sovereignty to obtain, such as a living wage, tenure security and security of housing, cultural rights, and an end to the dumping of goods below the cost of production, disaster capitalism, colonialism, imperialism, and genetically modified organisms (GMOs), in the service of a future where, among other things, 'agrarian reform revitalizes interdependence between consumers and producers'. (Patel, 2009, p. 669)

Food sovereignty's radical imperative is to consider social justice not simply as an additive property to a sustainable food system, but as the very foundation from which such a food system must be built; corrections to historical and structural injustices are among the essential 'preconditions before food sovereignty can be achieved' (Patel, 2009). The primacy of the social in the ideas and goals of food sovereignty, therefore, seems to suggest a reorientation in the critique of food systems toward the social, and the organization of society as a whole. It compels us not only to interrogate the juridical, economic, and legislative structures governing the production and consumption of food, but also to consider food systems first and foremost in terms of their social lives. It requires an examination of the transformations that capitalism has wrought on every level, from global macroeconomic structures to the most intimate spaces of everyday life. From that vantage point, it becomes possible to see how banal acts of daily subsistence reflect and reproduce capitalist social relations, express their contradictions, and contain the seeds of their overcoming.

Land Grabs and Big Macs: Food as a Modality of Living in Capitalism

An approach that starts with people at the center of a food system takes into account how space, power, and meaning are implicated within the system, engages with the particular struggles and histories of a community, and identifies the ways in which social transformations affect, and are affected by, the lived experience of food. It suggests a reconceptualization of food itself: from a discrete 'object' of research (e.g. as an economic commodity or ecological factor) toward a relational conception in which food—as material content and lived experience—is perceived as an *ensemble of relations*, a kind of nexus in and through which social processes at varied spatial and temporal scales converge and interact. This dialectical reformulation replaces 'the commonsense notion of "thing" . . . with notions of "process" and "relation"' (Ollman, 2003).

Thinking about food relationally is useful not only for an analysis of what went into its physical production, but also for the production of meaning through food practices, and their capacity to produce and reproduce social relations *in general* through the lived experience of obtaining, preparing, and consuming food. In this sense, the center of analysis shifts from the production of food (as in a commodity chain) to considering food as a kind of prism through which the underlying relations of society are revealed; a means of unpacking the different ways in which capitalist social relations are produced, reproduced, and articulated in particular places and historical conjunctures.

With an understanding of food as a historically and socially produced ensemble of interconnected processes, there now appears the question of *how* to connect larger scale processes (such as global political economy or historical oppressions) to the lived experience of food. What does racism, or land grabs, have to do with last night's dinner? How can we make a clear and credible account of these connections? And how can we use such an analysis to advance food sovereignty in a way that can speak to the linkages among the diverse, seemingly unrelated ways in which people are affected by these processes, up and down the food chain, in localities that seem worlds away from one another?

Stuart Hall's conception of *articulation* 'has the considerable advantage of enabling us to think of how specific practices articulated around contradictions which do not all arise in the same way, at the same point, in the same moment, can nevertheless be thought together' (Slack, 1996). In writing about the relation between race and class, Hall emphasizes the historically specific ways in which these social divisions are interlinked and come into being in and through one another. The articulation between race and class, or among any other social phenomena, is conceived as a dynamic link, constructed in myriad ways through concrete social practices in historical time. Articulation is the product and arena of struggle, as Hall asserts in his central thesis: 'Race is ... the modality in which class is "lived", the medium through which class relations are experienced, the form in which is appropriated and "fought through"' (Hall, 1996).

For a subject such as food systems—with its global scope, multiple mechanisms, and diversity of local effects— Hall's 'concept of articulation in its extended sense ... is useful not only in clarifying diverse and interrelated trajectories of sociospatial change but also in suggesting how struggles in different sociospatial arenas and across spatial scales might link with one another' (Hart, 2007). The bond between dispossessed peasants in the Global South and unemployed workers in South Chicago may not be readily apparent; their experiences, while both related to the global political economy of food, seem vastly different from one another. However, their articulations into a global 'food regime' (McMichael, 2009)—whose hunger for land on one continent, and markets for cheap fast food concoctions on another, swell the ranks of the poor and malnourished on both shores—could shed some light on how their situations can be linked together in a common struggle.

If 'race ... is the modality by which class is lived' (Hall, 1996), perhaps it can also be said that food is a modality by which capitalism is lived and made tangible in everyday experience. Throughout the roughly 500 years of its existence, the dynamics of global capitalist development have engendered deep transformations in social life, which has, as a consequence, transformed the ways people encounter and experience food. Aspects of everyday life that are structured by the demands of wage labor and the market—long work hours and/or strict time discipline (Thompson, 1967), pressures of market competition on small artisan producers (Bertaux & Bertaux-Wiame, 1981), spatial dislocations such as migration to urban centers or long work commutes (Coleman-Jensen, 2009), and even the transformation of rural communities through the growth of migrant labor and remittance economies (Hecht, 2010) can qualitatively affect and constrain people's options for the kinds of food they obtain on a daily basis.

For example, a study of low-wage women workers living in the northeast USA found that a majority of them 'made "quick stuff" or bought fast food because they did not have energy or time to cook' (Jabs et al., 2007). Often working two or three jobs to make ends meet, many workers do not have the time to obtain and prepare food at home, making them more dependent on cheap, unhealthy convenience foods. In urban communities of color—where the deleterious effects of deindustrialization and economic crisis are compounded by long histories of racial discrimination, redlining, and, more recently, epic rates of foreclosure—the strained relationship between economic circumstances, spatial–temporal production of deleterious environments, and everyday food choices is even more pronounced (Block, Chávez, Allen, & Ramirez, 2012).

Subsistence on the Side: Alienation and Resistance in Everyday Life

Seen in their eminently social, historical, and relational contexts, everyday experiences of producing, obtaining, and consuming food are, quite literally, visceral manifestations of multiple and intersecting processes that continually seek to subordinate the lives of human beings to the logic of accumulation, competition, wage labor, and the market. Struggles over food, therefore, can be seen as struggles over proletarianization and alienation; of the material and meaningful ways in which capitalism produces and transforms everyday life. These processes, however, are never quite as totalizing as their boosters, or their critics, purport them to be.

For Marx, the historical sine qua non for the development and maintenance of capitalist social relations is primitive accumulation: the separation of the producers from their means of subsistence, forcing dispossessed laborers into a dependent relationship with capital in order to survive. The capacity to produce food, or to access adequate sources of food, is an essential means of subsistence for human beings; one that is ripped away from the producer in the violent course of capitalism's 'original sin' (Marx, 1968). Processes of primitive accumulation are generally associated with the separation of peasants from the land that provides their immediate means of subsistence.

But Marx's definition alludes to a second dimension in which primitive accumulation entailed much more than separation from land. It was also a radical attempt to close off all possibilities for non-capitalist forms of life through the violent erasure of myriad forms of self-reliance and social subsistence, in order to present wage labor as the only survival strategy available to human beings. As Michael Perelman observes,

> Primitive accumulation cut through traditional lifeways like scissors. The first blade served to undermine the ability of people to provide for themselves. The other blade was a system of stern measures required to keep people from finding alternative survival strategies outside the system of wage labor. (2000, p. 14)

This highlights capitalism's imperative to continually reproduce the conditions by which capitalist social relations are established and maintained, naturalizing those relations in its drive to 'colonize all life' (De Angelis, 2004).

Henri Lefebvre, in his *Critique of everyday life* (2002), saw capitalist modernity as characterized primarily by the subordination of real life to the 'brutally objective power' of the abstract logic of capitalism. This logic produces and reproduces itself through everyday social practice in profoundly material as well as ideological ways; it is 'a practical illusion, with its basis in everyday life and the way everyday life is organized' (Lefebvre, 2002). Thus humanity, in all its infinite fullness and potential, becomes transformed through its subordination to abstract economic categories and functions into something not quite human:

> a tool to be used by other tools (the means of production), a thing to be used by another thing (money), and an object to be used by a class, a mass of individuals who are themselves 'deprived' of reality and truth (the capitalists). (Lefebvre, 2002, p. 166)

Lefebvre notes that 'there is a name for this fixing of human activity within an alien reality which is at one and the same time crudely material and yet abstract: *alienation*' (2002).

However, Lefebvre notes that the domination of abstractions over everyday life is necessarily limited; alternative social practices continue to exist and thrive because of the inimitably creative and untamable nature of everyday life. Central to Lefebvre's analysis is the relationship between the real world, experienced and lived as a totality, and the necessary but limited abstractions we use to make sense of it:

> Everyday life, in a sense residual, defined by what is 'left over' after all distinct, superior, specialized, structured activities have been singled out by analysis, must be defined as a totality … [these] activities leave a 'technical vacuum' between one another which is filled up by everyday life. Everyday life is profoundly related to *all* activities, and encompasses them with all their differences and their conflicts; it is their meeting place, their bond, their common ground. And it is in everyday life that the sum total of relations which make the human—and every human being—a whole takes its shape and its form. (2002, p. 97)

This, he argued, was a fundamental contradiction in capitalist life: necessarily limited by the categories it seeks to impose, the abstract logic of capitalism can never truly encompass the totality of everyday life. Everyday life as an ongoing, living process is continually 'leaking out the sides', so to speak, of capitalist structures; its 'residue' confounding the attempts of abstraction and alienation to contain it. In this residue, one can catch fragmented glimpses of possibilities for a life not dominated by alienated social relations: the 'substance of everyday life—"human raw material" in its simplicity and richness—pierces through all alienation and establishes "disalienation"' (Lefebvre, 2002). Real life, in a sense, is always running one step ahead of capitalism, which is constantly pursuing, but never fully achieving, its goal of colonizing all life.

The twofold character of primitive accumulation—physical separation from land as a means of subsistence and the suppression of alternative forms of social production that challenge the absolute primacy of wage labor—also helps us think about different aspects of the contemporary food system in relation to one another. On the one hand, the restructuring of global, national, and local economies as a result of the 2008 financial crisis—which precipitated dramatic increases in food prices worldwide (McMichael, 2009) —crucially impacted food security for working people and the poor at both ends of the food chain. In the Global South, the 'triple crisis' of food, energy, and finance (McMichael, 2009) spurred a wave of accelerated land consolidation and rural dispossession, characterized as 'new enclosures' (White, Borras, Hall, Scoones, & Wolford, 2012); while in the cities of the Global North, the decimation of living-wage employment and social safety nets undermined the purchasing power of urban populations.

On the other hand, the consequences of the food crisis have perhaps opened up conditions of possibility for re-articulating social relations around food, allowing alternatives to the 'corporate food regime' (McMichael, 2005) to proliferate. Lefebvre's expansive notion of 'everyday life' as a creative and undisciplinable universe of social praxis, simultaneously produced through capitalist development and developing in ways that move beyond the purview of capitalist logics, gains particular relevance in the current era of mass dispossessions and the proliferation of 'wageless life' (Denning, 2010). The sheer scale of unemployed, superfluous labor in urban peripheries the world over has created vast spaces where self-reliance has become a vital necessity; as African urbanist Abdoumaliq Simone notes, 'Self-responsibility for urban survival has opened up spaces for different ways of organizing activities' (Simone, 2004).

These not-quite-proletarians are engaging, inventing, and jerry-rigging an untold number of experiments and strategies for survival and resistance within the liminal spaces in which processes of primitive accumulation have left them. These could include rediscovering long-forgotten practices that reveal deep connections to rural places of origin, and learning new ones from people and groups they encounter. Political movements for land, rights, and urban citizenship can also be products of this conjuncture (Holston, 2008). In other words, in the spaces that capitalist development has left behind, people are forging new articulations with the system and helping each other out of whatever resources, skills, and social networks are available to them.

These everyday social forms of subsistence, especially as they relate to food, could be a fertile ground for building the kinds of self-determined food systems that food sovereignty seeks to champion. In the spaces where people resist, or are discarded by, the march of capitalist development, the diverse social networks, practices, and resources they have always marshaled for daily subsistence become salient building blocks for new social configurations of collective survival that—if recognized, cultivated, and defended by conscious political action—can potentially emerge as practically viable, culturally meaningful, and self-determined pathways to food sovereignty as a means of transcending life under capitalism.

Building an Ark: Resilience and Re-articulation in South Chicago

> Those who control food production and human reproduction have real power, have control over life and death. And we need to further our control, and build upon the foundation of our history and our ancestors, so that we make sure that we survive and come through this crisis, the way we came through the holocaust of the Slave Trade, slavery, Jim Crow, migration to the cities, the decline of industrial capitalism, and what the planet and society have in store for us in the future. (Healthy Food Hub member)

Seeing food systems in terms of their social lives—as sets of relations, articulations, and conveyors of meaning—helps food analysts and activists to avoid the universalisms that, unconsciously, attach food movement discourse and practice to a particular set of class and cultural subjectivities while alienating others (Guthman, 2008a). This approach, when applied to the empirical case study of the predominantly African-American members of Chicago's Healthy Food Hub, reveals the vexed relationship many Black folks have with mainstream food and environmental sustainability discourses. It also helps us to more fully appreciate what they have built, and why it resonates so powerfully with the community members who come into its orbit.

Located in an area once defined as both a 'food desert' (Gallagher, 2006) and an 'urban sacrifice zone' (Gottesdiener, 2013), the Healthy Food Hub was established in 2009 with the aim of pooling the resources of its members and surrounding communities to 'bring home healthier, tastier, fresher food for less'.[3] This is mainly achieved through collective purchasing of wholesale organic produce, as well as food production on rural farms in the historic Black farming community of Pembroke Township, Illinois, located about 60 miles south of the city. It is a membership-based organization, serving around 500 families in several South Chicago neighborhoods. The hub holds a Market Day every other Saturday at the Betty Shabazz Charter School, where members can pick up their orders, shop for additional food items, buy other sundries and gift items from vendors, and attend talks, workshops, and organizational meetings.

Preorders are the main mechanism by which the Hub obtains its food products; they also reinforce the cooperative and participatory culture that supports the Hub's aims for community building. There are two 'rounds' to the preorder process. Members submit the first round of orders on the Monday before Market day, over the website and over the phone. An email is then sent to members a couple of days later with details on what has been ordered, and how much more for each item must be acquired to receive the greatest bulk discount. Members can then choose to buy more, or recruit family and friends to add to their original order, so that everyone can receive the lowest possible price for their food. One of the Hub's volunteers described the collective buying process as a 'reverse CSA':

> It's not one farmer selling memberships, it's the eaters determining what they want to eat. And they're creating a system to support that . . . I know what you need, that way I only have to get what it is that my community recognizes they need.[4]

Market days, in contrast to the typical supermarket experience, are regarded as social events, fostering relationships among members and bringing together the diverse array of knowledge and resources they bring to the space. It is not unusual to spend the better part of an hour in the checkout line in conversation with fellow members and volunteers. Various presentations and workshops are held on diverse topics ranging from healthy cooking, herbal medicine, aquaponics (integrated fish and plant cultivation), disaster preparedness, and food growing techniques that stem from old farming traditions as well as newer forms of permaculture. This space allows members to share knowledge and ideas with each other, while also enhancing the scope of goods and services the Hub is able to provide.

The Healthy Food Hub also maintains a 40-acre production center and 'eco-campus' at the Black Oaks Center for Sustainable Renewable Living, located in Pembroke Township. At Black Oaks, organizers grow food, host school trips, and hold weekend seminars in ecology and permaculture for urban youth from the South Side. They have also launched a Rotating Apprentice Farmers' Training Program, an intensive agroecology summer course in which participants serve as apprentices to various Black farmers in the Pembroke community. By 2014, the program would have trained 40 mostly young new farmers in methods of crop and livestock cultivation.

The Healthy Food Hub's relative success stems not only from the goods and services it provides and the commitment of its membership, but also from an acute recognition of the material needs and cultural dilemmas faced by Black communities on the South Side. The neighborhoods from which the Hub derives its main membership are among the hardest hit by deindustrialization and the economic crisis: youth unemployment for Black males on the South Side approaches 50%, foreclosures have depopulated wide swaths of these neighborhoods, and in recent years, the area has endured unprecedented levels of violence (Malooley, 2013). The last Black-owned grocery store on the South Side closed down in 1995, and the lack of access to fresh, healthy food in those neighborhoods became the initial impetus for the creation of the Hub.

A historicized understanding of the articulations by which deindustrialization, economic marginalization, and the legacies of slavery and Jim Crow are implicated in food and everyday life in South Chicago is also essential for explaining the unique nature of the Hub's project, its particular difficulties, and its ultimate goals. Most of the Hub's older members are first- and second- generation migrants from four counties in the Mississippi Delta; as the children of sharecroppers, they fled the region with their families in the 1950s and 1960s to escape the racial violence following the murder of Emmett Till. Thus, the experience of agrarian life, in the collective memories of these urban transplants, appears to be less of a nostalgic feeling of transcendental connection to the land than that of being bound to a landscape of fear and oppression. One woman, venting her frustration at the well-intentioned but naive efforts of white food and environmental activists, expressed it thus:

> You want me to go plant a tree, but you hung us from a tree. A tree is not a symbol of life; you hung our brothers from it, took our lives with it. No. I won't dig my own grave; that's what nature is to us, a grave.[5]

The legacy of slavery has perhaps been the most powerful influence shaping the difficult relationship between food, land, and the Hub's Black constituency. Land—a material symbol of autonomy and freedom for agrarian communities around the world—carries painful and traumatic connotations for former slaves who fled to the cities to escape bondage from the land. Fred Carter, co-founder of the Healthy Food Hub and the Black Oaks Center, highlights the contradictory relationship between food and slavery when considered in the context of its deep history:

> It's a challenge not just confined to Pembroke, it's a challenge for us as a group, as a race of people, in this country and in the world. We entered slavery because of our ability to grow food, and because of our capacity to grow food and feed people, we were enslaved. That was one of the driving factors why they were importing us over here; we knew how to grow rice, we knew about this land . . . we were the powerhouse, we fed the planet. And because we were violated, enslaved and beat to serve whites, to feed them, it's a painful memory.[6]

However, just as poverty and oppression followed Black populations from the rural South into South Chicago, so did ways of surviving and coping, as a community, with the multiple forms of crisis imposed upon them. Along with the pain of their experience and social conditions in the rural South, positive and creative forms of collective endurance and resistance to those conditions also came with them, deeply embedded in social memory. These everyday food practices, derived from agrarian pasts, became essential parts of the Hub's toolkit for building collective means of community empowerment.

Collective purchasing—pivotal to the Hub's community project—carries particular importance as a household food practice for the Hub's founders, who migrated from rural Mississippi to Chicago as children. As Fred Carter recalls:

> We always had a food buying club, that's how we ate as a family . . . when we got to Chicago, our whole extended family, or people from our hometown, would all live together on a block. And we would all put our money together to buy a cow, and divide it up amongst ourselves. It was just cheaper that way . . . I guess maybe that is where the Healthy Food Hub came out of.[7]

Collective food buying in Mississippi has historical roots in the complex and largely forgotten history of Black farmers' resistance to white capitalism. In the first few years of Reconstruction, 1 in 10 African-Americans settled in the Delta region hoping to climb the 'agricultural ladder' to the 'poor man's promised land' (Willis, 2000; Woods, 1998). These Black yeoman farmers pursued a number of individual and collective strategies for utilizing the advantages of land ownership, including efforts to build new kinds of agrarian society based on solidarity, self-reliance, and collective uplift.

As the encroaching power of white creditors began to subordinate the nascent Black farming class into the 'second slavery' of sharecropping, Populist organizations such as the Colored Farmers' Alliance formed, buying cooperatives in the region and imploring Black farmers to 'discover how the united purchasing power of Black agrarians can reduce your debts and end your reliance on white creditors' (Willis, 2000). By the twentieth century, these efforts had been violently crushed by the Klan and Jim Crow, their political importance largely forgotten by Delta farmers and their descendants. But the idea of pooling resources to acquire basic necessities at lower prices persisted; it simply made good economic sense to large rural households struggling to make ends meet.

Collective buying, born in a moment of economic resistance, thus found its way to Chicago, tucked away in individual memories and households until, in another time of crisis, it became a keystone for developing a new articulation between food and community power. How the Healthy Food Hub redeployed this household practice on a community level, in a post-industrial urban context, may appear rather different in practice from its agrarian antecedent. The mechanisms for pooling and using resources are articulated through modern technologies, its infrastructure extends over rural and urban space, and—importantly—it does not isolate itself, spatially or economically, from the larger system in which it operates.

The ultimate objective of this practice—to build social formations based on solidarity, self-reliance, and collective uplift and to avoid and replace relations of dependency on forces that are oppressive and exploitative of them—is more than an artifact of the 'blues development tradition' (Woods, 1998) advanced by Black agrarians in Reconstruction-era Mississippi. It is a contemporary re-articulation of that tradition, one in which African-Americans, for over a century, 'have continuously experimented with creating sustainable, equitable, and just social, economic, political, and cultural structures ... the constant reestablishment of collective sensibility in the face of constant attacks by the plantation bloc and its allies' (Woods, 1998).

The collective aspect of the Hub's economic operations—inspired by the African socialist concept of *ujamaa*, or cooperative economics—serves as a powerful basis for re-inscribing understandings of community, sustainability, self-reliance, and resilience in and through cultural and material practice. In a city where the competitive, predatory dynamics, and ideologies of neo-liberal capitalism have left communities devastated, fragmented, and vulnerable, Healthy Food Hub members are struggling to rethink and redefine concepts of wealth and exchange along collective and self-determined lines. The members who contribute their money, material resources, time, skills, and knowledge to the Hub all do so with the intention of building, maintaining, and retaining control over their 'community wealth'. As a Healthy Food Hub core organizer describes it, 'We introduce economic opportunity, and then we try to circulate and grow that opportunity so that everyone can benefit from it.'[8]

The efforts of the Healthy Food Hub stem directly from an intimate understanding of Black communities' historical experience: of slavery, racial oppression, the fallout of deindustrialization, and the 'urban crisis' in which foreclosures, unemployment, infrastructural decay, and gang violence have been devastating consequences. For them, the shattering of false hopes for gaining individual prosperity through capitalist means becomes an impetus for reclaiming cultural values of collectivity through building resilient forms of social subsistence. While the Hub is, essentially, a type of 'social enterprise', the manner in which its members consciously aim to protect the community from alienation and privation meaningfully distinguishes its practices from mainstream politics of market-based 'conscious consumption' that reproduce neo-liberal values of competitive individualism in the production and consumption of food.

The Hub's commitment to collective self-reliance and self-determination has become all the more salient in the face of external pressures—not only from larger economic processes, but also from powerful nonprofit and political interests within the city who seek to impose their own models of sustainable development on the 'food deserts' of South Chicago. Healthy Food Hub members are

> literally determined to hold their ground ... to be able to transform the food deserts from within themselves, not from external inputs from people who don't live in their communities and carry the majority of the wealth out of their communities. Our standing commitment for all of us has been to keep the wealth in our community, on every level—whether it's social, intellectual, natural, political—we literally can create something different and new.[9]

Conclusion: Burying the Pain, Picking Up Power

> If the city is a huge intersection of bodies in need . . . how can permutations in the intersection of their given physical existence, their stories, networks, and inclinations, produce specific value and capacity? (Simone, 2004, p. 3)

In the interplay of ideas, debates, and movements struggling to define the 'big tent' (Patel, 2009) of food sovereignty, critique of the prevailing food system remains a dominant mode through which aspirations for a better food system—and by extension, a better world—is expressed. This is absolutely crucial: we must be clear about what we are against before we can proclaim what we are for. But critique, as such, places food sovereignty movements in an essentially defensive position. For urban dwellers in the heart of the industrialized world—primarily food consumers whose histories and articulations with advanced capitalism have produced a far more alienated relationship with food production, land, and nature—a proactive route to building and advocating for alternatives is far more difficult to imagine. What we are often left with is a host of utopian visions, constructed around the quality and value of food as a commodity; abstract models of 'sustainability' that often, in practice, end up reinforcing the social divisions and structures of alienated capitalist life.

Shifting the lens of analysis from food to the people and everyday social life at the heart of food systems suggests, perhaps, new strategies for research and action. It encourages a shift away from 'deficit thinking' in community-based research, toward a renewed focus on the resourcefulness and oppositional sensibilities that people sustain and develop in conditions of adversity. In terms of building and advancing alternatives through action, a 'people-centered' approach not only illuminates the power relations and injustices that lie at the heart of the food system, but also shows how the infinite array of relationships, resources, histories, struggles, and aspirations that express themselves in the everyday experience of food are the raw material from which many possible paths to a just and sustainable food system can be built.

The Healthy Food Hub is an example of one such path, a pragmatic reconfiguration of the memories, histories, resources, and knowledge of their members to build culturally grounded, self-determined, and resilient infrastructures for community survival and independence from the economic forces that have enslaved, exploited, and ultimately left them behind. At the time this research was undertaken, the Healthy Food Hub did not explicitly invoke concepts or ideas from the global food sovereignty movement; but their everyday practices reflected a critique of the corporate food system, engaged the community's specific needs and histories, and incorporated available elements and strategies in ways that *worked for them*. Even though Healthy Food Hub members did not necessarily 'talk the talk', I argue that they have 'walked the walk' in terms of practicing food sovereignty. The act of re-articulating the relations of subsistence, to create and 'own the pathways to healthy living', becomes an act of building community power; a form of sovereignty collectively developed from the intimate spaces of everyday life.

I hope that a people-centered approach to food systems can also help us envision strategies for food sovereignty that go beyond invoking essentialist utopias of 'sustainable urban living'. In contexts where the imaginary of an idealized agrarian past is not accessible, or, in the case of African-American descendants of slaves and sharecroppers, an extremely painful and undesirable option, a relational and historically grounded approach can help us recognize the actually existing, novel, ad-hoc food practices in these communities as potential grounds for social transformation. Instead of proposing blanket prescriptions for change, we can perhaps envision political trajectories for food sovereignty that engage diverse communities on their own historically and geographically specific terms, articulated in and through long-embedded processes of social struggle. These trajectories could not only transform the food system as a whole, but also actualize the very notion of food sovereignty into a living, breathing global process where food producers and consumers, rural and urban, North and South, can, as Dr J from the Healthy Food Hub put it, 'release our colonization and our suffering, and regain our power again'.

Disclosure Statement

No potential conflict of interest was reported by the author.

Notes

1 Remarks by Fred Carter, Healthy Food Hub Sustainability Address, 5 February 2011.
2 Black Oaks Community Center Newsletter, Vol. 1, No. 1.
3 Healthy Food Hub website, http://www.healthyfoodhub.org
4 Interview with Healthy Food Hub volunteer, 26 June 2011.
5 Radio interview with Kellen Marshall, Practically Speaking Radio Episode 11: Blacks in Green, 20 May 2013.
6 Television interview with Fred Carter, PCC Network Forum, 11 April 2012.
7 Interview with Fred Carter, 16 June 2011.
8 Michael Tekhen Strode, Healthy Food Hub promotional video. Posted at http://livesharelearn.com/our-stories.
9 Radio interview with Dr Jifunza Wright, Practically Speaking Radio, 20 May 2013.

References

Alkon, A. H., & Agyeman, J. (2011). *Cultivating food justice: Race, class, and sustainability*. Cambridge: MIT Press.

Altieri, M. A. (2009). Agroecology, small farms, and food sovereignty. *Monthly Review, 61*(3), 102–113.

Bertaux, D., & Bertaux-Wiame, I. (1981). Artisanal bakery in France: How it lives and why it survives. In F. Bechhofer & B. Elliott (Eds.), *The petite bourgeoisie: Comparative studies of the uneasy stratum* (pp. 155–181). London: Macmillan.

Block, D., Chávez, N., Allen, E., & Ramirez, D. (2012). Food sovereignty, urban food access, and food activism: Contemplating the connections through examples from Chicago. *Agriculture and Human Values, 29*(2), 203–215.

Brown, S., & Getz, C. (2011). Farmworker food insecurity and the production of hunger in California. In A. H. Alkon & J. Agyeman (Eds.), *Cultivating food justice: Race, class and sustainability* (pp. 121–146). Cambridge: MIT Press.

Coleman-Jensen, A. J. (2009). *Time poverty, work characteristics and the transition to food insecurity among low-income households* (Ph.D. dissertation). Pennsylvania State University, University Park. ProQuest/UMI (Publication No. AAT 3380890).

De Angelis, M. (2004). Separating the doing and the deed: Capital and the continuous character of enclosures. *Historical Materialism, 12*(2), 57–87.

Denning, M. (2010). Wageless life. *New Left Review, 66*, 79–97.

Gallagher, M. (2006). *Examining the impact of food deserts on public health in Chicago*. Chicago: Mari Gallagher Research and Consulting Group.

Goodman, D., Goodman, M., & Dupuis, M. (2011). *Alternative food networks: Knowledge, place and politics*. London, UK: Routledge.

Gottesdiener, L. (2013, August 1). The great eviction. *The Nation*.

Guthman, J. (2008a). 'If they only knew': Color blindness and universalism in California alternative food institutions. *The professional geographer, 60*(3), 387–397.

Guthman, J. (2008b). Neoliberalism and the making of food politics in California. *Geoforum, 39*(3), 1171–1183.

Hall, S. (1996). Race, articulation, and societies structured in Dominance. In H. A. Baker Jr, M. Diawara, & R. H. Lindeborg (Eds.), *Black British cultural studies: A reader* (pp. 16–60). Chicago, IL: University of Chicago Press.

Hart, G. (2007). Changing concepts of articulation: Political stakes in South Africa today. *Review of African Political Economy, 34*(111), 85–101.

Hecht, S. (2010). The new rurality: Globalization, peasants and the paradoxes of landscapes. *Land Use Policy*, *27*(2), 161–169.
Holston, J. (2008). *Insurgent citizenship: Disjunctions of democracy and modernity in Brazil*. Princeton, NJ: Princeton University Press.
Jabs, J., Devine, C. M., Bisogni, C. A., Farrell, T. J., Jastran, M., & Wethington, E. (2007). Trying to find the quickest way: Employed mothers' constructions of time for food. *Journal of Nutrition Education and Behavior*, *39*(1), 18–25.
Lefebvre, H. (2002). *Critique of everyday life: Foundations for a sociology of the everyday*. London, UK: Verso Books.
Malooley, J. (2013, August 20). Chicago kids go back to school surrounded by violence and cops. VICE.
Marx, K. (1968). *Capital: A critique of political economy*. New York, NY: International Publishers.
McMichael, P. (2005). Global development and the corporate food regime. In F. H. Buttel & P. McMichael (Eds.), *New Directions in the Sociology of Global Development (Research in Rural Sociology and Development)*, (Vol. 11, pp. 265–299). Bingley, UK: Emerald Group Publishing Limited.
McMichael, P. (2009). A food regime analysis of the 'World food crisis'. *Agriculture and Human Values*, *26*(4), 281–295.
Ollman, B. (2003). *Dance of the dialectic: Steps in Marx's method*. Durham, NC: University of Illinois Press.
Patel, R. (2009). Food sovereignty. *Journal of Peasant Studies*, *36*(3), 663–706.
Pelletier, D. L., Kraak, V., Mccullum, C., & Uusitalo, U. (2000). Values, public policy, and community food security. *Agriculture and Human Values*, *17*(1), 75–93.
Perelman, M. (2000). *The invention of capitalism: Classical political economy and the secret history of primitive accumulation*. Durham, NC: Duke University Press Books.
Perfecto, I., Vandermeer, J. H., & Wright, A. L. (2009). *Nature's matrix: Linking agriculture, conservation and food sovereignty*. London: Earthscan.
Pollan, M. (2006). Vote with Your Fork. *The New York Times*.
Simone, A. M. (2004). *For the city yet to come: Changing African life in four cities*. Durham: Duke University Press.
Slack, J. D. (1996). The theory and method of articulation in cultural studies. In D. Morley & K.-H. Chen (Eds.), *Stuart Hall: Critical dialogues in cultural studies* (pp. 112–127). London, UK: Routledge.
Thompson, E. P. (1967). Time, work-discipline, and industrial capitalism. *Past & Present*, *38*, 56–97.
Valencia, R. R. (1997). *The evolution of deficit thinking: Educational thought and practice*. London, UK: Routledge.
White, B., Borras Jr, S. M., Hall, R., Scoones, I., & Wolford, W. (2012). The new enclosures: Critical perspectives on corporate land deals. *Journal of Peasant Studies*, *39*(3–4), 619–647.
Willis, J. C. (2000). *Forgotten time: The Yazoo-Mississippi delta after the civil war*. The American South Series. Charlottesville: University Press of Virginia.
Wittman, H., Desmarais, A. A., & Wiebe, N. (2010). *Food sovereignty: Reconnecting food, nature & community*. Winnipeg: Fernwood Halifax.
Woods, C. A. (1998). *Development arrested: The blues and plantation power in the Mississippi Delta*. Haymarket Series. London: Verso Books.

'Quiet Food Sovereignty' as Food Sovereignty without a Movement? Insights from Post-socialist Russia

OANE VISSER*, NATALIA MAMONOVA*, MAX SPOOR* & ALEXANDER NIKULIN**

**Erasmus University, Rotterdam, The Netherlands*
***Center for Agricultural Studies of the Russian Presidential Academy of National Economy and Public Administration, Moscow, Russia*

ABSTRACT *What does food sovereignty look like in settings where rural social movements are weak or non-existent, such as in countries with post-socialist, semi-authoritarian regimes? Focusing on Russia, we present a divergent form of food sovereignty. Building on the concept of 'quiet sustainability', we present a dispersed, muted, but clearly bottom-up variant we term 'quiet food sovereignty'. In the latter, the role of the very productive smallholdings is downplayed by the state and partly by the smallholders themselves. Those smallholdings are not seen as an alternative to industrial agriculture, but subsidiary to it (although superior in terms of sociality and healthy, environmentally friendly produce). As such, 'quiet food sovereignty' deviates from the overt struggle frequently associated with food sovereignty. We discuss the prospects of 'quiet food sovereignty' to develop into a full food sovereignty movement, and stress the importance of studying implicit everyday forms of food sovereignty.*

1. Introduction

What shape does food sovereignty take in settings where rural social movements are weak or non-existent, such as in countries with post-socialist and (semi)-authoritarian regimes?[1] Food sovereignty is generally seen as something tightly connected to social movements, which are able to formulate a food sovereignty discourse and follow it up with collective action.

The expanding studies on food sovereignty have until now focused on the Global South and the West but have left Eurasia's post-socialist states—such as Russia, Ukraine, the Central-Asian states, and China, accounting for a large share of the world's countryside and population—out of the picture. Russia and most of the former Soviet Union's other major agricultural producers (i.e. Ukraine and Kazakhstan) constitute an area where the discourse on, and practices of, food sovereignty strongly diverge from the global understandings of it as defined by Via Campesina and the Nyéléni forum. Although the Global South and West already feature varying definitions and approaches to food sovereignty (Patel 2009), we contend that the Russian take is radically different from the basic premises of the food sovereignty variants studied until this time.[2] Therefore, a closer look at the post-Soviet space—and Russia in particular—may contribute to the critical examination of food sovereignty, which is registering a global rise in popularity.

With no study conducted on food sovereignty in Russia until now, and virtually none in the post-socialist area,[3] the first question that arises is whether food sovereignty exists at all as a concept or practice in the country. Food sovereignty is hardly used in government policy and media in Russia, and even then it is mostly as a synonym for 'national food security' (e.g. Super 2012). Government policy is focused on food security and in particular national food self-sufficiency, through the development of large-scale farming. Although food sovereignty rarely figures in Russian debates in its literal translation (*prodovolstvenniy suverinitet*), the concept is certainly not irrelevant.

We argue that a kind of food sovereignty does exist in Russia, but in a less pronounced form—as it practically thrives without any organizations that could formulate outspoken discourses or coordinate actions. However, some of the actions and implicit ideas related to the concept are widespread among the population and clearly emerge bottom-up. We term these practices and implicit ideas 'quiet food sovereignty', building upon the concept of 'quiet sustainability' introduced by Smith and Jehlička (2013). We argue that food sovereignty in practice plays an important role in Russia, with smallholdings producing a large share of the food consumed, in or near their local places of living, and in a largely ecologically friendly way. These elements match well the vision of food sovereignty advocated by global social movements. We reveal that a rights discourse, which is an important element in the food sovereignty concept (Claeys, 2013; Nyéléni, 2007), is rather implicit in 'quiet food sovereignty'. Moreover, the agricultural and environmental importance of Russian smallholdings—which produce, for instance, more potatoes than all the commercial farmers in the US and UK put together (Ries, 2009)—is grossly overlooked and downplayed by the government. Even more strikingly, it is also partly overlooked by the smallholders themselves. We will demonstrate that this extraordinary productivity and 'quiet food sovereignty' are primarily linked to: first, longstanding concepts and practices of household security and self-reliance, which date back to the Soviet era food deficits; and, second, the symbiosis between large farm enterprises (LFEs) and smallholdings, which consisted of the LFEs providing smallholders with large farm assets, and the smallholders' pilfering from the LFEs.

The paper is structured as follows. Section 2 sketches the theoretical (and methodological) approach for studying settings with weak or non-existent movements. Section 3 explains the weakness of rural social movements in Russia. Section 4 describes the Russian food system and the symbiosis between large-scale and small-scale farming. Section 5 deals with the discourses and practices of Russian smallholdings, and explains how they constitute 'quiet food sovereignty'. Section 6 discusses the implicit political dimension of quiet food sovereignty. Section 7 discusses the perspectives for the emergence of a genuine food sovereignty *movement*. Section 8 presents the conclusions and discusses the wider relevance of 'quiet food sovereignty'.

2. Rural Social Movements in Russia

In Russia, the policy space for social movements is very limited. In the Soviet era, virtually all social organizations were established top-down. After the fall of the Soviet Union in 1991, it became legally possible to establish social movements. However, due to 70 years of socialist reign without genuine social movements, the population starkly distrusted new collective endeavors and ideologies and lacked the experience of grassroots collective action. In addition, it was too distracted by the 'shock-therapy' reforms of the 1990s, with their sudden price liberalization, widespread privatization, and drastic reduction of state spending (Mamonova & Visser, 2014). Faced with such a context, Russians did not mobilize to resist changes collectively, but instead coped with (food) shortages by intensifying the Soviet practices of smallholder farming and informal exchange networks (Mamonova & Visser, 2014).

As a consequence, in the 1990s only a limited number of social movements emerged in the cities, and virtually none in the countryside. We refer below to 'rural movements', although some of them also represent urbanites with smallholdings. From the mid-2000s onwards, some rural movements emerged (Mamonova & Visser, 2014). However, due to increasing constraints imposed on civil society organizations by the Putin regime, practically all these movements became either strongly state led, with very weak links to their supposed constituency, or 'phantom movements', without substantial activities (Mamonova & Visser, 2014). The only movement that remained closely connected to rural dwellers was the countrywide movement *Krestyansky Front* (Peasant Front), which defended rural dwellers faced with land grabbing. However, due to mounting constraints by the state and the lack of social will to mobilize, the movement was disbanded in 2013. Thus, it is hardly an overstatement to characterize rural social movements in Russia as extremely weak or virtually non-existent. Moreover, it is increasingly problematic to call these organizations social movements: they are weak in terms of both their lack of popularity among the population and their lack of power (Mamonova & Visser, 2014).

3. Studying Food Sovereignty without a Movement: Analytical Tools

Food sovereignty is generally seen as something tightly connected to a social movement, which is able to formulate, promote, and execute a food sovereignty discourse, and convert it into collective action. The emergence of food sovereignty in the global policy arena is clearly strongly connected to the rise of Via Campesina as a transnational social movement, and various other peasant and farmer associations and networks (such as members of the International Planning Committee on Food Sovereignty). The study of food sovereignty, aside from being (among others) a response to the limitations of the food security studies, is very much a branch of social movement studies, with its focus on discursive aspects (discourses, visions on farming) and organizational issues (leadership, transnational alliances, and open/massive collective action).

Recently, some studies have explored food sovereignty beyond the node of social movements. Particularly relevant here are the studies that have gone beyond the 'global summitry' of large social movements, by looking at localized forms of resistance against the global food system (Ayres & Bosia 2011). But so far, the localism of such micro-encounters 'is still overshadowed by protest summitry and large-scale mobilizations' (Ayres & Bosia 2011).[4] Even with the growing attention for the various actors operating beyond social movements and the study of actors (or scales) in food sovereignty issues as 'multiple sovereignties' (McMichael, 2009), the social movements still remain the touchstone of analyses. This raises the question of what food sovereignty looks like (or might become) in settings where social movements are extremely weak or non-existent. Does food sovereignty exist in (semi)-authoritarian states where social movements are mostly forbidden (such as in China) or heavily restricted (as in Russia)?

For settings such as Russia as well as other post-socialist and/or semi-authoritarian settings with weak or non-existent movements, additional analytical tools are necessary to study food sovereignty. We propose to pay more attention to the level of everyday practices and customs (including the interconnections between large and small farms), 'everyday resistance' (Scott, 1985), as well as 'muted discourses' (Ardener, 1975). We advance these tools in contrast to the existing focus on outspoken discourses such as public speeches and declarations, and concepts from the social movement literature that are frequently used in the food sovereignty literature, such as 'framing', 'mobilization', and social movement strategies (e.g. Claeys, 2013; Desmarais, 2007; Torres, 2003).

The study of food sovereignty was initially very much a study of the framing, mobilization, and genealogy of the transnational movement La Via Campesina (Desmarais, 2007; Torres, 2003). This is, of course, fully understandable, taking into account the crucial role of the movement in defining and propagating—though not inventing (Edelman, 2014)—the concept. A focus on customs and everyday practices instead of social movements enables another approach to rights and entitlements. In the food sovereignty literature, the term 'right' appears frequently. The Nyéléni food sovereignty declaration (Nyéléni, 2007, p. 1) defines food sovereignty as:

> ... the *right* of peoples to healthy and culturally appropriate food produced through ecologically sound and sustainable methods, and their *right* to define their own food and agriculture systems. [emphasis added]

However, it is debatable whether this is about strict rights in the juridical sense, or about entitlements which would, for example, have a more social, informal character. Hospes (2014), for instance, argues that the choice of 'peoples' instead of 'humans' (individuals) as actors seriously complicates the conversion of food sovereignty claims into legally recognized rights, such as human rights (a more optimistic evaluation is provided by Claeys, 2013). As the legal impact of food sovereignty is (still) weak, it seems relevant to include 'entitlements' under the label of rights. Following up on Hospes' (2014) call for more attention to legal pluralism within food sovereignty, we will draw upon work in legal pluralism and anthropology (von Benda-Beckmann, von Benda-Beckmann, & Wiber, 2006), and view rights (for instance in the sphere of property) as multi-layered. von Benda-Beckmann et al. (2006) propose the analysis of property on four levels; ideology, legislation, social norms/customs, and (everyday) practices. The literature on property focuses mostly on the first two levels (which often fall together), while ignoring the latter two (von Benda-Beckmann et al. (2006). Applying this multi-layered analysis helps us to uncover the symbiosis between Russian smallholders and LFEs, which exists underneath the ideological and legal divergence between the two groups, and which is an important element for understanding 'quiet food sovereignty'. As mentioned above, this concept is inspired by the 'quiet sustainability' concept by Smith and Jehlička (2013). They argue, based on research in post-socialist central Europe, that healthy and environmentally sound agriculture can also be reached without explicit discourses and social movements, and therefore they call it 'quiet'. The concept does not incorporate a political dimension, as there is no mention of rights and entitlements. We will contend that quiet food sovereignty does include a political dimension—although a rather implicit one. In analyzing this implicit political dimension, we will draw on the earlier mentioned anthropological work on property relations and the concept of 'everyday resistance' (Scott, 1985).

Aside from interviews with rural social movement leaders (see Mamonova & Visser, 2014 for methods), the data collection for this article consists predominantly of qualitative interviews and observations among the rural population and *dacha* cultivators. In total, 60 interviews were used in this analysis (18 and 32 interviews with smallholders were conducted by Mamonova in the Vladimir and Moscow region, respectively (October–November 2013); 10 interviews and numerous informal conversations with smallholders and state and agribusiness officials were conducted by Visser in the Belgorod region (November–December 2013).

Before elaborating on (quiet) food sovereignty, we will describe Russia's large- and small-scale agriculture (and their interconnections), loosely based on the above-mentioned property relations framework.

4. Post-socialist Agrarian Reform and the Soviet Legacy of Symbiosis

Large-scale agrarian reform started in Russia after the Soviet Union's demise in 1991. Farmland privatization took place through a 'share-based' land distribution, as opposed to the 'plot-based', physical land distribution conducted in most Central and Eastern European countries. The rural population could choose to keep their shares in the privatized successors of the collective and state farms, or take out their paper shares and convert them into real land plots in order to establish a family farm.

Few rural dwellers established private farms, and the growth of such farms already stagnated by the mid-1990s due to insecure property rights, bureaucratic hurdles, and lack of market access (Pallot & Nefedova, 2007). As a result, the LFEs, successors of the collective and state farms, stayed largely intact. The number of LFEs, with an average size of several thousand hectares, remained remarkably stable. Moreover, so-called agroholdings emerged in the course of the 2000s—companies that consist of various integrated LFEs and/or other firms in the food chain. Rural dwellers largely remained employees in the LFEs, while simultaneously expanding (more than doubling) their 'subsidiary household plots' (Rosreestr, 2012).

Two opposing forms of production existed in the Soviet agriculture: on the one hand, the highly mechanized and subsidized, but inefficient, state and collective farms; on the other, the small, but highly productive, semi-private parcels of their employees. Although they only represented 5 percent of the total farmland (Rosreestr, 2012), the rural population—using manual labor on their tiny plots (of 0.10–0.25 ha)—nevertheless accounted for an astonishing 22% of the total agricultural production value of the Russian Soviet republic in 1989 (World Bank, 1992). Moreover, many households had (and still have) their *dachas* (summer houses with a garden around the cities); as *dachniks* (*dacha* owners), they cultivated several fruits and vegetables for own consumption and exchange. Currently, every second family has a *dacha* plot, with an average size of about 0.01 ha; 47% of them cultivate half or more of this land (Nefedova, 2008).

The impressive production on the household plots (further enlarged by *dacha* cultivators) was seen as a strong indication that—once Soviet-era restrictions on private production would be lifted—rural dwellers would establish fully independent farms. This expectation was based on a fundamental misunderstanding of the existing (informal) property relations.

Although, on the ideological and legislative levels, the state/collective farms and the household plots were opposite and fully separated, on the level of rural norms and daily practices, they were interlinked in a so-called symbiosis (Nikulin, 2003, 2009; Visser, 2006). Household plots could produce relatively large amounts of food because they were allowed to use a whole array of collective facilities: from obtaining young livestock and letting private cattle graze on collective pastures, to using machinery. As a result, households were able to ensure their own food security and get extra revenue through sales or exchange. The chairmen of the collectives were also interested in providing such support, as it was a way to motivate their low-paid workers. Finally, aside from the support *provided* to households, there was also a wide practice of goods being *taken* (pilfered) by the households.

The boundaries between the collectives and household plots were thus permeable—a situation which largely continued in the post-Soviet era (Visser, 2006). An LFE decline set in during the 1990s, and farm wages began not being paid for months. In reaction, rural households enlarged their plots and intensified pilfering from the collective. In the course of the 2000s, with some recovery in the LFEs and improved wage payment, households somewhat declined the intensified smallholder production, though it remained at a high level.[5] While towards the end of the Soviet era (1989) the Russian household plots produced 22% of the agricultural output value, in 2012 this was estimated to be 43.2% (Rosstat, 2013b). In sum, land reforms unintentionally led to a continued co-existence of LFEs and (intensified) smallholder production.

5. Quiet Food Sovereignty: Discourses, Importance, and Quietness

Although rural (and some urban) households are a fundamental part of the Russian food system, producing a large share of total agricultural output, their role in the pursuit of the national food security and sovereignty is overlooked or consciously ignored. This section will examine the state and agribusiness discourses on small-scale farming, discuss smallholder productivity and sustainability, and smallholders' own discourses.

5.1. *Discourse on Smallholder Farming by State and Agrobusiness*

The Russian government and the agribusiness elite regard the large-scale industrialized sector in a positive light, despite such social and environmental risks of large-scale, industrial farming as soil degradation (due to mono-cropping) (Nikulin 2009; Visser, Mamonova, & Spoor, 2012). The smallholder sector is largely depicted in negative terms—at least where its agricultural and economic functions are concerned. Descriptions like 'backward', 'relic of the past', 'without long-term perspective', 'low hygiene standards' abound. This statement by the vice-president of the Russian Grain Union, Alexander Korbut, illustrates this view:

> The reduction of the share of personal subsidiary farming is a normal process, because this farming is inefficient. And in the light of the forthcoming accession of Russia to the WTO, their fate seems pretty dismal.[6]

Western scholars have also frequently described the post-Soviet increase of the smallholders in such negative terms as 'muddling through transition with garden plots' (Seeth, Chachnov, Surinov, & von Braun, 1998). Pallot and Nefedova (2007, p. 202) correctly state that, in Russia, 'people's farms have been portrayed as the official "other" of the agri-food system'. They are seen as the opposite of the supposedly modern and efficient LFEs.

However, while smallholders are construed as backward and inefficient, and get little direct state support, they provide a substantial share of Russia's basic foodstuffs. Households produce 93% of the country's potatoes, 80% of the vegetables, 51% of the milk, and 54% of the meat (Rosstat, 2013a). It should be noted that smallholdings (especially *dacha* plots) are sometimes seen as positive by the state, but then as a 'healthy life style' (in terms of working with nature and consuming fresh produce) or 'recreation', and rarely in terms of its productive function and its role in the agrofood system.

5.2. *Productivity, Sustainability, and Localness*

Food self-provisioning in Russia is quite productive and resource-efficient (in terms of material inputs). Table 1 presents the yields of the most essential crops.

The table shows that rural households are currently nearly as productive (in terms of yields) as LFEs, having been even more productive until recently. The productivity of LFEs is primarily achieved through state support, use of chemical fertilizers, pesticides, and machinery. Households have comparable yields, with essentially no direct support from the state and with largely traditional methods.[7]

Those traditional methods result in environmentally friendly agriculture. Organic fertilizers (manure, compost) are used instead of agrochemicals, and fuel input is minimal as tractors are rarely used (occasionally for plowing) and much work is done by using animal traction (Pallot & Nefedova, 2007; Visser, 2009). These environmentally friendly practices do not emerge from wider concerns about sustainability or contributing to an environmentally sound or localized agricultural system. They arise mostly from the desire to grow healthy food (especially among *dacha* cultivators), the inability to buy expensive inputs, and self-interest in cultivating the small plots in a way that ensures longer-term fertility. The following quote by Tamara Semenova, a representative of the rural social movement 'Peasant Front', describes how the self-interest of smallholders brings about favorable environmental results:

> They are interested in maintaining the fertility of their land. (. . .). Peasants use predominantly organic fertilisers. They maintain the fertility of the land through the use of green manure. They also use crop rotations (. . .).[8]

Table 1. Yields of LFEs and rural households (ton/ha)

	1991	2001	2012
Large farm enterprises (LFEs)			
Grain[a]	1.44	1.83	1.69
Potatoes	9.24	9.95	16.64
Vegetables	13.59	13.58	21.44
Rural households			
Grain[a]	2.67	1.80	1.37
Potatoes	11.52	10.86	12.63
Vegetables	15.96	15.40	19.90

Source: Yields calculated based on output and cultivated land data (by producer and crop) from Rosstat (2013a).
[a]Includes legumes.

A 61-year-old inhabitant from Vladimir region we interviewed stated:

> Potatoes we plant for ourselves (. . .) not to buy the potatoes from the store! Look at those [latter] potatoes. They are 5 years old and still look gorgeous, clean, no rots, nothing! (. . .) It tells us that there are so many pesticides in those potatoes! And in the potatoes we plant—there is nothing.

Although the benefits of smallholder farming are not uncontested, globally, there is an increasing body of work arguing that smallholder farming is more ecologically sustainable (e.g. Altieri, Funes-Monzote, & Petersen, 2011). Relevant here is the fact that, while aversion of fertilizers (and in particular pesticides) is widespread in Russia, it is perhaps not surprising that some of the millions of smallholders do use chemical inputs. In a survey conducted in 2001–2002 among 43 LFEs, 12% of them indicated their provision of pesticides to households (Visser, 2009). This figure (as is the one for fertilizer) is much lower than that for other forms of support, such as ploughing plots (98%), fodder provision (79%), and use of pastures (53%). Overall, the intensification of household production from the early 1990s onwards was mainly achieved by expanding the small plots and, above all, by putting in much more labor (Visser, 2009).

Finally, smallholder production in Russia is highly localized, with a short food chain and distance from field to fork. Both the production and the wider food chain of these smallholders are rather sustainable. A large portion of the smallholders' produce is simply consumed by them and/or exchanged with fellow villagers. The sale of produce occurs within the district at market places, along roadsides, or via itinerant traders (Pallot & Nefedova, 2007). Much of the households' surplus, however, is exchanged via networks of relatives and acquaintances, and represents a sociality that is highly valued and has a long cultural history in the Soviet era (Zavisca, 2003).

5.3. *The 'Quiet' Discourse of Smallholders Themselves*

The discourse of the smallholders themselves is less pronounced and more implicit (with many adhering to the official view, but also some deviations), but it is also widespread. Essentially, they see their smallholdings as a means of survival when wages are not sufficient, or when one suddenly loses one's job—hence, responding to insecurity. The same holds for *dacha* cultivators. We agree with Ries (2009, p. 200) that the aspect of a fall-back option, a means to survive in times of sudden economic crisis or personal misfortune, trumps other elements such as recreation, health, and ecological values (Zavisca, 2003). A dacha cultivator interviewed by Ries (Zavisca, 2003) stated:

> You can trust that, if everything really falls apart, you have the skills and habits to survive.

A smallholder from the Prokuzino village of the Vladimir region we interviewed, who currently cultivates only half of his plot, stated:

> If there will be a year of famine, we will cultivate all our 10 sotkas (0.1 ha) with potatoes.[9]

There is a remarkable paradox that smallholdings are so important, in terms of both economic and ecological value, while at the same time the rural population is rather 'quiet' about these facts, and see them simply as a coping strategy. With the silencing of the smallholdings' role, the term 'quiet food sovereignty' – as inspired from the 'quiet sustainability' concept (Smith & Jehlička, 2013, p. 148) – would probably be the best way to characterize this muted, diffuse form of food sovereignty. The 'quiet' food sovereignty would then be one oriented towards coping with insecurity (also featuring a subsidiary function, as we will show below), instead of aspiring for a role as an independent mode of farming. As for the overlooked smallholding benefits to the environment (partly due to lack of income to buy fertilizers, herbicides etc.), the concept of 'quiet sustainability' seems apt. The concept of quiet sustainability was developed based on research in Poland and the Czech republic, and we should note the major differences between Central European Countries and (post-)Soviet countries regarding socialist agriculture and post-socialist land reforms (to name but a few). Particularly between Poland and Russia, an important difference is that the symbiosis between LFEs and smallholders is hardly found in Poland, where few state farms were established and independent farmers remained the mainstream. However, and most importantly for our argument, the countries do share a common post-socialist setting and a widespread practice of urban and rural dwellers engaged in smallholdings. Smith and Jehlička (2013, p. 148) have described 'quiet sustainability' as follows:

> This novel concept summarises widespread practices that result in beneficial environmental or social outcomes and that do not relate directly or indirectly to market transactions, but are not represented by their practitioners as relating directly to environmental or sustainability goals.

The practices are 'quiet' in terms of sustainability because 'the concern is with the state and quality of the food rather than the environmental impact of the food system per se' (Smith & Jehlička, 2013, p. 155). And they constitute:

> not a programme to be implemented, a future ambition for society or an exceptional contrast to the norm. Rather it is a quiet but purposeful parallel to the market economy of food. (Smith & Jehlička, 2013, p. 155)

In Russia, the quiet and parallel nature of smallholder production is clearly indicated by the widespread adherence of the rural population to the official categorization of rural smallholdings. As in the Soviet period, the smallholdings of the population are called 'subsidiary household plots'. The absence of terms like 'farm' or 'agriculture' is telling. The term 'household' has connotations of household chores (much of the work on the household plot is done by women, and seen as an extension of housekeeping).

Furthermore, the term 'subsidiary' is also crucial. In the Soviet Union, with its principle of full employment, rural smallholdings indeed functioned as a subsidiary income and food source, secondary to collective farm employment. However, during the slump in agriculture, with widespread wage arrears that came after the demise of the Soviet Union, smallholdings quickly rose in importance. Rural dwellers intensified smallholder production (and urbanites did likewise on *dacha* plots) (Visser, 2009). Even with a slight decrease in their share in the total agricultural production since 2009, these plots still constitute the main source of income for a substantial part of the rural population, and an important source of food and saved expenses for many urbanites (Visser, 2009). Thus, while the term 'subsidiary household plot' might have been appropriate during the Soviet period, it is now a stark understatement of its actual role in both agriculture and rural incomes.

However, as mentioned above, rural households still adhere to the idea of the subsidiary nature of their plots vis-á-vis LFEs.

While the personal smallholding is seen as crucial for survival, and few would do away with it completely, few rural dwellers actually aspire to expand their plots if they can get a salaried job that provides them with sufficient income (Nefedova, 2008). A considerable share of the rural households would in fact decrease production (although not fully, we suspect). Furthermore, few rural dwellers (or *dacha* cultivators) would see their smallholdings as a viable alternative to the large-scale food system. On the contrary, rural dwellers have strong nostalgia for the Soviet past and welcome the revitalization of former *kolkhozy* and *sovkhozy* (Pallot & Nefedova,

2007). The striking fact is that the state and agribusiness' negative view on smallholders partly resonates among the latter themselves.[10] While this is mainly the result of the longstanding subsidiary role of household plots, it is also caused by the longstanding stigmatization of rural dwellers (Ries, 2009), and reinforced by the official media discourse. However, while smallholders often expect a decline in the importance of smallholdings in agriculture, we rarely encountered smallholders who expect their complete disappearance.

6. The Political Dimension of Quiet Food Sovereignty

Many authors argue that the political dimension of food sovereignty is key (Claeys, 2013; McMichael, 2009; Patel, 2009). Desmarais (2007), for instance, speaks of 'a collective struggle to define the alternatives to the globalisation of a neoliberal, highly capitalised, corporate-led model of agricultural development'. Elements of the political dimension are: a clear vision to shift the control of productive resources to farmers, their subsequent claiming of rights, and finally their struggle (against state and/or agribusiness) to achieve those rights.

In Russia, at a first glance, the political dimension seems to be absent. There are no outspoken food sovereignty visions and claims. There is hardly any open struggle for food sovereignty. Could we then classify the Russian case as food sovereignty? In other words, in addition to quiet sustainability, can we call it quiet food sovereignty?

In terms of aims and claims, proponents and researchers of food sovereignty often state that it is, first a drive to roll back the mainstream large-scale food system (in terms of what it is against) and, second, a desire to gain democratic control over food production (and consumption) by establishing autonomous smallholder production (in terms of what it is in favor of) (Desmarais, 2007; McMichael, 2009; Nyéléni, 2007; Patel, 2009). We will discuss the relevance of these two aims for the Russian case.

Regarding the first point, it should be stressed that, whereas in many countries food sovereignty is inspired by the threats of the large-scale system for smallholders, this is has not been the case in Russia. Russian rural dwellers have traditionally experienced numerous benefits of the large-scale food system as rural workers and citizens (full employment, good social services, and support for their smallholdings have all been connected to their workplace in the LFE). As consumers, rural and urban dwellers' major concern constituted the frequent deficits of fresh and varied food. Long queues in front of half empty food shops became iconic images of this failure of the system. Thus, whereas elsewhere the dominance and pervasiveness (in terms of outcompeting other food options) of the large-scale food system is the main concern, in Russia the *lack* of pervasiveness and the resulting food insecurity have traditionally been the concern.

Second, are claiming more control by smallholders and striving for full autonomy essential criteria for acknowledging Russian practices as a form of food sovereignty? We would argue that the Russian smallholders see cultivating their own food as an important right. However, this right is implicit. It is hardly expressed as it is a longstanding tradition, and a substantial degree of control over their own production is seen as the natural order of things. Why would smallholders state the obvious?

Moreover, the right to cultivate (a part of) their own food does not necessarily mean that the right for autonomous food provision is claimed. As defined by the Peoples' Food Sovereignty Network (2002), food sovereignty is:

> the right of peoples to define their own food and agriculture; (..) to determine the *extent* to which want to be self-reliant. [emphasis added]

For Russian smallholders, a parallel existence of smallholdings next to LFEs seems to be the appropriate cultural form, with a symbiosis between LFEs and households preferred over full self-reliance.

As long as the right to produce their own healthy food is not threatened, smallholders will not have much of an incentive to protest. Rural dwellers 'have the core land resource, the household plot, in their inalienable property' (Pallot & Nefedova, 2007, p. 203), and this resource is hardly threatened as the plots are too small for LFEs. The access to LFEs' resources, however, has always been informal, and here 'the legal basis for their claims is often tenuous or non-existent' (Pallot & Nefedova, 2007, p. 106). Access to these resources seems to be based on an implicit social contract in which rural dwellers keep quiet as long as the symbiosis between LFEs and smallholdings is maintained by the former, or at the very least the smallholders are not restricted.

As the rights discourse is so implicit in quiet food sovereignty, it raises the question of whether the rights discourse is muted or in fact absent. In other words, does quiet food sovereignty have a potential for political struggle or is it intrinsically apolitical?

It seems that people will claim their rights and engage in struggle when the implicit social contract of the LFEs and smallholders' symbiosis (or at least co-existence) is threatened. A strong indication of this are the smallholders' fierce reactions to the state policy aimed at fighting swine flu in the autumn of 2013. After the outbreak of the disease in the swine herd of a household in the Belgorod region, the governor decided to slaughter all the pigs held by the households in the region and to pay them compensation. This policy triggered a widespread response: letters to newspapers, demonstrations, road blocks, and even the emergence of a small social movement ('Kolos') to counter it. The state policy was frequently interpreted by smallholders as a pretext to eradicate smallholdings—to the benefit of LFEs. As a smallholder stated;

> Initially pigs will be liquidated, then chickens, other birds. (. . .) In the end, by hook or by crook, the last peasants will be eliminated. (Park, 2013)

Furthermore, the current pilfering of farm assets by rural dwellers could be seen as a struggle in the form of 'everyday resistance' (Scott, 1985). It is not a form of resistance against LFEs as such, as rural households can hardly imagine a future without them; but it can be classified as resistance against the tendency of LFEs to curtail their support to smallholders in order to cut costs (Nikulin, 2003, 2009)—in other words, as resistance against the erosion of the 'implicit social contract' of symbiosis (cf. Pallot & Nefedova, 2007, p. 124).

These examples show that quiet food sovereignty is not apolitical. We agree with Pallot and Nefedova (2007, p. 106) that:

> . . . rural Russia has been the scene of a muted, but real, contestation of market reform on the part of the population intent on defending their access to resources and services to which they believe they are still entitled.

That active claim making and open struggle have been rare is caused first of all by the fact that, by and large, people are able to engage in producing and consuming 'healthy and culturally appropriate food' as they wish.

7. Preconditions for an Emerging Food Sovereignty Movement

To gauge how likely it is that a food sovereignty movement would emerge out of 'quiet food sovereignty', we discuss below various obstacles and opportunities.

One cognitive obstacle for a food sovereignty movement is that the rural population associates sovereignty exclusively with the state level (such as the 'sovereign' or 'guided' democracy propagated by the Putin regime, or the national food self-sufficiency—for which food sovereignty is occasionally used as a synonym. The rural dwellers' own food practices and narratives are mainly concerned with a secure food provisioning—control over food production is only a means to that end. Here we see a similarity with the situation in Honduras (Boyer, 2010), where Via Campesina's food sovereignty campaign failed because it did not take into account the understandings of the Honduran peasant. The latter associated food sovereignty with the powers of nation states, and the concept of food security with their deeply held peasant understandings of, and desire for, security in terms of their continued social reproduction in insecure social and natural conditions. This resonates with the Russian case, with its tradition of food deficits and smallholder farming as a vital survival strategy for coping with that.

Another obstacle is the low potential for mobilization among the rural population. This is related to the fragmentation of Russian rural society (with, for instance, numerous divisions between private farmers, household plot holders, and dacha cultivators (Pallot & Nefedova, 2007, p. 36–38), in addition to a demographic composition which is strongly skewed toward the elderly and economically inactive (Nefedova, 2008). Furthermore, there is a generally low proneness toward collective action (Mamonova & Visser, 2014).

Another major hindrance is the earlier discussed symbiosis between LFEs and household plots. This symbiosis, while favorable to the smallholders, at the same time hinders the further growth of independent family farming. What is more, it reinforces the status quo of the dominance of LFEs. More generally, this symbiosis precludes a more assertive, rights-based stance toward farm enterprises and the state, which could hold the seeds of a food sovereignty movement. When salaries or land rents are not paid, when a crisis strikes, the ingrained reaction is to seek refuge at the household/*dacha* plots. As a Russian farm director, interviewed by Visser in 2002, stated (cf. Ries, 2009, p. 201 on *dacha* cultivators):

> In France, farmers take to the streets to protest, but in Russia rural dwellers remain quiet because they can always get by on their household plots.

However, when the symbiosis is threatened, we might expect instances of sudden mobilization, as indicated by the earlier mentioned example of the smallholders' response to the state's swine flu policy. The ongoing modernization (read: further industrialization) of agroholdings, the sharpening of sanitary standards, and the rising influence of foreign agribusiness through Russia's recent accession to WTO might put additional pressure on the continuation of this symbiosis, and subsequently create incentives for a Russian mobilization around food sovereignty issues.

8. Conclusions

Normally, one would expect to find food sovereignty within rural movements; in Russia, genuine rural movements are extremely rare and weak. The food sovereignty term is rarely used in Russian debates in its literal translation.

However, the food sovereignty concept is neither irrelevant nor fully absent. Food sovereignty in its Russian guise is a more implicit, but widespread approach and clearly emerges bottom-up; we termed this 'quiet food sovereignty', building on recent insights regarding 'quiet sustainability' (Smith & Jehlička, 2013). We showed that food sovereignty in practice plays an important role in Russia, with the rural and urban population as smallholders being able to produce a significant share of the food consumed, in or near their local places of living, in a largely ecologically friendly and healthy way. Furthermore, the exchange of food from those smallholdings generates a sociality that is generally highly valued, and has a long cultural history (Ries, 2009), which presents a purposeful parallel to market exchange in agribusiness. These aspects match the vision of food sovereignty put forward by global social movements rather well.

However, at the same time, the productive and environmental importance of such smallholdings is grossly overlooked and downplayed by the Russian government, but even more strikingly, also partly by the smallholders (cf. Kitching, 1998; Pallot & Nefedova, 2007). Quiet food sovereignty does not challenge the overall food system directly through its produce, claims, or ideas, but focuses on individual economic benefits and ecological production for personal health, as well as a culturally appropriate form of sociality, generated by the exchange of self-produced food.

Furthermore, a rights discourse—which is so central in food sovereignty—while not absent, is rather implicit. It is grounded in the longstanding tradition of self-provisioning, and taken for granted.

Quiet food sovereignty is yet too diffuse to be classified as a genuine food sovereignty *movement*. Some emergent rural social movements do exist in Russia. However, for a national food sovereignty movement to take shape, there are many hindrances to overcome such as: the divergent understandings of food sovereignty and security among the Russian smallholders, and the low potential for mobilization among the rural population (due to, for instance, social fragmentation). The symbiosis between smallholdings and LFEs also impedes resistance; however, when this symbiosis is threatened—which we expect to happen increasingly—it might trigger sudden mobilization.

We contend that the Russian case is relevant for the wider food sovereignty debate and movement. Some media sources even heralded Russian smallholdings as offering a model that might be the key to feeding the world (NaturalNews.com, 2012). Our study suggests that food sovereignty as an everyday practice and discourse is more widespread in post-socialist and semi-totalitarian settings than one would suspect by evaluating food sovereignty by the presence of food sovereignty movements. Acknowledging this would further the global reach and inclusiveness of the food sovereignty movement, and build new transnational linkages with parallel struggles in non-democratic contexts.

Viewed critically, some might wonder whether considering ‘quiet food sovereignty’ a form of food sovereignty makes for a slippery slope, with the risk of weakening an already broad concept. We acknowledge this risk, and recognize that the inclusion of ‘quiet food sovereignty’ will be a major challenge, both conceptually and practically, for network building in settings without strong movements. However, the definition of food sovereignty has never been static over the past two decades, and the ambition to incorporate new local experiences to achieve ‘a fine balance’ between ‘local realities and global actions’ (Desmarais, 2007, p. 135) or visions is key to keep food sovereignty vital. Furthermore, we would argue that—for food sovereignty to constitute the global movement it claims to be—it should be inclusive of the large numbers of rural (and urban) people in non-democratic settings who in many ways practice the ideal of food sovereignty, even if they are less vocal in doing so.

Finally, we contend that the finding that ‘quiet food sovereignty’ has not (yet) turned into a solid social movement should not only be seen as a shortcoming. In fact, in less than democratic settings with limited open space for contention, the implicit practices and narratives, the strong orientation toward co-existing with large-scale farms, and the hidden or ad-hoc struggles of ‘quiet food sovereignty’ might be more effective than full-blown movements. Russia’s ‘sovereign’ or ‘guided democracy’ approach does not offer much space for social mobilization. It is very likely that a sizeable food sovereignty movement would face state opposition and restrictions, as is currently happening with various urban NGOs and emerging rural movements (Mamonova & Visser, 2014). Alternatively, the Russian government might take up the concept if food sovereignty would become more popular, but would likely do so in a tightly controlled manner. It might do so, for instance, by molding the concept ingeniously—taking out the elements that challenge the status quo—as it has previously done with various rural and urban movements and their notions, by creating state embedded civil society organizations (Mamonova & Visser, 2014). Thus, it would be less likely for a Russian food sovereignty *movement* to be close to the term's global understanding (in the vein of a social movement like *Via Campesina*), and more likely for it be something of a state-captured '*Via Kremlina*'.

Acknowledgements

This article benefited from Daniela Patru and Martha Jane Robbins' editing assistance.

Disclosure Statement

No potential conflict of interest was reported by the authors.

Funding

The article received financial support from European Research Council (ERC) [grant number 313781].

Notes

1 This applies also to urban food movements.
2 For varying definitions, see e.g. Desmarais (2007), Edelman (2014), Nyéléni (2007), Peoples' Food Sovereignty Network (2002).
3 An exception is DeMaster (2013).
4 Alternatively, some argue more recently that food sovereignty is becoming too locally focused (Iles & Montenegro, 2013).
5 Furthermore, though they mostly continued offering some support to household plots, LFEs gradually reduced the range of goods and/or beneficiaries (Nikulin, 2003, 2009; Visser, 2009).
6 See: Subsidiary farming—a relic of the past or the reality of the Russian countryside? http://altapress.ru/story/80477.
7 Some of the state support to LFEs may 'leak' to the plots through the symbiosis between the two; but this would be a small percentage, especially as the monitoring of large farm property became more strict from the late 1990s onwards (Visser, 2009).
8 Interview 21 October 2010, Moscow.
9 Interview 5 November 2013.
10 There are also differences between regions and households, with the small group of somewhat larger, commercial household plots likely to be more positive. For a slightly more positive view on smallholdings, see Alekhin (2012); for negative views, see Kitching (1998), Pallot and Nefedova (2007, p. 205).

References

Alekhin, I. (2012, February 18). Podvor'e: atavism ili shans? *Kuzbass*. Retrieved from http://www.kuzbass85.ru/2012/01/18/podvore-atavizm-ili-shans/

Altieri, M. A., Funes-Monzote, F. R., & Petersen, P. (2011). Agroecologically efficient agricultural systems for smallholder farmers: Contributions to food sovereignty. *Agronomy for Sustainable Development*, *32*, 1–13.

Ardener, E. (1975). Belief and the problem of women. In S. Ardener (Ed.), *Perceiving women* (pp. 1–17). London: Malaby Press.
Ayres, J. & Bosia, M. J. (2011). Beyond global summitry: food sovereignty as localized resistance to globalization. *Globalizations*, *8*(1), 47–63.
Boyer, J. (2010). Food security, food sovereignty, and local challenges for transnational agrarian movements: the Honduras case. *Journal of Peasant Studies*, *37*(2), 319–351.
Claeys, P. (2013, September 14–15). *An overview of La Via Campesina's right-based claims over the last 20 years.* Paper for the conference 'Food Sovereignty: A Critical Dialogue', Yale University/ISS.
DeMaster, K. (2013, September 14–15). *Navigating de- and re-peasantisation: Potential limitation of a universal food sovereignty approach for Polish Smallholders.* Paper for the conference 'Food Sovereignty: A Critical Dialogue', Yale University/ISS.
Desmarais, A.-A. (2007). *La Via Campesina. Globalisation and the power of peasants.* Halifax: Fernwood Publishing.
Edelman, M. (2014). Food sovereignty: Forgotten genealogies and future regulatory challenges. *Journal of Peasant Studies*, 1–20. doi:10.1080/03066150.2013.876998.
Hospes, O. (2014). Food sovereignty: The debate, the deadlock and a suggested detour. *Agriculture and Human Values*, *31*, 119–130.
Iles, A., & Montenegro, M. (2013, September 14–15). *Building relational food sovereignty across scales: An example from the Peruvian Andes.* Paper for the conference 'Food Sovereignty: A Critical Dialogue', Yale University /ISS.
Kitching, G. (1998). The revenge of the peasant? The collapse of Russian agriculture and the role of the peasant 'private plot' in that collapse, 1991–1997. *Journal of Peasant Studies*, *26*(1), 43–81.
Mamonova, N., & Visser, O. (2014). State marionettes, phantom organisations or genuine movements? The paradoxical emergence of rural social movements in post-Soviet Russia. *Journal of Peasant Studies.* doi:10.180/03066150.2014.918958
McMichael, M. (2009). Food sovereignty, social reproduction and the agrarian question. In A. Haroon Akram-Lodhi, & C. Kay (Eds.), *Peasants and globalization. Political economy, rural transformation and the agrarian question* (pp. 288–312). New York: Routledge.
Natural News.com. (2012). Russia's small-scale organic agriculture model may hold the key to feeding the world. http://www.naturalnews.com/037366_russia_home_gardens_food_production.html
Nefedova, T. (2008). Russian rural areas by the eyes of its inhabitants. In N. E. Pokrovskiy (Ed.), *Ugric project: the environment and the people of the North* (pp. 98–120). Moscow: Society of professional sociologists.
Nikulin, A. (2003). The Kuban Kolkhoz between a holding and a Hacienda. *Focaal*, *41*, 137–152.
Nikulin, A. (2009). *The Oligarkhoz as successor of Post-Kolkhoz.* Paper presented at the Max Planck Institute for Social Anthropology, Halle/Saale.
Nyéléni. (2007). Declaration of Nyéléni, 27 February, Selingué Mali. http://www.nyeleni.org/spip.php?article290
Pallot, J., & Nefedova, T. (2007). *Russia's unknown agriculture: Household production in post-soviet Russia.* Oxford: Oxford University Press.
Park, N. (2013). Chuma unichtozhaet Rossiiskoe svinovodstvo. *TTP Inform.* Retrieved from http://www.ttp-inform.ru/security/3588.html
Patel, R. (2009). What does food sovereignty look like? *Journal of Peasant Studies*, *36*(3), 663–706.
Peoples' Food Sovereignty Network. (2002). *Statement on peoples' food sovereignty.* Retrieved from http://www.peoplesfoodsovereignty.org/statements/new%20statement/statement_01.htm
Ries, N. (2009). Potato ontology. Surviving postsocialism in Russia. *Cultural Anthropology*, *24*(2), 181–212.
Rosreestr (Federal Service for State Registration, Cadastre and Cartography). (2012). *State (national) report on the status and use of land in the Russian Federation in 2012.* Retrieved from: https://rosreestr.ru/site/activity/gosudarstvennoe-upravlenie-v-sfere-ispolzovaniya-i-okhrany-zemel/gosudarstvennyy-monitoring-zemel/sostoyanie-zemel-rossii/gosudarstvennyy-natsionalnyy-doklad-o-sostoyanii-i-ispolzovanii-zemel-v-rossiyskoy-federatsii/
Rosstat. (2013a). *Russian federal statistical service.* Retrieved from http://www.gks.ru/wps/wcm/connect/rosstat_main/rosstat/ru/statistics/enterprise/economy/
Rosstat. (2013b). *Structure of agricultural output by farm types in the Russian Federation.* Retrieved from http://www.gks.ru/free_doc/new_site/business/sx/tab-sel2.htm
Scott, J. C. (1985). *Weapons of the weak: Everyday forms of peasant resistance.* New Haven, CT: Yale University Press.
Seeth, H. T., Chachnov, S., Surinov, A., & von Braun, J. (1998). Muddling through economic transition with garden plots. *World Development*, *26*(9), 1611–1623.
Smith, J., & Jehlička, P. (2013). Quiet sustainability: Fertile lessons from Europe's productive gardeners. *Journal of Rural Studies*, *32*, 148–157.
Super, E. (2012). Harvest 2012. Retrieved from http://odnako.org/blogs/show_21679

Torres, F. (2003). The via campesina. Peasant-led agrarian reform and food sovereignty. *Development*, *54*(1), 49–54.

Visser, O. (2006). Property, labour relations and social obligations in Russia's privatised farm enterprises. In K. von Benda-Beckmann, F. von Benda-Beckmann, & M. Wiber (Eds.), *The changing properties of property,* (pp. 205–234). London: Berghahn.

Visser, O. (2009). Household plots and the symbiosis with the large farm enterprises in Russia. In M. Spoor (Ed.), *Land, peasants and rural poverty in transition. The political economy of rural livelihoods* (pp. 76–98). London: Routledge.

Visser, O., Mamonova, N., & Spoor, M. (2012). Oligarchs, megafarms and land reserves: Understanding land grabbing in Russia. *Journal of Peasant Studies*, *39*(3–4), 899–931.

von Benda-Beckmann, F., von Benda-Beckmann, K., & Wiber, M. (2006). *Changing properties of property*. New York: Berghahn Books.

World Bank. (1992). *Food and agricultural policy reforms in the former USSR. An agenda for transition. Background working paper, vol.1.* Washington, DC: The World Bank.

Zavisca, J. (2003). Contesting capitalism at the post-soviet dacha: The meaning of food cultivation for urban Russians. *Slavic Review*, *62*(2), 786–810.

Return to Freedom: Anti-GMO Aloha ʻĀina Activism on Molokai as an Expression of Place-based Food Sovereignty

CLARE GUPTA*,**

*Yale University, New Haven, CT, USA
**The Kohala Center, Waimea, HI, USA

ABSTRACT *This paper explores the concept of food sovereignty on the island of Molokai, where the Hawaiian value of aloha ʻāina, or love for the land, guides local efforts to preserve and promote local food production. This organizing concept also has political undertones—food sovereignty requires access to land and resources, both of which Native Hawaiians have historically been dispossessed of since colonial contact. In the paper, I examine current anti-genetically modified organism (GMO) activism as one example of the uniquely Hawaiian food sovereignty efforts taking place on Molokai. I present two key arguments. First, I show how the anti-GMO platform, which has garnered support from both native Hawaiians and more recent settlers, reflects a strategic alliance that gives greater momentum to Hawaiʻi's food sovereignty movement, which in turn is viewed by a growing number of Native Hawaiians as a pathway toward Indigenous sustainable self-determination. I also draw from the Molokai case to illustrate a perceived tension between community-based work and political engagement that exists within both the food sovereignty paradigm and the contemporary Indigenous sovereignty framework. I argue that aloha ʻāina as a cultural and political praxis suggests 'ways out' of this apparent paradox, by showing how Hawaiians have historically engaged simultaneously in both community-based practices and political activism as a means to care for their land and people. While food sovereignty on Molokai calls for the privileging of place-based knowledge, there are lessons to be learnt for social movements elsewhere that are also struggling internally to deconstruct and define what is meant by food sovereignty, and how best to achieve it.*

Introduction

'Before there was this term "sustainability", there was aloha 'āina', Native Hawaiian and long-time activist Walter Ritte explained to me, as we sat discussing the current challenges Molokai faces. For Uncle Walter, aloha 'āina holds meaning beyond its literal translation—'love of the land'. To him and other Hawaiians it also refers to the political movement that developed in the 1970s in which the term aloha 'āina re-emerged as a catchphrase for a solution to the problems of Hawaiian dispossession of land and resources (Morales, 1984). Within aloha 'āina is the notion that if you take care of the land, the land takes care of you—a relationship partially severed for Hawaiians by settler colonialism. In the 1970s, aloha 'āina came to mean the restoration of that reciprocal relationship between Hawaiians and their land, both through political means to regain land rights and through a resurgence of traditional conservation-oriented land stewardship and subsistence practices.

Aloha 'āina refers to both values and a movement that at their core are about food sovereignty. First defined by La Via Campesina in 1996 and then refined at a global summit in Mali in 2007, food sovereignty is 'the right of peoples to healthy and culturally appropriate food produced through ecologically sound and sustainable methods, and their right to define their own food and agriculture systems' (Nyéléni, 2007). It encompasses a set of policies and principles that provide an alternative to and directly challenge neoliberal economic development, industrial agriculture, and asymmetrical power relations (Glipo & Pascual, 2005). As Figueroa (this issue) notes, food sovereignty's radical imperative is to consider social justice not simply as an additive property to a sustainable food system, but the very foundation from which such a food system must be built.

Food sovereignty is a thread in the larger political debate on sovereignty that in many ways parallels, and in some cases is part of, Indigenous peoples' movements across the world (Pimbert, 2007). In Canada for example, Indigenous peoples have self defined Indigenous food sovereignty as a framework that includes the 'freedom and ability to respond to our own needs for healthy, culturally adapted Indigenous foods. It represents the freedom and ability to make decisions over the amount and quantity of food we hunt, fish, gather, grow and eat' (Morrison, 2011, p. 100). In Hawai'i, a conference on food sovereignty started annually on Hawai'i Island in 2007, called Hō'ea Ea ('return to freedom'), described food sovereignty oriented around Native agricultural practices as 'a spiritual, physical and cognitive pathway toward greater wellbeing and self-sufficiency' (http://handsturned.tripod.com/what.html). In this way, food sovereignty is about securing the rights necessary to achieve food self-sufficiency.

Aloha 'āina as a way of being in the world underlies this and other contemporary food sovereignty initiatives in Hawai'i, which in turn are viewed as a pathway toward greater economic independence and social health—what Native Hawaiian activists and scholars call sustainable self-determination (Corntassel, 2008). Food sovereignty, which is about radically restructuring the streams of power that control and distribute resources, is a movement that operates according to a logic akin to that which underlies the concept of sustainable self-determination for Native Hawaiians and other Indigenous communities. As Pimbert (2009) notes, farmers and peasants who have joined together under the banner of food sovereignty contest:

> liberal understandings in which citizenship is viewed as a set of rights and responsibilities granted by the state. Instead, citizenship in the context of locally determined food systems is claimed, and rights are realized, through the agency and actions of people themselves. (p. 48)

He concludes that communities striving for food sovereignty must realize and practice 'emergent' rather than conventional forms of citizenship. Similarly, self-determination, as enacted through practices such as cultivation of kalo (taro), an Indigenous Hawaiian staple crop, is a sovereignty of autonomous livelihoods and self-determining collective personhoods, achieved through controlling one's labor (inputs and outputs) (Lasky, 2008).

Recently, aloha ʻāina has been employed as the rallying cry by activists against genetically modified organisms (GMOs) who see the expansion of the biotechnology seed corn industry in Hawaiʻi as the newest iteration of corporate colonial-style land grabbing, and who want this industry to be more regulated or, for some, removed from the state entirely. Nowhere in Hawaiʻi is this issue more heated than on the small island of Molokai, known for its fierce defense of ʻāina (land), kai (ocean), and natural resources; and its tight-knit predominantly Native Hawaiian community. While not all anti-GMO activists on Molokai engage explicitly with the term 'food sovereignty', the growth of the seed corn industry and its associated practices, as an issue that is deeply tied to the politics of land, power, and food production, is linked to larger questions about self-determination of food systems and Native Hawaiian sovereignty more broadly.

Indigenous sovereignty is the subject of a wide-ranging body of scholarship, and research on the food sovereignty movement is burgeoning (e.g. see this issue and articles in 2014 special issue in *Journal of Peasant Studies* on this subject), yet few studies have explored the relationship between traditional Indigenous values such as aloha ʻāina, a concept laden with both spiritual and political meanings, and contemporary food sovereignty activism. This paper builds on this sparse but significant literature (Goodyear-Ka'ōpua, 2009; Lukens, 2013) in its analysis of anti-GMO activism in Hawaiʻi, and in particular on Molokai, as a way to think about the challenges and opportunities that face a food sovereignty movement rooted in part in Indigenous struggles. Here, it is important to make a distinction between those who explicitly use the term food sovereignty and those who do not, and between those whose engagement with aloha ʻāina as an expression of food sovereignty is linked to Indigenous resurgence and those for whom it is not. In Hawaiʻi, the discourse of 'food sovereignty' circulates among a relatively small circle of Hawaiian scholars and activists, many of whom are cited in this paper, while the growing anti-GMO movement in many places, Molokai included, is not a specifically self-identified food sovereignty movement. Yet as Desmarais and Wittman (2014) point out, in many places, communities may not use the language of food sovereignty but in fact are engaged in initiatives that fit within a food sovereignty framework. This is true in Hawaiʻi, where residents invoke aloha ʻāina in their grassroots resistance to GMOs, though arguably within two overlapping yet distinct 'communities'. The controversy over the GMO industry's presence in Hawaiʻi is linked on one level to desires for local control over agri-food systems by a community of concerned Hawaiian residents that include settlers and non-settlers alike, in the face of an expanding corporate agribusiness sector. On another level, the protests against the seed corn industry on the grounds that it re-inscribes historical and structural injustices against Native Hawaiians, and efforts to create alternative food systems based upon restored relations with the land, are by their very nature about *Indigenous* food sovereignty. Situating the strand of anti-GMO activism that is an expression of Indigenous food sovereignty, and understanding how it links to a larger project of sustainable self-determination for Native Hawaiians, is the primary focus of this paper.

Focusing on the example of the small island community of Molokai, I examine the ways in which Indigenous food sovereignty claims are articulated through a Hawaiian framework of aloha ʻāina. This is a subject that is relevant not only to those working on food issues in Hawaiʻi but also to agrarian scholars more broadly, given the potentially illuminating yet unexplored implications of the Hawaiian concept of aloha ʻāina for the international movement for food sovereignty. The case of Molokai is particularly interesting for exploring key questions within agrarian studies today—namely, what does food sovereignty look like in practice, in specific places (Desmarais & Wittman, 2014)? How do long-standing Indigenous claims for sovereignty articulate with newer food sovereignty discourses? And what spaces of possibility exist for food sovereignty within the global food system?

This paper begins by tracing the genealogy of the aloha ʻāina movement through to the current period of anti-GMO activism. In doing so, I draw attention to the history and politics of Indigeneity that underlie this anti-GMO activism, which is inseparable from questions of Hawaiian food sovereignty and independence. For Native Hawaiians, the presence and activities of GMO seed corn companies represent the latest affront in a long history of land expropriation, dispossession, and environmental degradation. I show how GMO-related activism illustrates a perceived tension within both the food sovereignty paradigm and the contemporary Indigenous sovereignty framework. Today, Indigenous political work in Hawai'i has become less about asking for rights to be granted by the state through policy activism and more about ʻāina-based projects to restore individual and community responsibilities and abilities to be economically self-sufficient. For example, for many organizations working on Native food issues in Hawaiʻi, Corntassel's 'community-based solutions' to Indigenous colonization take shape through the restoration and re-integration of kalo into local diets, and other ways of teaching communities to provide for themselves. Yet efforts to regulate (or remove) the GMO seed corn industry in Hawaiʻi, as a means to realize greater food sovereignty, necessitate engagement with the state. Uncovering the history of aloha ʻāina is helpful for offering a 'way out' of this paradox, by showing the ways in which Hawaiians have historically engaged simultaneously in both ʻāina-based activities and political activism as a means to care for their land and people.

Aloha ʻĀina Warriors: Situating Anti-GMO Activism in Hawaiʻi

Aloha ʻĀina Genealogy: An Hawaiian Ethic and Practice

Integral to Hawaiian management is the practice of aloha ʻāina. This is a concept that is generations old, and that has been at the root of Hawaiian resistance to imperialism for over 100 years (Goodyear-Ka'ōpua, 2013). Yet it is not a static term—its usage over time by new generations of Hawaiians reflects a re-working of traditional values in the context of historical dispossession. Tracing its genealogy reveals the political, economic, and social relations in which its meaning continues to be articulated.

The Hawaiian genealogical worldview is found in the Kumulipo, a cosmological chant/prayer which places humans as the younger siblings of Haloa (kalo) and the ʻāina (islands) in the family of life (Andrade, 2008). As an elder sibling, land cares for the Hawaiian people as long as the Hawaiian people care for it, in a reciprocal interdependent familial relationship (Kameʻeleihiwa, 1992). One literal translation of ʻāina is 'that which feeds', in terms of both sustaining the physical body and nourishing the mind and spirit (Andrade, 2008). This definition connotes a concept of the environment based on the interconnections of land and people, and a union between culture and ecosystem (Beamer, 2013).

Aloha ʻāina is at the core of Hawaiian traditional spiritual belief and custom. Shared ancestry with the natural environment gives Native Hawaiians a responsibility to protect the land and its resources for current and future generations. As Kame'eleihiwa (1992) writes,

> it is the ''āina, the kalo, and the Ali'i Nui who are to feed, clothe, and shelter their younger brothers and sisters, the Hawaiian people . . . Clearly, by this equation, it is the duty of Hawaiians to Mālama 'āina [care for the land], and as a result of this proper behavior, the 'āina will mālama Hawaiians. (p. 25)

Hawaiians view aloha 'āina as active and something that must be put into practice rather than a state of being (Beamer, 2013), or a mere feeling or belief (Goodyear-Ka'ōpua, 2013). Conservation in particular is an integral aspect to traditional subsistence activities that connect people to land and sea. For Native Hawaiians, the health of people and their social systems are deeply tied to the health of the 'āina (McGregor, Tanemura, Matsuoka, & Minerbi, 2003).

Aloha 'Āina as Embodied Layers of Responsibility

Molokai scholar McGregor (2007) writes that aloha 'āina embodies several layers of kuleana, or responsibility:

> At one level, it meant protecting the physical sustainability of the Hawaiian lands as natural resources. At another level, it meant organizing and rallying for Hawaiian native rights and sovereignty to achieve the political standing necessary to protect the ''āina. At the deepest level, it meant a spiritual dedication to honor and worship the gods who were the spiritual life forces of nature. (p. 265)

The island of Molokai has been at the heart of Hawaiian efforts to practice aloha 'āina according to these multiple layers of responsibility. It was on Molokai where a movement developed in the late 1970s to protect the island of Kaho'olawe from military bombing practice, which led to a revival of the traditional Hawaiian value of aloha 'āina. The leaders of this movement came to realize that absence from the land was the common thread linking many of the problems that Hawaiians had (Morales, 1984). They formed the Protect Kaho'olawe 'Ohana (PKO) and began using the phrase aloha 'āina well before realizing its historical significance. Only later did they find out that aloha 'āina was a common term used around the time of Queen Lili'uokalani's overthrow in 1893—used as a password by counter-revolutionaries loyal to the Queen and as part of the title of the newspaper, *Ke Aloha 'Āina* (Morales, 1984). In those years, petitions circulated by a group called Hui Aloha 'Āina gathered nearly 40,000 signatures, essentially the number of Hawaiians alive at the time, who attested to widespread opposition to annexation and support for restoration of the monarchy. These petitions were delivered to deposed Queen Lili'uokalani in Washington where she was lobbying the US Senate against annexation. In this way, the meaning of aloha 'āina extended beyond familial love to the idea that Hawaiians must strive to control their own government in order to provide life to the people and to care for their land properly (Silva, 2004).

Kaho'olawe and the inspiration of the PKO leaders then sparked a broader cultural revival that embraced the environmental, political, and spiritual meaning and directive of aloha 'āina (McGregor, 2002). The 1970s marked the beginning of a cultural renaissance for Native Hawaiians, reviving the cultural practices of hula, Hawaiian music, lā'au lapa'au (traditional Hawaiian healing), traditional Hawaiian voyaging, and kalo farming. At the same time, mobilization around struggles for resources and cultural access at Kaho'olawe and evictions of farmers (both Hawaiian and non-Hawaiian) in Waiahole/Waikane, and Kalama Valley reflected a reigniting of a Hawaiian political spirit rooted in aloha 'āina (Lukens, 2013). The synergy of ostensibly purely cultural initiatives—notably the rebirth of open-sea canoe travel with the voyages of the Hokule'a throughout Hawai'i and Polynesia—and those viewed as simply political, such as PKO, served as the catalyst for the development of a cultural nationalist movement (Tengan,

2008). By the 1980s, many Hawaiian movement leaders were articulating an explicitly nationalist agenda calling for Hawaiian sovereignty (Goodyear-Ka'ōpua, 2013). Aloha 'āina thus provided (and continues to provide) space to link issues of social, cultural, and ecological justice (Beamer, 2013).

Aloha 'Āina and Sustainable Self-determination

Today, aloha 'āina has in part come to manifest itself in farming and cultural practice-based projects that are oriented around food sovereignty as a pathway toward sustainable self-determination. As Native Hawaiian scholar Meyer (2014) wrote recently, 'There is a food sovereignty movement in Hawai'i!' She describes youth garden projects as one small link in a larger chain of gardens, communities, and creative ideas oriented around a Hawaiian view of the land, 'āina momona (fertile land), which are surfacing in Hawai'i's food sovereignty and Indigenous education movements. Indeed, the failure of the 'Apology Resolution' by the US Congress and President Clinton in 1993 to produce substantive change revealed the limits of political recognition as a strategy for self-determination (Coulthard, 2007). Instead, and as a response, various cultural groups (e.g. Ma'o Organic Farms, Waiahole Poi Factory and Farm, and Waipa Foundation) have sought to restore many of the self-sufficiency and sustainability practices of traditional Hawaiian culture (Loke & Leung, 2013), and regain control over their means of production. In short, Hawaiians recognize that advocating for political recognition without addressing economic dependency relations is unsustainable.

The concept of 'sustainable self-determination', like that of food sovereignty (Pimbert, 2009), shifts the focus of Indigenous mobilization from a state-centric entitlements discourse to projects and practices that enable greater Indigenous economic independence, spiritual regeneration, and social health (Corntassel, 2008). This shift away from the state reflects a concern that in seeking settler state recognition for self-governance. Indigenous communities may reaffirm rather than transform the colonial relationship, by reinvesting power within the settler state apparatuses (Coulthard, 2007). Within this re-envisioned framework, non-state, community-based solutions rooted in Indigenous responsibility take precedence over rights-based movements (Corntassel, 2008). As Native Hawaiian scholar and political scientist Goodyear-Ka'ōpua (2009) describes,

> The hallmarks of sustainable self-determination include focusing on individual, family and community responsibilities, regenerating local and regional Indigenous economies, and recognizing the interconnection of social, spiritual, environmental and political aspects of self-determination. The ultimate goal is for Indigenous people to have the freedom to practice Indigenous livelihoods, maintain food security and apply natural laws on Indigenous homelands in a sustainable manner.

Like the concept of aloha 'āina, self-determination is a term that 'can encapsulate structural changes such as political struggles for decolonization and independence as well as personal struggles to perpetuate cultural practices' (Aikau, 2011). Self-determination manifests itself as a struggle to protect 'the heart and soul of [I]ndigenous nations: a set of values that challenge the homogenizing force of Western liberalism and free-market capitalism' (Alfred, 1999, p. 60). In the context of food, sustainable self-determination in Hawai'i translates into efforts to restore sustainable and prolific Indigenous food production, so that Hawaiian populations can survive and thrive (Goodyear-Ka'ōpua, 2013; Lasky, 2008). By re-building physical structures that feed people, Hawaiian farmers aim to dislodge overdependence on a corporate-dominated transnational market economy for basic nutritional economic needs (Goodyear-Ka'ōpua, 2013). The politics of aloha 'āina thus rests upon restoring the ability to access the land and natural resources that are so crucial to community and individual well-being, and of which native Hawaiians have historically been dispossessed. In this way, aloha ʻāina as a practice of sustainable self-determination is a strategy for both economic and political autonomy, and is a concept that brings personal and state-level responsibilities together in one framework. To practice aloha ʻāina thus is to engage in a struggle to counter the interwoven political, economic, and environmental injustices that Native Hawaiian communities face today.

II Aʻole GMO![1]

History of Seed Corn Industry in Hawaiʻi

While the popular image of agriculture in Hawaiʻi is still that of sugar cane and pineapples, today industrialized corporate agriculture in Hawaiʻi has shifted to biotech crops—namely, genetically modified corn seed research. This transition took place as tropical plantation agriculture lost its economic edge and ability to compete on the global market. The seed corn industry was established in Hawaiʻi in 1966 with relatively humble beginnings—a five-acre winter nursery was founded on Molokai in order to conduct initial corn breeding trials. The industry grew rapidly, stabilizing in value by the mid-1980s. As new lands became available with the closure of sugar plantations in the 1990s, this industry continued to expand (Brewbaker, 2003). After commercialization of the first transgenic crops in 1996 and the widespread adoption of these seeds by farmers throughout the USA, biotech firms began to acquire even more land in Hawaiʻi (Callis, 2013). Because Hawaiʻi's climate is suitable to year-round production, seed research can be accelerated three- or fourfold, giving Hawaiʻi a competitive advantage over US mainland and international locations for a seed crop industry.

Today, several thousand acres are occupied annually by the seed industry. As of 2010, the primary biotech companies in Hawaiʻi—Monsanto, Syngenta, BASF, Pioneer Hi-Bred International, and Dow AgroSciences—own or lease 25,000 acres, and exported annually 9.7 million pounds of seed, almost all of it corn and at least half of it genetically modified (Callis, 2013). The most profitable Hawaiʻi seed crop, corn, is valued at $230 million (2011/2012, National Agricultural Statistics Service, 2012) and accounts for 95% of the total value of Hawaiʻi's seed industry ($243 million in 2011/2012, National Agricultural Statistics Service, 2012), which as of 2009/2010 in turn comprises 36% of Hawaiʻi's $627 million agricultural sector.[2] This transition has happened quickly, though largely unbeknownst to many residents and visitors until recently (Voosen, 2011). The seed business is now one of the fastest growing agricultural industries in Hawaiʻi (Wu, 2007). On Molokai, there are two main companies—Monsanto and Dow AgroSciences—that are growing GMO corn seed on approximately 1850 and 385 acres, respectively. These two companies are the largest private employers on the island, and employ roughly 210 people.

Controversy over genetic modification of agricultural crops is not new to Hawaiʻi. In 2003, the University of Hawai'i began genetic engineering of taro, which led to widespread protests among the Native Hawaiian community, who view kalo as sacred. Native Hawaiian leader Walter Ritte compared the patenting of taro to a 'Second Mahele'—a reference to the Great Mahele in 1848, which established private ownership of land in Hawaiʻi (Kameʻeleihiwa, 1992) and provided the necessary preconditions to dispossess Native Hawaiians of much of their land. Native Hawaiian attorney Trask wrote (2006) that 'For Hawaiʻi's Indigenous peoples, the concept underlying genetic manipulation of life forms is offensive and contrary to the cultural values of aloha ʻāina'.

The rapid growth of the seed corn industry on the state's prime farmland in recent years has re-ignited concern and controversy over agricultural biotechnology's presence in Hawai'i. Bubbling tensions rose to the surface in 2013, when coordinated anti-GMO marches were organized across the islands, a GMO labeling rally (featuring renowned anti-GMO activist Vandana Shiva) took place at the State Capitol, and two island counties established GMO regulatory legislation.

The Island of Molokai

Molokai, situated squarely in the middle of the chain of Hawaiian Islands, was historically known as the land of 'fat fish and kukui nut relish', and produced enough surplus food to feed the neighboring isles. In recent decades, this island has been nicknamed the 'Last Hawaiian Island', because of its 72% Native Hawaiian population, lack of urban development (there are no stoplights or buildings taller than a coconut tree), and its residents' continued subsistence practices. While the community is certainly not homogenous, on Molokai, many residents take pride in their ability to provide food for themselves and sustain their families and neighbors.

Historically, the pace of cultural change on Molokai was slower than on the other major Hawaiian Islands, largely because Western trading vessels and whaling ships bypassed it. Molokai was considered a barren land with a sparse population, limited freshwater resources and lacking in adequate protected harbors. As a result, Molokai Hawaiians continued traditional farming and fishing subsistence activities throughout the nineteenth century and well into the twentieth (McGregor, 2007). However, the growth of the pineapple industry on Homestead land (designated solely for Native Hawaiians) starting in the 1920s meant that Homesteaders quickly became integrated into and dependent upon a cash economy based on wage earning and marketing of cash crops (McGregor, 2007).

Today, Hawaiian Homesteaders and the broader Molokai population still rely heavily on Molokai's reefs, streams, and forests to survive. When the pineapple agri-business closed on Molokai in the mid-1970s, subsistence became a more vital aspect of the economy (McGregor, 2007). A recent study in 2012 found that 40% of Molokai families' food came from subsistence activities and that 72% felt subsistence was very important to them (Akutagawa, Han, Noordhoek, & Williams, 2012). Subsistence living on Molokai is not merely utilitarian. Indigenous livelihoods are considered a tradition that creates a strong sense of a unified community and binds the social elements necessary for cultural perpetuation together (McGregor, 2007). A vision statement designed by a broad cross-section of the island population[3] envisions Molokai as a community that 'takes pride in its resourcefulness, self-sufficiency and resiliency'. It states that 'the values of aloha 'āina and mālama 'āina guide our stewardship of Molokai's natural resources, which nourish our families both physically and spiritually' (Molokai Enterprise Committee, 1998). Molokai residents reaffirmed these values in an updated vision statement that envisions a Molokai that leaves for its children a visible legacy: 'an island momona (abundant) with natural and cultural resources, people who kokua (help) and look after one another' (Molokai Community, 2008).

Molokai residents' sense of aloha 'āina, articulated in numerous community documents, has been displayed visibly through a long history of island-based activism against development, particularly tourism. Residents have organized on numerous occasions to stave off tourism development, which they believe would threaten the natural resource base (McGregor, 2007). Community activism halted plans by the Molokai Ranch, a private landowner, to develop 200 luxury lots on the southwest corner of Molokai, a fragile ecosystem known as Lau'au Point. In 2008, the Ranch closed ranch facilities, its golf course and hotels, which have since sat idle. Residents say that reliance on subsistence practices has increased since the closure of the hotel (the largest employer at that time on the island), which raised an already high rate of unemployment to 17.5% (as of 2012) on the island (Busch, Cortez, & Srivastava, 2012; Stephenson, 2013, unpublished research). Most recently, Molokai kupuna and cultural practitioners have begun to revitalize the Aha Moku, the traditional Hawaiian system of natural resource management, in order to ensure best practices for sustainable management of the natural and cultural resources upon which Molokai livelihoods depend.

Moms on a Mission

Like its neighboring islands, a segment of Molokai's population vocally opposes the expanding presence of the seed corn industries on their island. Residents worry that chemical companies 'are becoming the main farmers on [the] island', as was voiced by Walter Ritte (Star Bulletin March 24, 2007). These Molokai residents see the seed corn industry as the latest iteration of a plantation style economy that has characterized Hawaiian agriculture for the past two centuries. Like sugar and pineapples, corn seed is grown and shipped to the mainland. However as Ritte noted, unlike sugar and pineapples, GMO seed corn is not even edible in a crisis situation.

After spearheading the battle against the patenting of taro, or Hāloa, Ritte became aware of the quiet but steady growth of the seed corn companies on his home island, Molokai, and began campaigns to raise awareness and influence political decision-making on O'ahu (Black, 2012). As he explains,

> For Hawaiians, the focus has expanded to look at what these GMO companies are doing to the land ... [and] recognizing that the 'āina is what feeds us and keeps us alive. The GMO issue now is not just about taro, it's about aloha 'āina. (quoted in Black, 2012)

As an Aloha 'āina warrior,[4] he has taken two tacks, simultaneously fighting the seed corn companies and initiating the restoration of ancient fishponds on Molokai as a way to rebuild the capacity of Hawaiians to feed themselves (personal interview 9 January 2013). Ritte is well known throughout Hawai'i as a long-time champion of Native Hawaiian rights, but apart from his activism, the seed corn industry's presence on Molokai has until recently been an issue of 'quiet resistance' (Black, 2012), as the lack of alternative employment opportunities means many households depend on these companies for their income.

Indeed, not all Native Hawaiians are against the presence of the GMO seed corn industry. As one Native Hawaiian Homesteader on Molokai explained, Monsanto 'has kept people working and kept the lands open and in agriculture ... it has helped prevent overdevelopment with lots of people coming in from happening'. While the number of people opposing the seed corn industry on Molokai is growing, the silent majority see the companies as providing jobs without changing the agrarian lifestyle on Molokai (Interview with Mercy Ritte, 24 July 2013). One could argue that their support for the GMO industry is circumscribed by a broader political economic system in which jobs at the seed corn companies are better than the alternative of unemployment. Also, not all those who disagree with the practices of the seed corn companies are actively or visibly protesting their presence.

However, a more organized movement against the presence of the seed companies on Molokai has developed. Moms on a Mission (MOM) was formed in 2012 by Molokai resident and mother Mercy Ritte (daughter-in-law of Walter Ritte), after her son became ill from what she believes to be pesticide drift from the nearby Monsanto fields. This group has gained traction and has been featured prominently on a number of anti-GMO campaigns across the state. Their organizing culminated in a march against Monsanto in March 2013, which attracted state and national media attention. The organization has now developed into a statewide group, called the MOM Hui, with chapters on the five major islands. Their mission supports 'sustainable agriculture which includes farming practices and principles that improve soil and plant life, preserves Hawai'i's limited natural resources and enhances the quality of life and health for farmers and consumers' as well as 'the right for people to define their own food system and policies, rather than corporations and marketing'.

Those who oppose GMOs on Molokai feel deeply that the presence of the corn seed industry on the island is antithetical to notions of aloha 'āina. As one Native Hawaiian activist on Molokai explained, 'George Helm [father of the aloha 'āina movement in the 1970s] would not see this [pointing to Monsanto fields] as aloha 'āina' (June 2013). This same activist has also helped create and co-star in homespun videos by the ''āina warriors' documenting the seed corn companies' alleged negligent practices, which have gone viral on YouTube. Mercy Ritte of MOM explained that as a Native Hawaiian, she knew her culture was intimately linked to the 'āina, but that it was not until the GMO issue arose that this connection between the health of the land and its people become real and immediate for her.

The MOM group and others also worry that the expansion of the seed companies—namely their increased use of land and water—will compromise the ability of the island to move toward feeding itself, and achieving greater food self-sufficiency. Molokai is currently designated to be in 'severe drought' and as water usage increases (primarily due to the seed companies), the State has placed a mandatory reduction of irrigation water by 20% and increased water rates for all agricultural users other than Hawaiian Homesteaders.[5] A recent agricultural needs assessment by Sust'āinable Molokai concluded that while biotech seed crops have proven economically lucrative for Hawai'i agriculture, 'allocating precious acreage and limited water resources to GMO seed crop research would in the long-term compromise the State's overall food security and limit the State's ability to provide locally grown healthy and nutritious foods' (Akutagawa et al., 2012). For Native Hawaiians, food self-sufficiency is a key component of sustainable self-determination. One Native Hawaiian community leader on Molokai explained that 'we want to keep open space and keep the island sustainable by feeding ourselves. Recently we have gotten the word "sustainable" but that's just how we live—our parents taught us to live off the land' (Interview, January 2013). In this way, residents who understand aloha 'āina to be predicated upon a reciprocal relationship with the land that provides localized food self-sufficiency feel threatened by the growing seed corn industry.

For many Molokai residents involved in anti-GMO organizing, the seed company's use of pesticides is of greatest immediate concern. These residents fear the potential risks to human and environmental health associated with pesticides applied by the seed corn companies. They describe run off and dust storms associated with soil erosion (a result of what they say is poor soil conservation on the part of GMO companies) and worry about the potential hazardous chemicals that may be transmitted through the air and water sources. Several interviewees who hunt deer, a common subsistence activity on Molokai, questioned the risk of eating deer that may have broken into GMO fields and grazed on sprayed crops. One activist cited greater resentment toward Monsanto than Mycogen, because Monsanto's fields are in close proximity to residential housing and schools, while Mycogen's fields are downwind from most settlements and pose less of a health risk. Other members of the MOM group worry about the type of genetically modified seeds the companies are growing and the possibility of genetic drift. For Mercy, the goal of her organizing was not just to move seed fields farther away from town or improve pesticide management, as some have suggested, but to evict the companies entirely from the island and replace them with a 'better' alternative. To this end, she is working to promote local farmers by creating a distribution center on island where local produce can be consolidated for purchase. In that vein, another grassroots organization, Sust'āinable Molokai, has chosen to avoid engaging in GMO-related activism and instead is pursuing a strategy of supporting local farmers to make diversified agriculture a viable livelihood. By increasing the economic viability of small-scale agricultural production on the island, the organization hopes to bypass the current scenario in which the seed corn industry, the largest private employer on the island, is seen by some as a 'necessary evil' for the island economy. Indeed, the founder of this organization has compared gardening to 'passive resistance' and growing food self-sufficiency as 'an activist act'—highlighting the way in which aloha 'āina as a praxis to combat the seed corn industry involves both political engagement with the state and community-based solutions.

These non-state centered community-based approaches range from the restoration of the fishponds by Walter Ritte and his family to high school agricultural programs that teach kalo planting. They aim to promote communal empowerment, personal and interpersonal fulfillment, self-determining collective personhood, shared autonomous agency, re-connection and re-assertion of Indigenous culture and traditions, and self-sustaining livelihoods—what Lasky (2008) identifies as the enactment of a Hawaiian form of sovereign agency. As she notes, activities like kalo cultivation are explicitly contemporary political practices as well as revitalized cultural practices that reflect 'a legacy of Hawaiian resistance and the resilience of a non-state, non-modernist "everyday" sovereign agency in *response to* and in *interaction with* state forms of sovereignty struggle'.

In sum, the protests against the seed corn industry reflect on one level a citizenry's concern over the risks to environmental and human health that are perceived to be associated with genetically modified agriculture. On another level, the grievances run deeper. For the Native Hawaiian community, the succession of settler-based forms of industrial agriculture—from sugar to pineapple to macadamia nuts and now to seed corn—represents a continuing process of accumulation by dispossession that has profoundly impacted the ecological and social conditions of the local food system (Lukens, 2013). Activists' use of the phrase aloha 'āina implicitly and in some cases explicitly relates past efforts to restore the independent Hawaiian nation to current desires for Hawaiian sovereignty and independence from corporate interests. On O'ahu, for example, at the first of the series of anti-GMO marches, protestors on the north shore held signs saying: 'De-occupy Hawai'i'. As journalist Altemus-Williams (2013) has noted, 'when protesters chant "aloha 'āina" at anti-GMO marches, they are alluding to the fact that this fight isn't only over competing visions of land use and food creation. It's also a battle for the islands' political sovereignty'.

Implications for the Global Food Sovereignty Movement

Food sovereignty is situated, in that it unfolds in particular places through unique articulations of historical, social, political, ecological, and cultural dynamics (Desmarais & Wittman, 2014). As such, food sovereignty on Molokai calls for the privileging of place-based knowledge that is inherent in the idea of aloha 'āina. Yet this does not preclude the opportunity for cross-learning to occur between the residents of Molokai who want greater access to and control over the means of producing food, and food sovereignty movements elsewhere. Indeed, highlighting the historical context and socio-political dynamics of claims for food sovereignty on Molokai provides insight for social movements elsewhere that are also struggling internally to deconstruct and define what is meant by food sovereignty, and how best to achieve it. Centered on the key example of current controversy over the GMO seed industry, the case of Molokai illustrates both inherent challenges to and possibilities for realizing food sovereignty in the state of Hawai'i and beyond.

There are several lessons to be learnt from studying the unfolding of the anti-GMO movement on Molokai, and in Hawai'i more broadly. First, an examination of food and land politics on Molokai serves as a reminder that food sovereignty is necessarily place based. There is no one food sovereignty movement; rather, the desire for greater control over how and what one eats manifests itself in different forms in different places, based on unique histories and geographies that produce a particular set of circumstances. This historical and geographical specificity is well illustrated by the example of food sovereignty demands in Hawai'i as currently articulated through anti-GMO activism—a movement that is rooted in the concept of aloha 'āina and that is inseparable from a history of colonial land appropriation and Native Hawaiian dispossession. Acknowledging this history allows us to see that food sovereignty is not just about food—in many cases, it is also about broader claims for social and/or environmental justice as well as Indigenous rights, which often hinge upon a restored relationship with the land. This point is muddied by the fact that in practice, food sovereignty is a multivalent term that is used and deployed by different people for different purposes. In the case of Hawai'i, there is now a broad coalition of residents who are organizing against the seed corn industry under the banner of aloha 'āina, many of whom are not explicitly aware of the links between the current GMO issue and past grievances against Native Hawaiians and their land. As a multi-layered concept with political, ecological, economic, and cultural meanings, aloha 'aina serves as a powerful foundation for a movement of people motivated by different reasons.

This makes it tricky to evaluate the Hawaiian food sovereignty movement given the fact that food sovereignty holds different meanings to different people. Similarly, at a broader level, there is a disjuncture between food sovereignty in theory—as laid out by La Via Campesina and the various mission statements it has helped to produce—and food sovereignty in practice, which tends to be a slippery concept that varies dramatically depending on who is wielding (or some might argue appropriating) the term (Schiavoni, this issue). The diversity of communities that use the language of food sovereignty and its associated rhetoric defies a universal conceptualization of food sovereignty, which suggests challenges to building any kind of unified food sovereignty movement (Desmarais & Wittman, 2014).

At the same time, the case of Hawai'i suggests that the fact that food sovereignty, like aloha 'āina, can be broadly and variably defined means that it can serve as an umbrella organizing concept for a diverse set of actors, which in turn can allow for coalition-building. On Molokai and in Hawai'i overall, the broad-base support for aloha 'āina as a way to contest the seed corn industry can be understood as an opportunity for Native Hawaiians to align their agenda with that of other segments of Hawai'i's population. The debate over GMOs and the seed corn industry in Hawai'i is not strictly a Native Hawaiian issue, and strategic movement-building may allow Native Hawaiians to gain traction and build support for goals that advance them toward sustainable self determination. A coalition between Native Hawaiians and 'environmentalists' is not a new story to Hawai'i, or to a number of other parts of the world where Indigenous populations and conservation-minded groups form unholy alliances to fight 'development' or other threats to a natural resource base (Brosius, 1997; Hecht & Cockburn, 2010). Similarly, food sovereignty movements elsewhere may be strengthened as they grow beyond 'peasant' movements to include a broader support base of individuals and communities who contest globalized corporate agriculture on various grounds.

Second, food self-sufficiency initiatives and anti-GMO activism on Molokai illustrate a tension inherent in the broader food sovereignty paradigm. This tension exists between, on the one hand, a desire for autonomy from the state and, on the other, the necessity of engagement with the state in order to change policy. In Hawai'i, the process of sustainable self-determination, particularly in the context of contemporary food system issues like the growth of the seed corn industry, must address a similar tension. Sustainable self-determination is premised upon the idea of individual and community responsibility as a pathway to greater independence, rather than rights-based engagement with the state. Yet as Lukens (2013) has pointed out, a refusal to engage with the law eclipses the ways in which law and policy can affect everyday living conditions and cultural practices. In the context of food sovereignty, ignoring the way in which the state plays a powerful role in governing and regulating the food system limits the ability to carve out and maintain autonomous and self-determined spaces for Indigenous communities. Indeed, current anti-GMO activism, much of which is lobbying the state for greater regulation of the GMO industry, illustrates that 'tactical policy activism' (Lukens, 2013) is required in order to enable practices of community-based self-determination by Indigenous communities.

In places like Molokai, it is the material and discursive practices of aloha 'āina that may offer a historical roadmap out of this apparent contradiction, and provide lessons for the global food sovereignty movement. Aloha 'āina embodies several layers of kuleana, or responsibility, and has always been a dialogical process that operates on multiple fronts, as both a political endeavor, necessitating engagement with the state, as well an individual and community-based restoration of Indigenous livelihoods, responsibilities, and ethics. Aloha 'āina as the backbone of a Hawaiian social movement means that cultural practice is always political. As Goodyear-Ka'ōpua (2013) writes,

> one of the most powerful ways to challenge the settler state . . . [is] to help make space for Indigenous-led communities to keep practicing and transforming ancestral knowledges on their own terms. The pedagogies of aloha 'āina . . . are just a few examples of the ways Hawaiians are enacting ea [sovereignty, or life] in ways that recognize that sovereignty is not just a political status but a way of living in relation to land and others. (p. 246)

Within the framework of aloha 'āina, the efforts of those working on grassroots projects to restore Indigenous agriculture and other livelihood activities both support and are supported by political activism oriented around Native Hawaiian land claims, demands for better infrastructure for small farmers and for tighter regulation on the seed corn industry, and a host of other policy and legal-related issues that influence the ability of Hawaiians to access natural resources, provide for themselves, and practice aloha 'āina.

Aloha 'āina as a concept provides space for multiple layers of personal and community responsibility and recognizes the different roles that individuals in a community may play. As the founder of Sust'āinable Molokai interpreted, 'whether people are actively protesting GMOs or just living aloha 'āina practices, they are both forms of protest against GMO'. In the context of Hawai'i, kalo cultivation, for example, *is* a practice of sovereignty (Lasky, 2008). These layers of responsibility associated with aloha 'āina do not hold in opposition a sense of personal responsibility rooted in project-based work with state-oriented engagement and activism, a trope often employed by geographers critical of a growing neoliberal sentimentality that places the burden of change on individual citizens. On the contrary, aloha 'āina is about putting one's hands in the soil as well as taking the political action necessary so that Hawaiians can access that soil in the first place.

Funding

This work was supported by National Science Foundation [grant number 1215762].

Notes

1 'A'ole GMO', meaning 'No, GMO' has been the rallying cry at many of the recent GMO marches in Hawai'i, including the Molokai march in March 2013.

2 Agriculture makes up as of 2009 1.1% of the state's GDP and 2.7% of the labor force (Bureau of Economic Analysis, US Department of Commerce).

3 Despite community documents that present a unified view, there are of course a diversity of perspectives held by Molokai residents as to their values and beliefs that defy any essentialized notion of 'the Molokai community'. These micro-politics are recognized but beyond the scope of this paper, which focuses on the articulation of long-standing vocalized values (exemplified by various community mission statements) with current anti-GMO organizing on the island by a prominent segment of Molokai's resident population.

4 'Aloha 'āina warrior' is a term that has been used to describe Uncle Walter and more recently other activists fighting against GMOs. While the exact origin of this phrase is uncertain, it harkens back to resistance to the American overthrow of the Hawaiian Kingdom. As a community organizer working to 'build our nation' (Sanburn, 2007), Ritte is viewed widely as a key 'warrior' in the fight to restore Hawaiian sovereignty.

5 Under the Hawaiian Homes Commission Act, Molokai Homesteaders are entitled to two-thirds of the water from the Molokai Irrigation System for their agricultural lands without charge.

References

Aikau, H. (2011). Personal correspondence cited in *Goodyear-Ka'ōpua, N. 2013.*

Akutagawa, M., Han, L., Noordhoek, E., & Williams, H. (2012). *Agricultural needs assessment.* Unpublished report by Sustainable Molokai.

Alfred, T. (1999). *Peace, power, and righteousness: An indigenous manifesto.* Toronto: Oxford University Press.

Altemus-Williams, I. (2013, April 10). The struggle to reclaim paradise. *Waging Nonviolence: People-Powered News and Analysis.*

Andrade, C. (2008). *Ha'ena: Through the eyes of the ancestors.* Honolulu: University of Hawai'i Press.

Beamer, K. (2013). Tutu's grace. In N. Goodyear-Ka'ōpua (Ed.), *Values of Hawai'i 2* (pp. 11–17). Honolulu: University of Hawai'i Press.

Black, C. M. (2012). Engaging the grassroots: "Uncle" Walter Ritte takes on GMOs. In C. M. Black (Ed.), *Facing Hawai'i's future: Essential information about GMOs* (pp. 66–69). Hong Kong: Palace Press International.

Brewbaker, J. L. (2003). *Corn production in the tropics: The Hawai'i experience.* Honolulu: College of Tropical Agriculture and Human Resources, University of Hawai'i at Mānoa.

Brosius, J. (1997). Endangered forest, endangered people: Environmentalist representations of indigenous knowledge. *Human Ecology, 25*(1), 47–69.

Busch, J., Cortez, R., & Srivastava, C. (2012). *Molokai material flow analysis.* Unpublished paper. Yale University.

Callis, T. (2013, June 9). GMO: $243 million seed industry largest in state's ag sector. *West Hawai'i Today.* Retrieved February 15, 2014, from http://westhawaiitoday.com/sections/news/local-news/gmo243-million-seed-industry-largest-state%E2%80%99s-ag-sector.html#sthash.lu1bNc8Q.dpuf

Corntassel, J. (2008). Towards sustainable self-determination: Rethinking the contemporary indigenous-rights discourse. *Alternatives: Global, Local, Political, 33,* 105–132.

Coulthard, G. S. (2007). Subjects of empire: Indigenous peoples and the 'politics of recognition' in Canada. *Contemporary Political Theory, 6*(4), 347–460.

Desmarais, A., & Wittman, H. (2014). Farmers, foodies and first nations: Getting to food sovereignty in Canada. *The Journal of Peasant Studies.* doi:10.1080/03066150.2013.876623

Glipo, A., & Pascual, F. (2005). *Food sovereignty framework: Concept and historical context*, 1–23. Retrieved February 22, 2014, from http://www.nyeleni.org/spip.php?

Goodyear-Ka'ōpua, N. (2009). Rebuilding the 'Auwai: Connecting ecology, economy and education in Hawaiian schools. *AlterNatives*, *5*, 46–77.

Goodyear-Ka'ōpua, N. (2013). *The seeds we planted: Portraits of a native Hawaiian Charter School*. Minneapolis: University of Minnesota Press.

Hands turned to the soil. Retrieved February 15, 2014, from http://handsturned.tripod.com/what.html

Hecht, S. B., & Cockburn, A. (2010). *The fate of the forest: Developers, destroyers, and defenders of the Amazon*. Chicago, IL: University of Chicago Press.

Kame'eleihiwa, L. (1992). *Native land and foreign desires: Pehea Lā E Pono 'Ai?* Honolulu: Bishop Museum Press.

Lasky, J. (2008, March 26–29). *Cultivating sovereignties: The taro-farming movement in Waiahole, Hawai'i*. Conference paper presented at the International Studies Association Annual Convention in San Francisco, CA.

Loke, M., & Leung, P. (2013). Competing food concepts—implications for Hawai'i, USA. *Food and Energy Security*, *2*(3), 174–184.

Lukens, A. (2013). *Legalize Pa'i'ai: Tactical policy activism in a settler state*. Unpublished paper.

McGregor, D. (2002). Kaho'olawe: Rebirth of the sacred. *Amerasia Journal*, *28*, 68–83.

McGregor, D. (2007). *Na Kua'aina: Living Hawaiian culture*. Honolulu: University of Hawai'i Press.

McGregor, D., Tanemura, P., Matsuoka, J. K., & Minerbi, L. (2003). An ecological model of wellbeing. In H. A. Becker & F. Vanclay (Eds.), *The international handbook of social impact assessment: Conceptual and methodological advances* (pp. 108–128). Cheltenham: Edward Elgar Publishing.

Meyer, M. A. (2014). Ho'ea Ea: Land education and food sovereignty in Hawai'i. *Environmental Education Research*, *20*(1), 98–101.

Molokai Community (2008). *Molokai: Future of a Hawaiian Island*. Unpublished report.

Molokai Enterprise Committee (1998, October 9). *Moloka'i rural empowerment zone application submitted to the United States Department of Agriculture*.

Morales, R. (Ed.). (1984). *Ho'iho'i Hou: A tribute to George Helm and Kimo Mitchell*. Honolulu: Bamboo Ridge Press.

Morrison, D. (2011). Indigenous food sovereignty—a model for social learning. In H. Wittman, A. A. Desmarais, & N. Wiebe (Eds.), *Food sovereignty in Canada: Creating just and sustainable food systems* (pp. 97–113). Halifax: Fernwood Publishing.

National Agricultural Statistics Service (2012). *Hawai'i seed crops*. USDA report. Retrieved February 15, 2014, from http://www.nass.usda.gov/hi/

Nyéléni Forum for Food Sovereignty (2007, February 23–27). Selingue, Mali.

Pimbert, M. (2007). *Transforming knowledge and ways of knowing for food sovereignty*. International Institute for Environment and Development. Retrieved February 15, 2014, from http://pubs.iied.org/14535IIED.html?c=agric/food

Pimbert, M. (2009). *Towards food sovereignty: Reclaiming autonomous food systems*. London: International Institute for Environment and Development. Retrieved from http://pubs.iied.org/14585IIED.html?c=agric/food

Sanburn, C. (2007). A road less taken. *Hana Hou: The Magazine of Hawaiian Airlines*, *10*(1).

Silva, N. K. (2004). *Aloha betrayed: Native Hawaiian resistance to American colonialism*. Durham, NC: Duke University Press.

Tengan, T. (2008). *Native men remade: Gender and nation in contemporary Hawai'i*. Durham, NC: Duke University Press.

Trask, M. (2006). Hawaiian perspectives on GMOs. In C. M. Black (Ed.), *Facing Hawai'i's future: Essential information about GMOs*. Hong Kong: Palace Press International.

Via Campesina (1996, November 11–17). *Food sovereignty: A future without hunger. The right to produce and access to land*. FAO World Food Summit, Rome, Italy.

Voosen, P. (2011, August 22). King corn takes root in Hawai'i. *New York Times*.

Wu, N. (2007, March 24). Biotech firm grows on Molokai. *Star Bulletin*. Saturday, *12*(83).

Broadening the Land Question in Food Sovereignty to Northern Settings: A Case Study of Occupy the Farm

ANTONIO ROMAN-ALCALÁ

International Institute of Social Studies, The Hague, The Netherlands

ABSTRACT *Land access is an accepted corollary to food sovereignty, long promoted by the transnational agrarian movement La Via Campesina (LVC). LVC's land access politics have evolved with increased incorporation of diverse perspectives, but remain largely focused on achieving 'integral agrarian reform' in the global South. Here, I take a case where food sovereignty activists ('Occupy the Farm' (OTF)) occupied land owned by a public university in California, the USA, in order to broaden food sovereignty's land access considerations beyond the South, and to analyze conditions where political actions (including occupations) can help achieve changes in land access regimes. The OTF action was successful in challenging cultural norms about property and achieving access, partly due to the occupation having foregrounded multiple appealing narratives that invited participation and wider support. These narratives included agroecology versus biotechnologies; community/public access versus privatization; participatory versus bureaucratic governance structure; and green space/food production versus urban development. The article tests the use of the 'land sovereignty' frame in expanding food sovereignty's land politics, to encompass land contestation contexts globally and deal with the particular conditions surrounding lands. The case indicates that land occupations in the North are potentially useful—but uncertain, and very context-dependent—tactics to promote land and food sovereignty.*

1. Introduction

Land is a key pillar of food sovereignty, its centrality exemplified in the surge of concern by food sovereignty advocates over global 'land grabbing' (Via Campesina, 2011). Food sovereignty proponents argue that land use is key to economic, ecological, and social health (Rosset, 2006, p. 319). As a political movement, food sovereignty has been increasingly adopted by consumer and urban populations, and thus is no longer the exclusive purview of so-called developing countries or food producers (McMichael, 2014, p. 20). Yet, the food sovereignty discourse on land has not fully reflected this change, remaining focused primarily on the experiences and conditions of certain kinds of 'peasants' pushing for agrarian reforms (Rosset, 2006, pp. 310–312). The case described here shows the limitations of agrarian reform as a central discourse for a worldwide land access movement, and how 'land sovereignty', as elaborated by Borras and Franco (2012), can potentially serve as a better analytical and political frame. Land sovereignty's more focused strategizing based on *actual conditions of access and contexts for its achievement* is key to concretize and link the diverse struggles occurring around land. The article attempts to build on this preexisting evolution in food sovereignty, to illuminate the challenges to and conditions surrounding land occupations as successful tactics for land and food sovereignty in the North. The case concerns a 10-acre parcel of land in Albany, California known as the Gill Tract (GT), which contains some of the last remaining Class-1 agricultural soils left undeveloped in the Bay Area of California. In 2012, the GT was occupied by 'Occupy the Farm' (OTF), a direct action group that promotes 'a future of food sovereignty' and the idea of community management of land.[1]

The article will be arranged as follows. First, a brief review will present the need for and basis of the land sovereignty frame. Next, macro- and meso-scale cultural and political factors pertaining to the case are presented. These *conditions and contexts* of the occupation action are then related—through an exposition of the more micro-level material and discursive histories of the case—to *effective access and benefits* derived from the land. Here, I assess the influences of the occupation on access to the GT, and in relation to broader norms of land access and use. The conclusion considers how the OTF case relates to and builds on the land sovereignty framing, and posits the wider implications for advancing goals of food sovereignty through land occupations and land sovereignty.

2. Evolution of the Land Dimension in La Via Campesina

Food sovereignty movements have proposed redistributive land reforms to shift existing land concentration and the monocultural industrial agricultures associated with it toward the food sovereignty ideal of small-scale, peasant, family, and collective production of high-quality products intended mainly for community consumption and local/domestic markets (Rosset, 2006). The 2007 Nyéléni World Forum on Food Sovereignty Declaration called for 'integral agrarian reform that guarantees peasants full rights to land', and that such reform ensures 'respect for local autonomy and governance' (Nyéléni, 2007). This vision is in turn supported by notions that community management of resources is more environmentally sound, that there is an 'inverse relationship' of farm size with productivity, and that it is peasant producers—and categorically *not* industrial capitalist agriculture—who will 'feed the world' (McMichael, 2014; van der Ploeg, 2013). These positions point to how food sovereignty's vision for democratic, equitable access to land is premised upon a particular kind of agriculture, thus a particular kind of agriculturist, and thus a particular land politics. Through drawing in more diverse members (Torres & Rosset, 2014, p. 3), La Via Campesina (LVC) has had to adopt more complex perspectives on land, but its essential frame remains a 'right to land', achieved through 'integral agrarian reform' that includes other forms of state support, credit, technical assistance, and infrastructure (Altieri & Toledo, 2011, p. 607; Rosset, 2013, p. 724).

LVC's land politics have been developed alongside a heterogeneous history of state-led agrarian reforms (see MST, 2013, pp. 747–749), and to counter the increasing dominance of 'market-led' agrarian reform in the era of neoliberalism (Torrez, 2011). Because state-enforced private land titling often leads to land dispossession, concentration, and alienation (Akram-Lodhi, 2007), LVC emphasizes stable land tenure through individual but also *community* level property rights, often to community-managed 'commons'. During its first 20 years, LVC's land politics have been particularly influenced by the prominence of Brazil's Landless Worker's Movement (MST), perhaps the most emblematic instance of 'from below' land reform. In the absence of meaningful redistribution of land 'from above', the MST occupied millions of hectares of land, converting the land into farm communities under the auspices of a clause in the Brazilian constitution demanding 'social use' of underutilized or neglected lands (Wright & Wolford, 2003). The fact that the MST were able to successfully settle so much land, and gain legal titles to that land, has inspired many others to see land occupations as a hopeful tactic for achieving land access.

2.1. *Land Sovereignty as Potential Unifying Frame?*

The long-standing land discourse in food sovereignty movements—focused on agrarian reform 'from above' and 'from below'—is not misdirected. While apposite, this discourse may neglect inconvenient complexities within land struggles, and struggles that fall outside of the typical (and powerful) narrative of land access for 'emblematic' peasants who are assumed to be able to form a new production base for a sovereign food system globally (Bernstein, 2014, p. 2). 'Land sovereignty' has been proposed by Borras and Franco (2012) as a frame with which to nuance food sovereignty's answers to questions of land politics, and more effectively promote a unified vision for a desired land politics that encompasses a plurality of struggles, North and South. In contrast to institutionalist assumptions that legal rights are sufficient to ensure land access, or populist assumptions that 'local' control is sufficient for justice, land sovereignty utilizes an inductive, realist approach to uncover the conditions (within land titling and state politics but also beyond them) that affect real, effective, sustained access to land. Differentiating between 'access' and 'property rights', land sovereignty also reminds us that the '*ability* to derive benefit' from land is not equivalent to 'ownership' (Ribot & Peluso, 2003).[2] Even assuming that there is a need for agrarian reform, it is important to analyze specifically the form and content of reforms necessary to achieve *access* beyond simply property rights (Borras & Franco, 2012, p. 7).

Land sovereignty describes 'the right of working peoples to have effective access to, use of, and control over land and the benefits of its use and occupation, where land is understood as resource, territory, and landscape' (Borras & Franco, 2012, p. 6).[3] In this framing, commons are 'privileged' but not 'romanticized' (Borras & Franco, 2012, p. 1). In addition, the land sovereignty frame treats the role of the state non-dogmatically, accepting that states both facilitate land dispossession and concentration, and offer potential opportunities for increased land access for non-elites (Borras & Franco, 2012, p. 7). Land sovereignty addresses redistribution, for economic (*but also gender*) justice; recognition and protection of the land rights and cosmologies of indigenous peoples; and attention to the intra-community inequalities around land that exist (Rosset, 2013). Land sovereignty's 'access' orientation focuses on *what works* with regard to democratizing land resources, and opens up food sovereignty to encompass a wider array of avenues toward land access. While the political strategies built from analyses may very likely take precedents of agrarian reform and land titling as starting points, they need not, and they may find it more useful to start elsewhere (De Schutter, 2010). Land sovereignty is thus an important step toward understanding how struggles over land ownership, management, and use can be unified discursively, given diverse circumstances.

Importantly, the benefits derived from resource contestation may be 'immaterial' (i.e. discursive) as well as 'material' (Rosset & Torres, 2012, p. 17). This is especially important for vetting the usefulness of land occupations, insofar as the narrative force and discursive influence of such occupations may be significant and, depending on political and cultural circumstances, as important a foundation for food sovereignty as the ability to derive material rewards from the occupied land. Material gains are, of course, important, but not the only gains worth tracking. Since peoples' values and words have impact on the 'real world', land property regimes are shaped in part by discursive struggles; land sovereignty is framed by the constant interaction of material and discursive conditions. Discursive changes may (though do not necessarily) lead to material changes, while material changes—by altering the material grounds on which discursive battles are fought—may open up opportunities for further material advances. Because ideological hegemony and physical force both underpin the legitimate and sustained control of land, land sovereignty is most likely constructed via interlinked material and discursive actions.

3. Contexts of Land, Farming, Culture and Politics

Macro-scale characteristics of the USA would not seem to support land occupations as a tactic for land sovereignty construction; yet, the *particular* meso- and micro-scale conditions surrounding the GT were conducive to achieving access through occupation. This section and the next explore these contexts, before assessing what the case indicates for land sovereignty and land occupations in the North. Though conditions of farmers and farmer movements and the national cultural politics of land do not seem conducive to 'radical' land action or national land reform, occupations are found to still have a potential contribution, insofar as they contest property norms, construct agrarian subjectivities, and improve movement capacity. An OTF organizer explains the context as he sees it:

> Developed capitalist economies have almost completely divided us from land. . . . Food sovereignty is coming out from people with preexisting relationships to land, not people creating that connection. This creates an interesting dynamic in our society, because how can we implement food sovereignty if people don't even understand the issue? . . . We had a lot of people at the occupation saying they had never done something like that before. That doesn't happen in other movements I imagine, and that's the difference between us and agrarian societies. Their tactic is the cultivation of a political process, community-based and revolutionary . . . changing the relationships of power and space through the control of land. One of our tactics and goals is to just reestablish relationships to land.

In general, US legal and cultural structures privilege private property rights to land, and systems of property enforcement are legitimized and functional. Private property is equated with individual and family liberty, and land property in particular has long been linked to the ideals enshrined in the US Constitution and the 'Declaration of Independence'. Especially due to the demonization of communism throughout the twentieth century, Marxist notions that dispossession and alienation are the corollary of private property are not encountered in everyday political theorizing. Many US citizens feel that respect for private property is paramount and are generally skeptical of political action that threatens it. Ascendant 'libertarian' ideologies have further constrained efforts to conceive of and administer property rights in social or collective rather than individual terms. Just as 'the broader public is unlikely to comprehend' a land reform campaign (Borras & Franco, 2012, p. 5), land occupations and commons—even if historically relevant—do not sit well with the dominant land property regime, which strongly links private ownership with access and use.

According to census data, smallholder farms in the USA are the most common farm type, but comprise a small percentage of total farm income; a majority of these farmers do not make a full living from farming (USDA, 2014b). The proportion of farmers altogether is low (compared with farming populations in the global South), around 1% of total population (USDA, 2014a). This low proportion is one factor in the lack of smallholder political power in the country. Furthermore, farmer communities are more often failing to reproduce themselves, as younger generations from rural backgrounds increasingly seek urban lifestyles.

The average person in the USA eats not directly from the land itself but via mediating systems of production, distribution, and the monetary effective demand crucial for consumer access to foods-as-commodities. There is reviving interest in food sources that are not part of monetary economies such as foraged or home garden produce and barter systems to distribute such produce, but these sources are currently minuscule in relation to the sources required to feed the population of cities like San Francisco (Zigas, 2012, p. 8). Hunting, gathering, and sustenance relationships to land remain, but likewise in very limited form.

The US 'food movement' is an amalgam of environmental NGOs, the small organic and family farm sector, voluntary initiatives like community gardens, consumer groups, and (social) entrepreneurial projects (see Allen, FitzSimmons, Goodman, & Warner, 2003, p. 64). Composed of diverse sectors that do not necessarily share the same goals, strategies, or campaigns, these movements have been largely ineffective in substantially shifting federal policies. While there have been mainstream cultural advances for food movement ideas (such as localism) in the past 10 years, the US federal government has been historically unresponsive to these movements of food producers and consumers. National farm politics are fraught, skewed toward corporate agribusiness lobbies, and unappealing to smallholder farmers and their interests, though certainly there are NGOs and networks advocating for small-scale, local, and sustainable agriculture in federal farm policy. Judging from the occasional and minor concessions achieved by such advocates in this context, 'land reform' appears as an extremely remote possibility, and as a political demand does not make much sense. Also, those who *might* push for reform may be linked by ideological ties and common subjectivities, but they lack the 'material autonomy'—based in relationships to land—that Zibechi (2012, p. 15) refers to as central to the effective political force of many of Latin America's peasant-based movements. That is, in contrast to grassroots, mass, farmer-based social movements like most LVC national member organizations and historic movements for land reform (particularly the emblematic MST), US national policy networks are looser, more urban, and less mass in character.

That said, there has been an increase in discussion on land reform recently. In April 2014, the NGO 'Agrarian Trust' convened a symposium at University of California at Berkeley (UCB) called 'Our Land', where the nation's 'dilemma of farmland succession' was assessed through 'historical, ecological and political economy perspectives' by a multitude of food movement actors. This event is just one indication that there *are* efforts focused on land reform and land rights in the USA, and that land issues may be becoming more central to the food movement. Yet, presently, such efforts lack much cohesion and power. This process of rethinking land relations stems from a nationwide revival of interest in agriculture exhibited by young and urban agrarians (like the organizers of Agrarian Trust), but also a general trend toward cynicism of capitalism and its norms of private property. This latter trend has been indicated (and perhaps deepened) by the 2011 countrywide Occupy Wall Street (OWS) movement, which opposed capitalism's effects on social equality and democratic functionality.

These more macro-scale factors are linked to the meso scale and micro scale. While some movement organizations and participants work on federal policy to achieve land-use changes, others find local, direct, and discursive action more effective. Even if private property is primary, social movements have made 'social use' critiques that have discursively tempered this primacy with non-private and non-monetary values. Such movements include 'environmental justice' struggles presenting land use (among other environmental issues) as matters of democratic rights and responsibilities (Schlosberg, 2004), organic farming movements contesting the meaning and impacts of various forms of agriculture (Vos, 2000), and urban agriculture movements bringing these issues into the city (Tornaghi, 2014). All these movements have specific and important histories in California and the Bay Area, and have influenced the struggle over the GT.

Since US residents tend not to see access to land as a means to subsistence, agrarian reform may make less sense than a re-politicization of land and property relations more broadly. Pre-existing gentrification processes and additional dispossessions and evictions in the wake of the 2007 financial and housing crisis are more prominent land issues weighing on marginalized communities in the Bay Area than access to farmland.[4] Yet, while rural youth are abandoning farming, and urban residents have land concerns beyond farming, some of the greatest renewed interest in farming is urban or semi-urban (McClintock, 2014). Operating on the belief that food production must be re-localized and democratized, OTF—along with this upsurge of other urban agricultural projects—seeks to expand the ranks of farmers and commoners by starting with the urban populations who have previously been separated from farming.

In US conditions, land sovereignty activism becomes about creating experiences of farming in common and increasing the narrative legitimacy of the right of communities to land, including for local food production (cf. St. Martin & Hall-Arber, 2007); the OTF occupation's narratives deployed and participant experiences engendered reflect this. Yet, activism as a choice is informed partly by politics and partly by social position, as understood by one OTF organizer:

> Not knowing enough about the people who make up movements in other parts of the world, I don't know what the mix of immediate necessity and political ideology is. I imagine it's a mix of both. But in OTF, we don't really have the immediate visceral needs that require those politics and choices.

Food sovereignty as conceived by peasants is a project that has a role in improving those peasants' lives, even if it also contains more ambitious political aspects (Guttal, 2013, pp. 739–746). To OTF, these more ambitious political aspects are important, but only accomplishable with greater food movement cohesion and size. Building 'material autonomy' and discursive legitimacy for food sovereignty movements are thus strategies to reach for more transformative goals while achieving improvements locally, in the here and now. Though many may stand to gain from increased access to land, not everyone can (or is willing to) act in the same ways to go about gaining that access, especially with weak cultural connections to farming. Furthermore, housing struggles may be the more pertinent land issue for urban marginalized communities. OTF organizers recognized that land occupations are particularly difficult for many to participate in, due to political, economic, and legal reasons, but still, they are a way to advance this material/discursive strategy. In starting locally and advancing material and immaterial goals toward the building of farmers, commons legitimacy, 'the right to land', and social movements that can fight these battles (Borras, 2007, p. 73), OTF offers a new emblem of food sovereignty action—one that merits continued study, support, and critique.

3.1. *OTF Case*

3.1.1. *GT: a space for disputed priorities.* The GT's legal owner, the UCB, is a 'land grant' college, founded in the mid-1860s in order to spread agricultural knowhow across the western frontier. Though long used for agricultural research, the university had by 2012 sold off or developed more than 90 acres of the original 104-acre parcel. From 1945 to the late 1990s, the GT was utilized for research in Integrated Pest Management and other forms of biological pest control, under UCB's Division of Biological Control (DBC). However, developments in biotechnologies and molecular genetics research precipitated a shift in funding for DBC and the GT's use (Jennings, 1997). After a UCB research agreement made with biotechnology corporation Novartis in the late 1990s, DBC was displaced from the Tract. DBC was defunded, and has not used any part of the GT since 2001. One faculty member who was part of the DBC, Professor Miguel Altieri, continues to use part of the GT, but funds his own research. As support from the university waned for such ecologically focused farming research, funding increased for research with product-outcome potential, like genetically engineered seeds (Jennings, 1997; Kloppenburg, 2005). This kind of research often began with 'basic' genetic research, and often used corn as a subject. As an investigative journalist with the local newspaper East Bay Express learned, most of the research conducted on the GT for the past 10 years has benefited the university and its researchers through patent development; these patents have gone into biotechnological applications and many have been used by biotechnology companies in their products (Bond Graham, 2012).

By the 1990s, environmental justice organizations in the Bay Area were looking to expand on their practice of urban agriculture, seeking institutional support to enhance their impact. A coalition of organizations approached UCB in 1997 with a proposal to convert the remaining GT into a site for urban and sustainable farming education. Supported by 30-plus community-based and non-profit organizations, the Bay Area Coalition for Urban Agriculture (BACUA) proposal attempted to integrate the local community's interest and pursuit of food security and economic justice with UCB's existing resources at the GT. BACUA was also driven by a vision of collaborative governance, a process described well as the bringing of 'public and private stakeholders together in collective forums with public agencies to engage in consensus-oriented decision-making' (Ansell & Gash, 2008, p. 543). According to a longtime community gardening organizer in Berkeley and participant in BACUA, the contentious issue that caused UCB to back out was the role and involvement of the 'public' in managing the GT (Turman, personal communication with author, August 14, 2013).[5] For the next 15 years, members of BACUA and other local urban agriculture advocates continued to request access to the GT from UCB.

Professor Altieri was the only remaining biological control researcher on the GT when the UC Regents' Master Plan for the University Village development was published in 2004. In the plan, the Capital Projects division of UCB announced plans to develop the remaining portions of the GT. The plan stated that the remaining GT would likely become little league ball fields, in addition to grocery retail and market-rate housing developments. These developments required a re-zoning of the land and for the development agreement with UCB to be approved by the Albany city council. Between 2004 and 2012, genetic research continued as the main use of the GT while Capital Projects prepared for the development legally and financially. Albany residents and others involved in BACUA and subsequent attempts to access the GT felt unable to stop the development. The novel action of OTF—occupation contested the seemingly inevitable nature of the GT's development.

3.1.2. *Occupation: events and narratives.* The OTF group formed in late 2011 and clandestinely organized for months. Organizers, aware of the GT's contentious history and emboldened by the impact of OWS, corresponded with various local food justice organizations and activists regarding the idea of occupying the GT. Finding support for the idea, OTF mobilized on Earth Day (22 April) 2012; hundreds of participants (mainly made up of UCB students and alumni, organizers and participants from Occupy Oakland, and other urban farming advocates) marched from a nearby park, broke the locks on the GT's gates, entered, and proceeded to remove weeds and replace them with over 15,000 vegetable starts. The occupying group included some neighbors of the GT, but the majority came from other nearby parts of the Bay Area. The initial organizers of OTF also spearheaded a media campaign to spread information about the GT and its importance to food sovereignty in the Bay Area, and supported/participated in lawsuits by local Albany residents that disputed the Environmental Impact Report (EIR) approved by the Albany city council for the proposed Capital Projects development. However, in the larger struggle over the GT, the occupation received and sustained the most attention, indicating the narrative power of the action.[6]

According to one OTF participant:

> The story of how there is a higher use of the [GT], that it is a common resource that should be governed together, that development was not ideal, and that we were not afraid of hard work, were key elements of broadcasting a new vision.

During the occupation of the GT, OTF strove to create narrative resources for questioning land use, at the GT specifically and more generally in relation to 'misused' private and public properties. Workshops and open meetings were organized on various topics relating to the land's history, UCB's collaboration with biotechnology corporations, and food sovereignty alternatives. Banners, interviews with media, slogans, and ceremonies at public events all contributed symbolic resources against UCB's development plans, and for a 'community farm' alternative. When journalists asked how people could support OTF's efforts, organizers sometimes responded: 'Take more land: there is a destructive development project planned on arable land somewhere near you,' showing how OTF's actions sought material access to the GT, but also (in the words of one later participant) 'focused on restructuring relations to property' in a more general sense.[7]

While OTF worked toward their narrative of what the occupation was about and meant, UCB promoted an opposing narrative. Police were deployed to film participants and threaten anyone on the GT with arrest for trespassing, attempting to disincentivize, stigmatize, and demonize participation. Editorials in the UCB school paper repeated the administration's spokesperson Dan Mogulof's narrative that OTF was attempting to 'unilaterally' decide what the land should be used for. Mogulof consistently referenced the stake that existing researchers had in the GT, in order to argue the illegitimacy of OTF's contestation of the space. UCB's most consistent public relations campaign trope, aside from painting OTF as selfish and naïve interlopers, was that OTF had trampled on researcher's 'academic freedom'. Yet, researchers would have been kicked off the GT had development moved forward. Additionally, OTF left already planted research crops alone, and attempted to convince GT researchers that their efforts—aside from differing positions on biotechnology—should be aligned to 'save' the GT, to no avail.

Local television coverage was uncharacteristically positive (for coverage of illegal political actions) and supportive of OTF, stacking interviews with participants and supportive neighbors against Mogulof's claims.[8] Coming off of the heels of OWS, media interest in the action was strong, providing OTF the opportunity to link that movement to the world of food sovereignty.

While utilizing OWS's 'radically inclusive' and non-hierarchical forms of decision-making (anyone could show up to the GT encampment and involve themselves in organizing), these more 'immaterial' aspects of embodying radical democracy in the process of action were bolstered by the 'material' changes they accompanied: a field once inaccessible to the public had become an open community farm. During the initial occupation, thousands of people visited and participated (evidenced by sign-in sheets), and OTF as a group expanded beyond its initial organizers.

The farm encampment was evicted after three weeks of tending the crops, resulting in nine arrests. After this, OTF alongside other local community organizations hosted a series of open public forums to elaborate a community-crafted set of principles and goals around future management of the GT. By a year after the first occupation, six GT re-occupations had occurred. Each time occupiers re-entered the land, they harvested produce from the part of the farm which had not been tilled in by UCB, distributing this according to what those in attendance agreed was the best use of the food. Hundreds of pounds of food were distributed to mainly low-income residents of nearby cities (a material and immaterial gain) while UCB's official positions were continually contested.

In September 2012, the dean of UCB's College of Natural Resources (CNR) announced that management authority over the northern portion of the GT had been transferred from Capital Projects to his college. Concurrently, a referendum by Albany residents forced a rescinding of City Council approval of the development agreement, citing an inadequate EIR. When the anchor tenant at the proposed development pulled out of the agreement citing too many delays, the development project seemed all but a dead deal.

Meetings with sympathetic faculty and staff at CNR brought OTF organizers into a process of negotiation with UCB. In July 2013, CNR offered a small piece of the north side of the GT ('Area A') for a 'community-based' project. This project was spearheaded by professor Altieri and in it, community groups (including members of OTF) planted equal area plots and gathered data on output in order to assess the efficacy of various agroecological approaches. The southern portion, however, remained under management of Capital Projects and slated for development. OTF's strategy for contesting this development was to organize a boycott of Sprouts Market (the ostensible retail tenant to replace the southern fields). OTF also attempted multiple guerrilla plantings of the southern portion, only to experience arrests and have the crops plowed under.

After this, some OTF members focused on Area A—now expanded to 1.5 acres and managed as 'Gill Tract Community Farm' (GTCF), through a 'collaborative governance' arrangement of students, OTF participants, Albany residents, and CNR faculty. However, UCB's plans to develop the southern portion faced continued opposition from OTF, UCB student group SEAL, and the resident-based Albany Farm Alliance (networks that emerged from the occupation), who continued to raise awareness, organize community opposition, and petition UCB authorities. This opposition has been marked by tensions between some UCB employees and GTCF participants who believe that opposition to south side development jeopardizes the GTCF and others who believe, like SEAL's co-founder, that 'how to fight for the future you want to live in is an intrinsic part of what we can teach in Area A'. Ongoing anti development action thus presents a narrative that political contention is a crucial learning opportunity, rather than merely a tactical choice, for constructing food sovereignty. At the same time, the struggle to produce 'community' management of land comes up against the reality that neither Albany residents nor GTCF participants hold unified positions on the GT's development.

Even considering these contradictions within 'community' and the challenges of US conditions, the OTF action was successful in challenging cultural norms about property and achieving access, partly due to the occupation having foregrounded multiple appealing narratives that invited participation and wider support. These narratives included *agroecology versus biotechnologies*; *community/public access versus privatization*; *participatory versus bureaucratic governance structure*; and *green space/food production versus urban development*. Even considering observers' potential pro-private property biases and concerns for the action's illegal nature, these narratives helped legitimize the occupation and turn observers into supporters. Part of OTF's effectiveness was due to its use of context-appropriate frames to contest the GT; relating the existing conditions of the land discursively to material and immaterial ends regarding its social use. Helping this was the previous history of 'legitimate' (i.e. legal, bureaucratic) efforts involving university professors, students, nearby community members, and established NGOs engaging with the university to secure the site for urban agroecology and community access, and the normative role that UCB was expected to play as a public, democratic agency and educational institution. Without this history and context, it is quite possible that the narratives created by the occupation would have been less effective in eliciting support, and that the outcome of the occupation might have been quite different.

4. The Relationship of OTF to Food and Land Sovereignty

In personal communication, OTF organizers made the partially joking claim that their strategy rested on a four-step process. The campaign was to include: (i) land occupation, (ii) media coverage and education, (iii) ' . . . ' and (iv) the achievement of a land trust or conservation easement for the GT that would preserve its use for ecological farming, in perpetuity. Step 3, the ' . . . ' indicates that OTF saw many possibilities for means of contesting land access, beyond just occupation. One organizer explained direct action as a central component to 'challenging the conditions of access to the GT' within 'a broad spectrum of tactics', toward the goal of community management of the land. As one OTF organizer asserted, in relation to the notion that occupation was all they planned for,

> The ' . . . ' is a creative and fertile space that I don't think we should presume to be able to trim neatly into a road map for change. There could be other avenues for the change energy a direct action cultivates. It may not be 'revolution' but it may also be something other than 'policy'. . . . [It is crucial] to hold first that undefined space, where new and creative social innovation that lies outside the spheres of state or market solutions can happen.

Much like LVC, OTF has oriented its rhetoric and actions against the state (as manifested in UCB) and market (as manifested in profit-driven development), and their dominance in determining land access and use. OTF fights against unyielding state/market private property regimes, and for a 'right to land' for 'communities', in order to support agroecological, community-based knowledge development—a key component of integral agrarian reform (Rosset, 2006). OTF is also linked to food sovereignty in its commitment to an egalitarian democracy (Patel, 2009, p. 670), in this case constructed via an urbanized 'agrarian citizenship' (Wittman, 2009). Although Wittman used the term to describe rural struggles specifically, 'agrarian citizenship' can equally describe urban populations undergoing a reassertion of agrarian identities, knowledges, positions, and political struggles. Much like the MST in Wittman's studies, OTF's prefigurative, process-oriented approach to making change relies on personal and collective transformations to build new agrarian citizenships from below. However, confusion remains about defining the 'community' of sovereign importance in urban cases of land sovereignty: are they delineated based on geographic proximity? Interest? Relative societal marginalization? In urban contexts, as in OTF, 'communities' are diverse, and rarely apparent (or cohesive) regarding questions of land sovereignty.

OTF's use of commons and food sovereignty rhetoric and the land occupation tactic may appear as an uncritical adoption of LVC's most dominant frames and land-related tactics. However, their strategies for bringing about food sovereignty were based on the tools available to achieve access given the context, and so they reflect the more context-specific land sovereignty frame. OTF desired to prevent the GT's development, and occupation was used because other means had failed. Yet, while fighting for community access to the GT, OTF also discursively challenged the existing property regime broadly. Through the narrative that non-monetary use values of land (such as education or food security) are more important than profit and development, OTF linked a land sovereignty frame to other topics of food systems, and the tactic of occupation. Members of the group have participated in other radical land reclamation projects, but none have prioritized national policy as an area of intervention or land reform as a frame. Besides a concern for protecting the GT from development in perpetuity, and ensuring agroecological, educational, community uses, OTF did not agree or fixate on a particular property designation goal. Most important was to loosen the hold of private property regimes by making land access conditions more porous and accountable to food sovereignty values, at the GT and beyond. The de-sanctification of private property as determinative of access and use is a difficult but important component to land occupation strategies in the North.

Many food sovereignty advocates recognize that industrialized agriculture is not just harmful but also tenacious. Though they might not work on national policy directly, OTF participants in interviews acknowledged how federal policy and multinational corporations constrain food sovereignty, and that 'direct action and mass mobilization are necessary to motivate any sort of significant policy changes'. Thus, OTF does not naively ignore federal policy, but sees dismantling state support for the hegemonic food system—and confronting fierce elite opposition in the process—as unfortunate yet necessary forthcoming battles. Members have engaged the UCB administration and the Albany city government as a complement to their direct actions, seeing a possibility in affecting policy locally—in contrast to the possibilities perceived at the federal level. If OTF members *do* address national land reform, it is as part of a movement building platform, based in local-level work: from its start, OTF has worked toward broader coalitions around the GT and to connect GT efforts and participants to land struggles more broadly.

5. Conclusions: Land Occupations—Steps Toward Land and Food Sovereignty?

The OTF occupation resulted in material gains and discursive advances for community rights to social land uses. OTF's material success (halting north side development; the transfer of management to CNR; the food, education, and subjectivities grown from the resulting GTCF) constitutes a narrative victory for those in favor of community control of land, and supports the narrative that 'direct action gets the goods'. In building 'the foundation for improved access to material and ecological resources' (Wittman, 2009, p. 811), the occupation supported tangible progress on community access to the GT, continued resistance to UCB's development plans, and further possibilities for food sovereignty action involving newly formed 'agrarian citizens'. OTF echoed LVC's agrarian reform strategy by leveraging state-directed 'right to land' frames but also deployed communitarian, prefigurative ideals of direct action to achieve the same (Guttal, 2013, p. 746), promoting 'from below' claims to land, but also the obligations of state managers to provide access and enable more 'social uses' of land. If seen as part of a long-term strategy that includes movement building, cultural change, and (eventual) policy-making—reflecting how land occupations everywhere occur in the context of many kinds of political action that non-elite actors pursue 'from below' (Borras, 2007, pp. 72–73)—occupations may be viable tactics toward food sovereignty.

For the agrarian reform discourse to succeed in the USA, there would need to be a viable population of existing and to-be 'small farmers', otherwise what would be the point of democratizing access to land? Existing small and 'family' farmers have not even formed the most visible proponents of a 'right to land' in the USA. More often, it has been urban people and younger agrarians who demand access to land, to create spaces to sustain them and others, to spread agroecology, and to increase the potential for movement autonomy. Encouraging food production 'wherever you are, whatever you do' is a broader discourse for food sovereignty's land pillar, and land sovereignty has an easier time underpinning this discourse than agrarian reform (which is often associated implicitly with creating full-time farm employment). As agrarian social movements of the USA develop and expand, the agrarian reform frame may become more appropriate, while food sovereignty struggles in the South may benefit from the strategic alliance opportunities these stronger agrarian movements would provide. Additionally, the potential to connect agrarian land issues to other issues such as housing (e.g. anti-gentrification) and environmental justice (e.g. anti-hydrofracking) remains underexplored.

Where non-elites' cultural and material relationships to land are tenuous, federal political systems intractable, and social movements weak, redistributive land reform and commons-like active management may be premature, perhaps unrealistic, ideals. Yet, even in these situations, land occupations contain the potential for gains. They can delegitimize hegemonic food systems and provide a legitimizing vision of alternatives, while contesting the material basis for the production of food and providing non-elites (potential participants in commons and social movements) with means of subsistence and reproduction. If uncritically deployed in emulation of emblematic food sovereignty movement members like MST, however, occupations may compromise the long-term success of food sovereignty (see Baletti, Johnson, & Wolford, 2008).

The OTF case does not prove that occupation is a certain route to land sovereignty. Occupations might be necessary, but are by no means sufficient, to achieve land sovereignty. Effective access to land often remains in contention, even in supposedly fixed property regimes, because this access is determined by the ability to enforce the 'bundle of powers' associated with land 'rights' (Ribot & Peluso, 2003) through material and discursive force—an ability dominantly but *not totally* commanded by the state (e.g. Malseed, 2008). The conviction that food sovereignty is premised on 'an alternative conception of rights that is more collective and decentralized, with implementation depending not just on states, but also on communities, peoples, and international bodies' (Desmarais & Wittman, 2014, p. 4) leads invariably to the need for masses of people and new institutions to be involved in enforcing those rights. While legal land tenure can improve access, it cannot secure it. Rights are not inviolable or unmoving and so movements must be prepared to fight physically for access, while they construct discursive force behind rights—broadly construed and in specific cases. Movements with mass characteristics are more able to defend land physically and through cultural/ideational struggle, and thus in the long-term achieve real, effective access to space. It is this work of culturally building mass movements and institutions, and provisioning these with resources that sustain them, that must be done with even more intention in polities that lack them.

Disclosure Statement

No potential conflict of interest was reported by the author.

Notes

1 This paper relies on qualitative interviews (conducted in 2012 and 2013) and personal communication with OTF's initial organizers and later participants. Quotes not attributed are taken from these interviews/communications.
2 State-backed titles can solidify—but do not guarantee—tenure security. Conversely, benefits of access can be achieved without legal title.
3 For the purposes of this article, I identify Borras and Franco's 'working peoples' as *non-elite* members of society: those who have less influence on politics and economics, as individuals and as classes, due to their positions in existing political and class structures.
4 This brings up the important and complex issues of race and class which play into the OTF case. Unfortunately, due to space constraints, these issues have been deferred from this article, but will form the focus of a forthcoming study by this author.
5 It has also been suggested that internal divisions among the coalition, particularly in regard to issues of race, precipitated UCB's hesitation. Neither 'state' (UCB) nor 'society' (BACUA) is monolithic, and tensions can exist within either.
6 This ongoing attention includes a feature-length documentary film on the occupation released in 2014.
7 Some OTF members also participated in the application of the occupy tactic to other social issues, as in the 'Occupy Housing' group that fought foreclosure evictions in low-income communities. This overlap also indicates how 'land sovereignty' may fit US subaltern struggles better than 'agrarian reform'.
8 Certainly, coverage was not uniformly positive. Local blogs hosted very contentious debates, with some Albany residents disparaging the action. Remarks on the local 'Albany Patch' news blog indicated that OTF was seen by some residents as outsiders interloping into the local issue of the GT; furthermore, some residents expressed support for the GT's development. Yet, the validation of OTF's narratives by news reportage, vocal resident support at public meetings, presence on the farm, and in organizing against the development belies the idea that the occupation was unable to build or sustain local community support. What is clear is that Albany residents are not unified in their positions on the GT and its development, and real tensions continue between OTF and some Albany residents.

References

Akram-Lodhi, A. H. (2007). Land, markets and neoliberal enclosure: An agrarian political economy perspective. *Third World Quarterly*, *28*(8), 1437–1456.

Allen, P., FitzSimmons, M., Goodman, M., & Warner, K. (2003). Shifting plates in the agrifood landscape: The tectonics of alternative agrifood initiatives in California. *Journal of Rural Studies*, *19*, 61–75.

Altieri, M., & Toledo, V. (2011). The agroecological revolution in Latin America: Rescuing nature, ensuring food sovereignty and empowering peasants. *Journal of Peasant Studies*, *38*(3), 587–612.

Ansell, C., & Gash, A. (2008). Collaborative governance in theory and practice. *Journal of Public Administration Research and Theory*, *18*(4), 543–571. doi:10.1093/jopart/mum032

Baletti, B., Johnson, T., & Wolford, W. (2008). 'Late mobilization': Transnational peasant networks and grassroots organizing in Brazil and South Africa. *Journal of Agrarian Change*, *8*(2/3), 290–314.

Bernstein, H. (2014). Food sovereignty via the 'peasant way': A sceptical view. *Journal of Peasant Studies*, *41*(6), 1031–1063. doi:10.1080/03066150.2013.852082

Bond Graham, D. (2012, May 16). Unclean hands at the Gill Tract? East Bay Express. Retrieved from http://www.eastbayexpress.com/oakland/unclean-hands-at-the-gill-tract/Content?oid=3204032

Borras, S. (2007). *Pro-poor land reform: A critique*. Ottawa, ON: Ottawa University.

Borras, S., & Franco, J. (2012). *A land sovereignty alternative?* Amsterdam: TNI.

De Schutter, O. (2010). The emerging human right to land. *International Community Law Review*, *12*, 303–334.

Desmarais, A., & Wittman, H. (2014). Farmers, foodies & first nations: Getting to food sovereignty in Canada. *Journal of Peasant Studies*, *41*(6), 1153–1173. doi:10.1080/03066150.2013.876623

Guttal, S. (2013). Porto Alegre, Nyéléni and Bukit Tinggi: Evolving views of agrarian reform. *Journal of Peasant Studies*, *40*(4), 739–747.

Jennings, B. H. (1997). The killing fields: Science and politics at Berkeley, California, USA. *Agriculture and Human Values*, *14*, 259–271.

Kloppenburg, J. (2005). *First the seed: The political economy of plant biotechnology (Science and Technology in Society)* (2nd ed.). Madison, WI: University of Wisconsin Press.
Malseed, K. (2008). Where there is no movement: Local resistance and the potential for solidarity. *Journal of Agrarian Change*, *8*(2–3), 489–514.
McClintock, N. (2014). Radical, reformist, and garden-variety neoliberal: Coming to terms with urban agriculture's contradictions. *Local Environment: The International Journal of Justice and Sustainability*, *19*(2), 147–171.
McMichael, P. (2014). Historicizing food sovereignty. *Journal of Peasant Studies*, *41*(6), 933–957. doi:10.1080/03066150.2013.876999
MST. (2013). The nature of struggle for agrarian reform in Brazil: Historical context and contemporary challenges. *Journal of Peasant Studies*, *40*(4), 747–755.
Nyéléni. (2007). *Declaration of Nyéléni*. Retrieved from http://nyeleni.org/spip.php?article290
Patel, R. (2009). Guest editor, food sovereignty. *Journal of Peasant Studies*, *36*(3), 663–706.
van der Ploeg, J. D. (2013). *Peasants and the art of farming: A Chayanovian manifesto*. Halifax: Fernwood.
Ribot, J., & Peluso, N. (2003). A theory of access. *Rural Sociology*, *68*(2), 153–181.
Rosset, P. M. (2006). Moving forward: Agrarian reform as a part of food sovereignty. In P. M. Rosset, R. Patel, & M. Courville (Eds.), *Promised land: Competing visions of Agrarian reform* (pp. 301–321). Oakland, CA: Food First Books.
Rosset, P. M. (2013). Re-thinking agrarian reform, land and territory in La Via Campesina. *Journal of Peasant Studies*, *40*(4), 721–775.
Rosset, P. M., & Torres, M. E. (2012). Rural social movements and agroecology: Context, theory, and process. *Ecology and Society*, *17*(3), 17–28.
Schlosberg, D. (2004). Reconceiving environmental justice: Global movements and political theories. *Environmental Politics*, *13*(3), 517–540.
St. Martin, K., & Hall-Arber, M. (2007). Environment and development: (Re)connecting community and commons in New England fisheries, USA. In S. Kindon, R. Pain, & M. Kesby (Eds.), *Participatory action research methods* (pp. 51–59). London: Routledge.
Tornaghi, C. (2014). Critical geography of urban agriculture. *Progress in Human Geography*, *38*(4), 551–567. doi:10.1177/0309132513512542
Torres, M. E., & Rosset, P. M. (2014). Diálogo de saberes in La Vía Campesina: Food sovereignty and agroecology. *Journal of Peasant Studies*, *41*(6), 979–997. doi:10.1080/03066150.2013.872632
Torrez, F. (2011). La Via Campesina: Peasant-led agrarian reform and food sovereignty. *Development*, *54*(1), 49–54.
USDA. (2014a). *Farm demographics*. Retrieved from http://www.agcensus.usda.gov/Publications/2012/Online_Resources/Highlights/Farm_Demographics/Highlights_Farm_Demographics.pdf
USDA. (2014b). *Farms and land in farms 2013 summary*. Retrieved from http://www.usda.gov/nass/PUBS/TODAYRPT/fnlo0514.pdf
Via Campesina. (2011). *Conference declaration: Stop land grabbing now!* Retrieved from http://viacampesina.org/en/index.php/main-issues-mainmenu-27/agrarian-reform-mainmenu-36/1127-stop-land-grabbing-now
Vos, T. (2000). Visions of the middle landscape: Organic farming and the politics of nature. *Agriculture and Human Values*, *17*, 245–256.
Wittman, H. (2009). Reworking the metabolic rift: La Vía Campesina, agrarian citizenship, and food sovereignty. *Journal of Peasant Studies*, *36*(4), 805–826.
Wright, A., & Wolford, W. (2003). *To inherit the earth: The landless movement and the struggle for a new Brazil*. Oakland, CA: Food First Books.
Zibechi, R. (2012). *Territories in resistance: A cartography of Latin American social movements*. Oakland, CA: AK Press.
Zigas, E. (2012). *Public harvest*. San Francisco, CA: SPUR.

A Recipe for Change: Reclamation of Indigenous Food Sovereignty in *O-Pipon-Na-Piwin Cree* Nation for Decolonization, Resource Sharing, and Cultural Restoration

ASFIA GULRUKH KAMAL*, RENE LINKLATER**, SHIRLEY THOMPSON*, JOSEPH DIPPLE*** & ITHINTO MECHISOWIN COMMITTEE****

**Natural Resources Institute, University of Manitoba, Winnipeg, Canada*
***Tommy Thomas Memorial Health Complex and Community Care, O-Pipon-Na-Piwin Cree Nation, South Indian Lake, Canada*
****Department of Native Studies, University of Manitoba, Winnipeg, Canada*
*****O-Pipon-Na-Piwin Cree Nation, South Indian Lake, Canada*

ABSTRACT O-Pipon-Na-Piwin *Cree Nation (OPCN), an Indigenous community in northern Manitoba, Canada, was flooded and forced to relocate from ancestral lands to a nearby settlement under such circumstances. Regaining strength from their inherent cultural values grounded in their relationship with the land, OPCN eventually formed a community-based food program called* Ithinto Mechisowin *(IMP) ('food from the land'). This article uses OPCN's concept of resource (*wechihituwin*) and decolonization (*pasekonekewin*) to present a nuanced understanding of Indigenous food systems in Canada. We argue that the ways in which IMP inspires reconnection with land, thereby improving access to culturally appropriate healthy food, are steps forward in strengthening Indigenous food sovereignty.*

Introduction

Hydroelectric projects in northern Manitoba, Canada, have undermined environmental, economic, and social welfare of Indigenous communities for decades (Kamal, Thompson, Linklater,

& Ithinto Mechisowin Committee, 2014; Liénafa & Martin, 2010; Martin & Hoffman, 2008; Waldram, 1988). In 1976, one such project, Manitoba Hydro's Churchill River Diversion (CRD), flooded many northern Manitoba Indigenous[1] communities (Waldram, 1988). CRD damaged Indigenous food and medicine, leading to food insecurity, negative health impacts and a legacy of poverty among the affected populations (Kamal et al., 2014).

The community of *O-Pipon-Na-Piwin* Cree Nation (OPCN), a small First Nation reserve located on the shore of Southern Indian Lake (SIL), was one of the most negatively impacted of all the communities affected (Waldram, 1988). Despite OPCN's appeal for cultural and livelihood rights, community concern was purposely undermined by Manitoba Hydro and the province (Waldram, 1984, 236). A number of studies were published attesting to the severity of socioeconomic and environmental damages occurring in northern Manitoba, particularly in OPCN (Waldram, 1984, 1985, 1988; Hoffman, 2008; Hoffman & Martin, 2012; Loney, 1995). In 2009, a household food security survey confirmed that an alarming 75% of residents in 14 different northern Manitoba communities were food insecure (Thompson et al., 2011, 14). Of them, OPCN had the highest rate of food insecurity—100% (Thompson et al., 2011, 24).

However, within the existing socioeconomic challenges, communities in northern Manitoba and elsewhere in Canada, including OPCN, have worked persistently to preserve local food systems and cultural rights (Kamal et al., 2014; Thompson, Wiebe, Gulrukh, & Ashram, 2012). The recent wave of food sovereignty discourse in North America acknowledges the need to address Indigenous organizing against the tactics of contemporary colonization (Corntassel, 2012a; Desmarais & Wittman, 2014; Grey & Patel, 2014; Kamal et al., 2014; Morrison, 2011). Few academic studies, however, have examined what Indigenous food sovereignty looks like as it is developed in practice.

Throughout this paper, we will argue that in Canada the practice of Indigenous food sovereignty through local food harvesting programs can provide an opportunity for decolonization. First, in order to gain a nuanced understanding of the current situation at OPCN, we must address the community's history and the establishment of hydropower production in northern Manitoba. Following this review, we will address the concepts of food security, food sovereignty and Indigenous food sovereignty. Finally, we describe the history of the *Ithinto Mechisowin* program, hereafter IMP, and its contribution to decolonization within the community. As a means of establishing our argument from the local point of view, we will introduce OPCN's contextually specific concepts of resource sharing and decolonization.

Community History

It is believed that Indigenous people started living in SIL region 6000 years ago (Waldram, 1988, 116). Much later, in early nineteenth century, a community was formed and named after the lake (Waldram, 1988, 117). People used to live well, with a thriving food system based on harvesting different seasonal foods and medicines from the land until 'colonization intervened in the form of trade and treaties' (Elder Thomas Spence, personal communication, September 22, 2013). In Canada, such treaties were made between the reigning monarch and Indigenous communities, most of which were signed between 1871 and 1921 (Waldram, 1988, 27). The initial conditions of agreement promised to guarantee mutual peace and friendship; Indigenous rights to trade, fish, and hunt in allocated reserve land; and to receive annual supplies of food, provisions, and ammunition from the Crown 'as long as the sun shines above and the waters flow in the ocean' (Morris, 1880, 96). However, in reality, the treaties were constructed under Canadian imperialist politics.

At the time of the treaty process in Manitoba, the community of SIL was meant to receive reserve land, named *Ithinoway Sagahegan* (People's Lake), and benefits (Steve Ducharme, personal communication, August 8, 2013). However, this plan never materialized and, in 1908, SIL residents were registered as members of the nearby community of Nelson House Cree Nation, now *Nisichawayasihk Cree Nation* (NCN), under Treaty 5 (Waldram, 1988, 116).

In 1942, a commercial fishery was established to take advantage of the quality and availability of whitefish in SIL (Waldram, 1988, 117). The lake became North America's second largest white fish fishery, producing approximately one million pounds of Grade A whitefish annually (Ducharme, 2013). Under contemporary measures of poverty in Canada, only 27.9% of the population at SIL would have been considered poor at the time (Hoffman, 2008, 113).

Beginning in the 1960s, Manitoba entered a phase of hydropower production directed towards the construction of mega projects along the Nelson River system (Liénafa & Martin, 2010; Hoffman, 2008; Hoffman & Martin, 2012; Waldram, 1988). The objective was to 'modernize' northern Indigenous communities with a 'hydro induced' program of 'modernization'and 'redevelopment' (Robson, 1993, 106). Under Premier Duff Roblin, the province proposed a project, known as the CRD that would divert the waters of the Churchill River through SIL, the Rat and Burntwood Rivers and into the Nelson River system (Waldram, 1988, 119). Overall, this project would raise SIL by approximately 10 meters, effectively flooding the entirety of the community (Waldram, 1988). Upon receipt of this information, the community began a vigorous battle against the province, ultimately leading to a change of government and promises to cancel the project (McClullum & McClullum, 1975, 107). Ultimately, the project moved forward. The new, low-level diversion 'only' project increased the level of SIL by 3 meters, forcing half of the community to relocate (McClullum & McClullum, 1975, 107–108). Eventually, the entirety of the community was forced to move in order to access infrastructure, including the school and nursing station (Hilda Dysart, personal communication, 2012). Construction of Missi Falls, the CRD control structure at the outlet of SIL into the Churchill River, effectively converted the lake into a reservoir that stores approximately 40% of the water used to power Manitoba Hydro's arsenal of generating stations (Dysart, 2014, 1).

In response to the environmental destruction wrought by the construction of the CRD, five First Nations communities in northern Manitoba formed an alliance known as the Northern Flood Committee (NFC) (Waldram, 1988, 147). Although the NFC did not include the community at SIL, it did include the communities from Split Lake, Nelson House, Cross Lake, Norway House, and York Factory First Nations (Waldram, 1988). These communities challenged Manitoba and Manitoba Hydro and ultimately brought about the Northern Flood Agreement in 1977 (NFA) (Waldram, 1988, 160). This agreement, termed a modern day treaty by Minister of Aboriginal and Northern Affairs Eric Robinson in 2000, established promises to the communities as a means of mitigation against the effects of hydropower production (Kulchyski, 2008, 134; Province of Manitoba, 2015). Most prominently, Schedule E of the NFA establishes the 'Substantive Purpose of Development Plan' and states it will affect 'the eradication of mass poverty and mass unemployment and the improvement of the physical, social and economic conditions and transportation' (NFA, 1977, 70). Strikingly, the SIL community was one of the most impacted by the CRD, but did not receive any compensation until much later, because they were not recognized as a reserve by the federal government and did not have title to the land (Hoffman & Martin, 2012, 37). A mitigation plan was needed to minimize social and environmental damages but never truly established (Dysart, 2014).

The timing of the formation of the contemporary OPCN reserve was influenced largely by hydroelectric dam construction (Hoffman & Martin, 2012). At that time, another hydroelectric generating station, called *Wuskwatim*, was proposed by Manitoba Hydro, in financial partnership with NCN to be built on the Burntwood River system, which would further impact SIL (Hoffman & Martin, 2012, 45; Kulchyski, 2008). In order to establish the partnership and complete the project, Manitoba Hydro's proposal required community support (Leslie Dysart, personal communication, August 8, 2013). Rather than risk a defeat of the proposed *Wuskwatim* partnership at the hands of NCN band members living at SIL, who were predominantly against further construction, the rules were changed drastically by the federal government in regards to the creation of a new reserve at SIL, called OPCN (Kulchyski, 2008, 143). The reserve was established in 2005, less than a year prior to the vote on the *Wuskwatim* Generating Station. The divide and conquer strategy of government effectively changed the outcome of the NCN referendum on *Wuskwatim* (Kulchyski, 2008), as creation of the OPCN reserve eliminated 400 highly probable no votes from the NCN band (Dysart, 2014, 4). Construction on the dam began in 2006 and went into operation in 2012, resulting in further fluctuation of water levels around the community and impacts to OPCN. These impacts are ongoing.

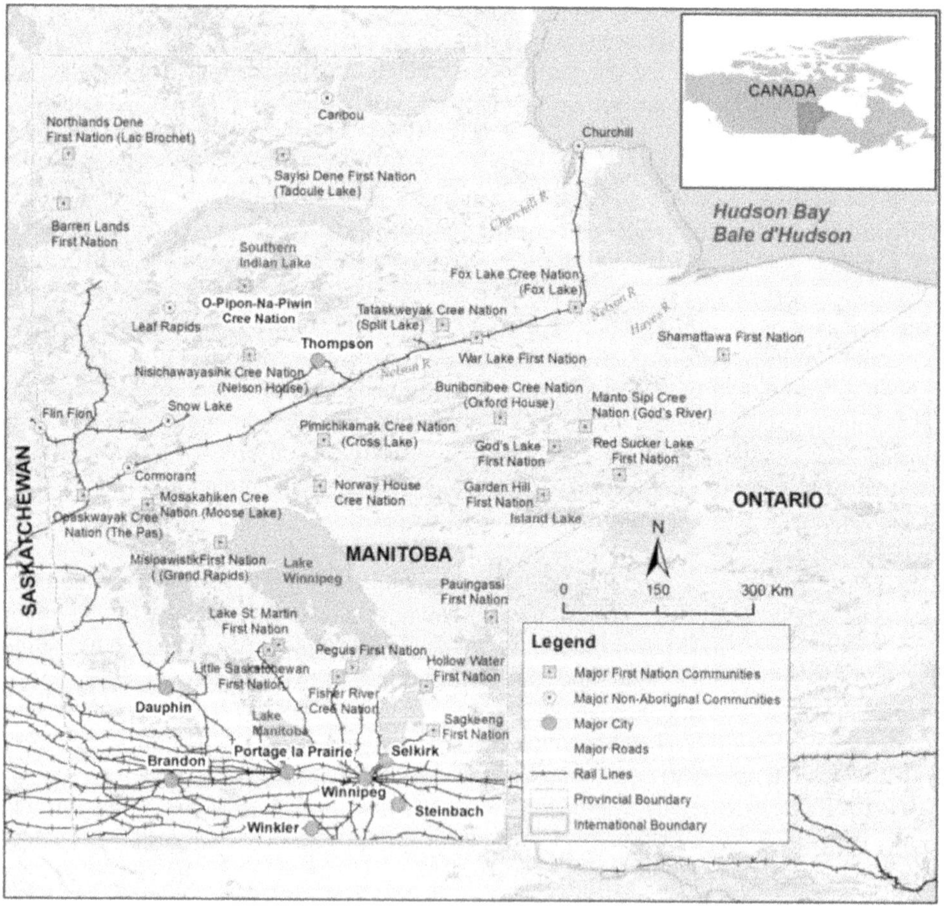

Map source: Kamal et al. (2014, 144).

Impact of CRD on OPCN

Cultural, social and physical well-being of Indigenous peoples in Canada are deeply integrated with their food system, a food system that culturally incorporates harvesting and sharing food with sustainable care for land (Desmarais & Wittman, 2014; Morrison, 2011). OPCN members lost regular access to both culturallyappropriate food and their livelihoods following completion of the CRD. Before the lake was flooded, people enjoyed diverse wild food harvested in different seasons (Hoffman & Martin, 2012). After the CRD flooding, wild food harvesting activitieswere compromised in all seasons. Continuous fluctuation of water levels created massive debris in the waterways, breaking the seasonal fish spawning cycle, and causing wild game migration to the inland (Kamal et al., 2014).

Indigenous people around the world value food as a source of medicine for numerous health benefits (Kuhnlein, Erasmus, Spigelski, & Burlingame, 2013). In Canada, land-based food is considered essential for 'identity, health and survival' (Power, 2008, 95). Following completion of the CRD, a lack of wild food has impacted all aspects of OPCN's community health. Wild food is important for physical nourishment, as it is rich in nutrients (Kuhnlein & Receveur, 1996; Mason, Dana, & Anderson, 2009, 347). It also inspires physical activities and health outdoor lifestyle (Kamal & Thompson, 2013, 6). Wild meat and fish can be both a source of protein and minerals and contain less fat and cholesterol than commercial meats (Waldram, 1985, 45). Environmental damage from the CRD caused mercury contamination in fish in OPCN and other flooded communities (Loney, 1995, 238). It also drowned the habitat for important medicinal plants. In addition, gradual dependency on poor quality store bought food and a lack of physical activity caused acute health disparities and chronic diseases such as diabetes in all CRD affected communities (Public Utility Board, 2014, 7).

Arguably, the most direct impact of CRD on OPCN's community was the near complete destruction of the fishery—to approximately 10% of its original capacity (Ducharme, 2013). As an outcome of this destruction, unemployment rates increased throughout the community (Waldram, 1985, 1988; Hoffman, 2008). Under these circumstances, people were forced to travel long distances by boat or floatplane to harvest wild food and medicine. A decade after CRD, Manitoba Hydro gave partial subsidy for harvesting activities, which they abruptly ended in 2013 without consultation or explanation (Dysart, 2014, 2). In addition, the high cost of living, particularly the cost of food and gas in the north, has contributed to the continuing impoverishment. The community was forced to rely upon government social assistance programs (Hoffman, 2008, 114–115).

Both food security and sovereignty over Indigenous food systems were severely impacted by the CRD. The following section presents an analysis of food security, food sovereignty and Indigenous food sovereignty in Canada. This will follow a discussion to reflect on the differences between colonial and Indigenous food systems.

Food Security, Food Sovereignty and Indigenous Food Sovereignty

Food security emerged in the 1970s and is defined as 'exist[ing] when all people, at all times, have physical and economic access to sufficient, safe and nutritious food to meet their dietary needs and food preferences for an active and healthy life' (FAO, 1996, 3). Household food security is taken as a technical measure to assess the severity of hunger, poverty and malnutrition in marginalized communities (Chandrasekera, 2008; Coleman-Jensen, Nord, Andrews, & Carlson, Steven, 2011; Council of Canadian Academics, 2014; Tarasuk, 2009; Thompson et al., 2011).

While the concept of food security has little to say about the means through which food is secured, it is often a part of a neoliberal framework that views food as a commodity most effectively delivered through the global market (Rudolph & MacLachlan, 2013, 1080).

Although food security and food sovereignty cover some common ground, they are considered to be different concepts (Jarosz, 2014; Menser, 2014; Rudolph & MacLachlan, 2013). The Via Campesina (1996) Declaration of Food Sovereignty defined food sovereignty as

> the right of each nation to maintain and develop its own capacity to produce its basic foods respecting cultural and productive diversity. We have the right to produce our own food in our own territory. Food sovereignty is a precondition to genuine food security. (Via Campesina, 1996, 1)

Put forward as a multidimensional rights-based political framework, food sovereignty situates contemporary resource depletion, economic crisis, and environmental degradation within the context of neoliberal trade and production, with negative consequences for peoples' access to healthy, sustainable, and culturally appropriate food. Besides a focus on the fundamental causes of hunger, other noteworthy and interlinked issues addressed in food sovereignty discourse include industrialization of agriculture, colonial strategies of (under)development, commodification of food, and protection of the rights of farmers, women, and Indigenous peoples (Declaration of Nyéléni, 2007, Desmarais & Wittman, 2014). As a growing social justice movement, food sovereignty offers alternative modes of producing and consuming food, suggesting participatory methods of intervention (Stédile & de Carvalho, 2011, 25). In short, the food sovereignty movement functions as a broad political alliance to rectify the problems wrought by the current food system at the local, regional, national, and global levels.

Food sovereignty distinguishes the concept of 'sovereignty' from its more rigid classical definitions (Menser, 2014). Traditionally, sovereignty has been understood as 'final and absolute authority in a political community' (Hinsley, 1966, 1) and is a concept related to a state's legal control over a particular geographical area and its population. It is connected to the notion of private property and resource accumulation, where nature is divided and extracted based on material value and state politics (Dean & Levi, 2003; Menser, 2014). In contrast, food sovereignty refers to increased control over the food system by both consumers and producers, who are seen as having shared collective interests contrary to the capitalist emphasis upon accumulation and privatization (Wittman, 2011). With influences ranging from Marxism to ecology, food sovereignty values growing food as a means of maintaining sustainable ecosystems and promoting cultural integrity as opposed to a means of maximizing and accumulating capital, resources, and property (Andree, Jeffery, Michael, & Marie-Jane, 2014; Desmarais & Wittman, 2014; Holt-Giménez & Altieri, 2013; Menser, 2014).

Within this context, food sovereignty is a large and diverse movement encompassing a variety of perspectives, goals, and approaches. Regarding the state, in some cases, the goal is achieving self-determination—and the freedom of a dignified life—without political intervention from state, while in other cases, states are called upon to fulfill certain rights while respecting the ability of communities to assert their rights in a meaningful way (Menser, 2014). In the postcolonial era, a state's control over the marginalized is re-established through the imposition of universal human rights over Indigenous peoples (Kulchyski, 2013; Dean & Levi 2003, 9). The concept of universal human rights is not entirely negative. However, when it is used to undermine cultural distinctions and remove rights established to protect these distinctions, it becomes problematic (Alfred, 2009b; Kulchyski, 2013; Dean & Levi 2003, 10). As Corntassel argues, 'rights-based approaches do not offer meaningful restoration of Indigenous homelands and food sovereignty' (2012a, 93). United Nations approved Declaration on the Rights of Indigenous Peoples in 2007 and Canada adopted it in 2010 (Lum, 2014). However, in practice Canadian state regulations follow the historical blindness that can come with United Nation's universal plea of human rights (Kulchyski, 2013; Lum, 2014). It creates further authority for the state to determine the benefits and limitations of an already colonized population.

In Indigenous understanding sovereignty is inherent and collective (Barker, 2005, 20). It is infused with interconnected autonomy nurtured through relationship with land. A community, for Indigenous peoples, includes both human and non-human beings, particularly natural entities (Adelson, 2000; Simpson, 2004) and in a sovereign space, all aspects of culture (language, sacred ceremonies, food system, livelihood, relationship, and stories with land) are preserved, as they are essential for community health and sustainability; for example, Cree concept of health and collective well-being, 'has everything to do with connections to the land and to a rich and complex past' (Adelson, 2000, 25). Thus sovereignty for Indigenous people, 'cannot be separated from people or their culture' (Kickingbird, 1977, 2). That is why restoring the culture of a particular region is fundamental for Indigenous food sovereignty, generally more so than to non-Indigenous food sovereignty. Indigenous food sovereignty addresses 'Indigenous' aspirations for collective well-being and prefers to rectify inequality and acknowledge peoples' rights to land and cultural integrity (Morrison, 2011).

Relatedly, achieving food sovereignty for Indigenous people requires the inclusion of Indigenous cultural values in state policies and Indigenous participation in the economy (Desmarais & Wittman, 2014; Morrison, 2011). In Canada, incorporation of Indigenous values is essential for the reclamation of Indigenous Treaty rights, as opposed to continued colonization under the guise of modernization, development and national prosperity (Kulchyski, 2013). To be more specific, the meaning of reclamation is not 'collaboration, partnership or infrastructural development' provided from the state, but the removal of discriminatory state regulations, land and title transfers and

> the stopping of practices that encroach upon the sovereignty of those territories (from active resource extraction to more passive but deadly forms of pollutions like the dumping of radioactive toxins proximate to watersheds, the siting of incinerators, overdrawing water tables, or damming rives). (Menser, 2014, 70)

In light of this argument, food sovereignty for Indigenous people in Canada is contributing to past and ongoing commitment of Indigenous political mobilization in North America.[2]

Working to make sovereignty over cultural and livelihood resources and relationships a reality is a major step towards regeneration of a long oppressed people in Canada (Corntassel, 2008, 2012a, 2012b). To achieve this reality, decolonization must start at a personal, intimate, and collective level and must be realized both in mind and action (Fanon, 1952; Waziyatawin & Yellow Bird, 2005). Indigenous food sovereignty advocates for decolonizing activities—reclaiming land for hunting, fishing, trapping, berry picking, community gardens, wild food programs, and other cultural activities, along with their cultural meanings. These activities involve restoration and development of cultural practices, values, and thoughts that were overpowered but are still important and necessary for the continuance and renewal of ideas, well-being and empowerment of colonized people. According to OPCN leaders, these activities help to re-build sovereignty.

Within this context we introduce OPCN's concept of resource, best expressed through the word *wechihituwin*. *Wechihituwin* refers to any means of livelihood that is shared and used to help another person, family, or the community. The term emphasizes the fact that food in the cultural tradition of OPCN is not a commodity; it is a set of relationships. Similarly, the concept of decolonization is defined as *pasekonekewin* which means taking the person by the hand and helping her or him stand. From this section, *wechihituwin* is used in place of 'resource' to provide a more nuanced and spiritual significance to land, water and food, as well as the life living within each. The term *pasekonekewin* is used to elaborate the integration of youth in food harvesting activities in OPCN. Using these concepts, we examine local food programs, understanding them not as isolated actions, but in the context of efforts to reestablish Indigenous sovereignty over resources, land and culture (Barker, 2005).

Research Background and Methodology

Following CRD, OPCN's food champions and Elders worked towards the maintenance and revitalization of their cultural livelihood and connection to the land, through community gatherings and individual efforts to train youth (Kamal et al., 2014). Upon receiving results from the 2009 survey on food insecurity, OPCN felt a need for an immediate response within the community. This study highlighted NCN's community-based country food[3] program as a probable cause for their significantly lower food insecurity (Thompson et al., 2011). From this realization, OPCN envisioned a wild food program that could subsidize some of the prohibitively expensive costs of harvesting. In return for this subsidy, food champions would share some of the *wechihituwin* with the community through the wild food program. In response to community interest, in 2010, Ph.D. candidate Asfia Kamal, who conducted the 2009 survey at OPCN, focused her doctoral thesis on helping to establish a wild food program. The study was proposed as a collaborative initiative between the University of Manitoba and OPCN.

In order to complete this study, and help establish the wild food program, both parties agreed to use OCAP (Ownership, control, access, and possession) principles as a foundation of the study. OCAP is a set of research guidelines adopted and proposed by the Steering Committee of the Aboriginal Regional Longitudinal Health Survey in Canada. The objectives of these guidelines are to add self-determination, collective ownership, and community control over research information to studies conducted with Aboriginal people or in Aboriginal territory (Schnarch, 2004). As the project progressed, members of a University of Manitoba research team, led by Kamal, participated in a multitude of community events and programs in relation to the establishment of the wild food program. She learned and gathered information through multiple visits to the community, helped to orchestrate youth educational experiences and was invited to a number of community gatherings. These opportunities provided her with a sense of community and relationship with the people of OPCN, a relationship that greatly informs her knowledge.

Relationships formed through the advancement of this program facilitated a total of 44 open-ended interviews, 2 participatory video workshops, and 8 focus groups. These interviews allowed for what were probably the most informative and impactful interactions of the research—storytelling and personal narratives from harvesters and Elders. Stories and narratives have an important place in Indigenous cultures, and provide a wealth of knowledge about a number of different topics that are necessary to gain a nuanced understanding of the culture and life of a particular group of people (Fitznor, 2012; Iseke & Moore, 2011; Simpson, 2011). Additionally, these stories and narratives helped provide understanding of community members' perception of Indigenous food sovereignty as well as the vision and establishment of the IMP ('food from the land').

IMP ('Food from the Land')

Hydroelectric power production in northern Manitoba removed the *wechihituwin* from the Cree people. As the community moves forward and attempts to assert its place as an Indigenous community, it must 'regain its *wechihituwin* from the destructive power of energy production' (Barb Spence, personal communication, November 8, 2013). IMP, as a program, has brought this option back to the community by supporting individual and community claims to the land surrounding, and including, SIL.

Community members decided to establish this program to support others within the community who are unable to access healthy, sustainable, and culturally appropriate food. From 2012 to 2013, the IMP evolved in three major phases. First, a committee was formed to discuss the needs of the program. OPCN's program is supported through sharing *wechihituwin*, in this case equipment, space, labor, skills from the community. In second phase, the community focused on local outreach, applied for funding to hire a community coordinator, and renovated the community's food handling area, as per Health Canada regulations (Kamal et al., 2014, 146). The program received funding from various local and provincial government organizations in January 2013. In the third phase, three industrial freezers were bought to store wild food and medicine. The program began distribution in June 2013. During the first four months of the program, the number of families receiving food from the program grew from 5 to 390 families. Money is provided to subsidize some harvesting costs if the food champion agrees to share the food through IMP. Food collected through program activities is labeled, stored in freezers, and distributed once a week to single mothers, low-income families, and Elders (Kamal et al., 2014, 147).

Pasekonekewin: Empowering Youth in OPCN

Youth programs are of paramount importance to the IMP, and as such have been established in multiple occasions throughout the year. These programs consist of hunting, fishing, berry picking, preparation of wild food, gardening, and education on the health benefits of different wild foods. OPCN's Oscar Blackburn School plays an integral part of the educational aspect of the program and has helped instill culturally important principles in the community's youth through a life skills class. This class requires youth participation in the IMP, creates outdoor activities for food harvesting and involves Elders who teach youth about 'the Cree principles of responsibility, respect, focus, patience, sharing, listening and generosity', says class instructor Shirley Ducharme. Such activities contribute to community initiatives of *pasekonekewin* and youth empowerment. Applauding IMP's collaboration with the school, community members recommend the use of both educational methods as a means of continuing decolonization while remaining true to community heritage. 'My son should learn to read and learn to hunt, we need both to fight and stay close to our roots' (Dysart, personal communication, 2013).

IMP also uses storytelling, in Cree, throughout program activities, to engage the community through culturally appropriate educational methods. 'Each food harvested from the land has a story that teaches something to us', explained program advisor Steve Ducharme. Additionally, the program instills an understanding of the relationship and responsibilities community

Table 1. The importance of seasonal local food harvesting and the impact of the Churchill River Diversion[4]

Season	Seasonal traditional food and method of consumption	Health significance as understood by OPCN members	Cultural significance of harvesting and consuming the food	Stories of traditional food-related activities	Perceived damage due to CRD
Summer and winter	Fish (smoked, boiled and fried, dry fish with berries, fish head boiled, fish broth for soup)	White fish is good for diabetes and blood pressure. Jack fish guts are cold medicine. Fish head and broth are good sources of and calcium. (Jennifer Linklater)	Act of fishing teaches us that we need to work hard. (Fisherman Wilbur Wood)	'In summer spending time in the fish camp was like a ritual in the community. Youth loved playing by the beach and chasing fish.' (Louis Dumas)	Continuous fluctuation of water hampers fish egg spawning. Fish taste mushy. People need to travel to inland lakes to fish
Spring	Beaver and muskrat (smoked and boiled meat)	Beaver meat has pain relieving and anti-inflammatory element Muskrat meat is quality protein. (Roger Moose)	Trapping teaches focus, hard work, and respect for elders. Beavers are hard-working and youth must be too. (Elder Ross Moose)	'Trapping beaver and muskrat was a favorite past-time for us before the CRD. We used to catch hundreds of muskrats, now we can only catch a few if we are lucky.' (Steve Durcharme)	Continuous fluctuation of water froze and killed many beaver and muskrat
Spring	Ducks, geese, and other waterfowl (boiled meat and broth for soup with oats)	Duck and goose meat is good for heart health and high blood pressure. (Roger Moose)	Hunting ducks and geese can teach about determination, focus and is a form of meditation. (Barb Spence)	'We always like to save some of our birds for feasts and gatherings. Goose broth with oatmeal is a favorite dish in every gathering.' (Delia Dysart)	Loss of marsh and shoreline changed waterfowl migration paths
Summer	Seagull eggs(boiled)	Good sources of protein and is good for bones. (Barb Spence)	Harvesting seagull eggs teaches the rules of conservation. (Elder Vivian Moose)	'In summer before CRD fishermen used to bring baskets full of seagull eggs. It was a treat for us.' (Barb Spence)	Seagulls lay eggs in small rocky islands in Southern Indian Lake. After CRD many of these islands were drowned

(*Continued*)

Table 1. Continued

Season	Seasonal traditional food and method of consumption	Health significance as understood by OPCN members	Cultural significance of harvesting and consuming the food	Stories of traditional food-related activities	Perceived damage due to CRD
Summer	Berries (Blueberry, moss berry, raspberry, and cranberry)(mixed with dry meat and fish, raw and making jam with sugar)	Medicines for colds, diarrhea and other stomach problems, diabetes and detoxifying body. (Elder Florence Donkey)	Berry harvesting teaches sharing and caring for family. (Linda Baker)	'Women used to go out for berry picking with their families and children, make tea and socialize all day long sharing their harvest.' (Hilda Dysart)	Erosion of shoreline damaged and drowned berry patches.
Summer	Tea (Labrador, wild mint)	Medicine for cold and headache. (Elder Vivian Moose)	Spending time with medicinal plant is healing, and teaches generosity, peace, kindness and respect for the land. (Roger Moose)	'After you use a medicinal plant, you need to throw it on fire or somewhere safe where people will not walk on it. You also need to leave something behind when you pick them. I still do that. People leave tobacco when they pick wild mint.' (Shirley Ducharme)	Loss of land; shoreline drowned many medicinal plants
Fall	Moose (meat, lard from bone marrow, nose) (Boiled, smoked, dry)	Dry moose meat with berries is good for stomach and bones. (Elder Helen Moose)	Hunting moose teaches responsibility for feeding family and allows for sharing. (Shirley Ducharme)	'The common saying is one should not eat his first kill. This is to teach the young hunter about kindness and sharing.' (Shirley Ducharme)	Erosion creates debris and requires long travel to hunt moose.

members have with the land and waters of their homeland. Indigenous people in Canada use storytelling and knowledge sharing as an essential part of education and empowerment for youth (Iseke & Moore, 2011, Simpson, 2011). Storytelling has been a cultural framework for maintaining Cree collective memory in Canada for generations (McLeod, 2007). Scholars consider activities on the land with Elders and youth together as decolonizing, essential for Indigenous knowledge transmission and community cohesion (Alfred & Corntassel, 2005, 613; Simpson, 2004, 374).

OPCN's concept of decolonization, in particular, is inherently one of support and communal strength. Both Cree terms used in this paper; *wechihituwin* and *pasekonekewin*, have a common theme, communal support. Table 1 addresses this theme related to food.

Re-establishing *Wechihituwin*

IMP is an outcome of OPCN's growing spirit to reproduce and reuse *wechihituwin* within the community. The table above gives a contextual account of OPCN's existing practices that address life on the land. These practices are primary determinants of food sovereignty and community well-being. Being on the land and participating in any bush related activities resonates with Cree peoples' distinct culture, concepts of health and well-being and ratifies history of 'the connections between identity and personal, social, and political well-being' (Adelson, 2000, 99). The stories told to youth connect past with present and contribute to a future where food is a source of cultural strength. In this future, food, as *wechihituwin,* represents more than sustenance, it contains stories and memories that can heal the community. Similarly a food program building is not just infrastructure, it is a catalyst to regenerate *wechihituwin*, to inspire new ideas and collective will. The program's success has motivated other local organizations in OPCN to implement different youth focused programs. The program office itself is slowly becoming a place of community gathering, reinventing social bonds and collective well-being.

Conclusion

The OPCN wild food program is decolonizing, providing both practical control over resources and cultural restoration. Indigenous food sovereignty, which emphasizes the importance of cultural practices, is a pathway in this case towards decolonizing land and peoples. Through the IMP case study, we provide evidence that community defined programs similar to this can be beneficial in a number and variety of social and cultural domains. Additionally, Indigenous regional programs and organizations can work as a political actor to turn (sovereignty) theory into practice. For example, Inuit Circumpolar Council has been helping mobilizing Inuit sovereignty in the Arctic (Shadian, 2014).

The way in which OPCN's food champions use the term food sovereignty, neither 'food' nor 'sovereignty' retains their classical meanings. OPCN contested the predominant understanding of 'food'—understood as 'consumable commodities'—and struggled to restore its cultural meaning as the bond between people, health and land. IMP is OPCN's active vision to go beyond this struggle, becoming more food sovereign through the process of Elders and food champions sharing stories and teachings with youth, and through the process of sharing wild foods with those in need. The intention is to 'step out of the box' and make these stories and teachings as lived experience to 'remove our colonial blinders' (Simpson, 2011, 148).

Sovereignty is redefined by OPCN as a re-establishment of relationships with the land and *wechihituwin* of their area. OPCN does not perceive sovereignty as control over land, water, or wildlife, but a relationship with these entities that allows for the mutual benefit of all parties. The community does not perceive sovereignty as an ability to take from others or the environment, but to support the community through engagement and sharing of *wechihituwin*.

IMP has been successful as an outcome of the existing *wechihituwin*, as opposed to establishing a program on the basis of importing a predefined framework. However, it has faced challenges since its inception. Ensuring a food handling area as per Health Canada regulation was the primary challenge. Health Canada regulations are meant for good health, hygiene and food safety. However, in remote Indigenous communities, receiving external support to make any kind of change is time consuming and costly. Additionally, financing such programs can be immensely difficult, and at times when a budget is not available, community cohesion and support is necessary to provide the required equipment. Lack of infrastructure can also hamper attempts at supporting wild food programs.

Furthermore, establishing this case study as a permanent framework from which all communities are able to establish Indigenous food sovereignty can be problematic. Challenges within each and every community vary in type and severity, making a predefined framework difficult to implement. The impacts of colonization are so grave and continuous that long-term healing is required.

IMP shows that youth empowerment, through the practice of *pasekonekewin*, is one means of supporting the long-term healing of the community, which can be a combination of both Indigenous and Western education which is a welcoming approach present in Canadian Indigenous communities (Ball, 2004, 459–460). Additionally, transmission of knowledge through Elders and youth engagement in land-based activities is highly encouraged as a step towards Indigenous cultural regeneration (Alfred, 2009b, as cited in Corntassel, 2012a, 97). The IMP is a testament to Indigenous strength against colonial forces. Actions such as these call for a reinforcement of contemporary research with Indigenous wisdom and community driven projects. Related to policy, governments and corporations, for example, Manitoba Hydro, should accommodate Indigenous sovereignty cultural restoration in its policy and activities and consider issues surrounding natural resource extraction and exploitation, land-based industries and food production.

Outside researchers can provide a number of benefits to community programs, through grant writing and establishment of external relationships and partnerships. However, these programs must be community based and centered on the wants and needs of the community within which it will be situated Any community hoping to establish Indigenous food sovereignty must find an approach that is right in their particular situation, though this case study can be used to help guide initial planning and decision-making. Communities must find their own spirit 'to cause a mental awakening' (Alfred, 2009a, 282). To quote Alfred and Corntassel (2005), we need

> to start to use our Indigenous languages to frame our thoughts, the ethical framework of our philosophies to make decisions and to use our laws and institutions to govern ourselves. (614)

Acknowledgements

The authors give special thanks to OPCN Elders as well as the *Ithinto Mechisowin* committee members, OPCN and all community members who stood by us during this effort. The authors thank Bethann G. Merkle (www.commnatural.com) for editorial support. Heartfelt thanks to Steve, Annie, Christina, Saydia and Wahid.

Disclosure Statement

No potential conflict of interest was reported by the authors.

Funding

This research received financially support through Dr. Shirley Thompson's SSHRC Insight Grant Award and the SSHRC partnership grant called 'Sharing the Feast of Ithinto Mechisowin (Food from the Land) and Grow North: Food-based Community Development at O-Pipon-Na-Piwin Cree Nation and Northern Manitoba communities'. We also acknowledge funding from SSHRC through the Manitoba Research Alliance grant: Partnering for Change – Community-based Solutions for Aboriginal and Inner-city Poverty.

Notes

1 Under Canadian constitution 1982, Section 35, Aboriginal refers to First Nation (recognized by constitution), Métis (cultural and ethnic identity of individuals who are the result of relationships between Indigenous and Europeans), and Inuit (Indigenous people from northern Canada considered "Indian" in Canadian constitution) people (Asch, 1984). OPCN is composed of both First Nations and Métis individuals who speak both Cree and English. This paper uses the term Indigenous to situate the community in the dialogue of Indigenous food sovereignty.

2 Indigenous resistance against colonial policies of the USA, Canada, and Central and South America to achieve sovereignty and cultural regeneration has been consistent. From the longest walk in early 70s to the most recent Idle No More movement there are many noteworthy examples of political mobilization (Johansen, 2013, 178–179; The Kino-nda-niimi Collective, 2014).

3 Country food refers to locally harvested fish, mammals, plants, birds, and berries; however as a result of community preference wild food will be used in its place throughout this article.

4 Information obtained from OPCN community members through interviews and personal correspondence. Sources are noted following each section of information. Only texts in quotations are directly quoted; all other statements are paraphrased.

References

Adelson, N. (2000). *Being alive well: Health and the politics of Cree well-being*. Toronto: University of Toronto Press.

Alfred, T. (2009a). *Wasáse: Indigenous pathways of action and freedom*. Toronto: University of Toronto Press.

Alfred, T. (2009b). Colonialism and state dependency. *Journal of Aboriginal Health*, *5*(2), 42–60.

Alfred, T., & Corntassel, J. (2005). Being indigenous: Resurgence against contemporary colonialism. *Politics of Identity*, *9*, 597–614.

Andree, P., Jeffery, A., Michael, B., & Marie-Jane, M. (Eds.). (2014). *Globalization and food sovereignty: Global and local change in the new politics of food*. Toronto: University of Toronto Press.

Asch, M. (1984). *Home and native land: Aboriginal rights and the canadian constitution*. Agincourt: Methuen.

Barker, J. (2005). For whom sovereignty matters. In J. Barker (Eds), *Sovereignty matters: Locations of contestation and possibility in indigenous struggles for self-determination* (pp. 1–32). Lincoln: University of Nebraska Press.

Ball, J. (2004). As if indigenous knowledge and communities mattered: Transformative education in aboriginals communities in Canada. *The American Indian Quarterly*, *28*(3), 454–479.

Chandrasekera, U. (2008). *We're hungry, truth about food security in North America*. Toronto: Toronto Community Health Centres' Food Security Network. Retrieved December 9, 2014, from http://www.srchc.ca/downloads/FoodSecurityLiteratureReviewMay12008.pdf.

Coleman-Jensen, A., Nord, M., Andrews, M., & Carlson, S. (2011). *Household food security in the United States in 2010*. Economic Research Report 125. United States Department of Agriculture. Retrieved January 31, 2015, from http://ssrn.com/abstract=2116606.

Corntassel, J. (2008). Towards sustainable self-determination: Rethinking the contemporary Indigenous rights discourse. Alternatives: Global, Local, Political, *33*(1), 105–132.

Corntassel, J. (2012a). Re-envisioning resurgence: Indigenous pathways to decolonization and sustainable self-determination. *Decolonization: Indigeneity, Education and Society*, *1*(1), 86–101.

Corntassel, J. (2012b). Cultural restoration in international law: Pathways to Indigenous self-determination. *Canadian Journal of Human Rights*, *1*(1), 94–125.

Council of Canadian Academics. (2014). *Aboriginal food security in Northern Canada: An assessment of the state of knowledge*. Ottawa: The Expert Panel on the State of Knowledge of Food Security in Northern Canada, Council of Canadian Academics.

Dean, B., & Levi, J. (Eds). (2003). *At the risk of being heard: indigenous rights, identity and post-colonial states*. Ann Arbor: University of Michigan Press.

Declaration of Nyéléni. (2007). *Declaration of Nyéléni*. Retrieved January 5, 2015, from http://nyeleni.org/spip.php?article290.

Desmarais, A. A., & Wittman, H. (2014). Farmers, foodies and first nations: Getting to food sovereignty in Canada. *Journal of Peasant Studies*, *41*(6), 1153–1173.

Ducharme, S. (2013). Fighting for fishery: The Churchill river diversion swamped lucrative whitefish fishery. *Winnipeg Free Press*. Retrieved August 4, 2014, from http://www.winnipegfreepress.com/opinion/analysis/fighting-for-a-fishery-235187641.html.

Dysart, L. (2014). *Summary of South Indian lake history*. OPCN: CASIL.

Fanon, F. (1952). *Black skin, white masks*. New York: Grove Press.

FAO. (1996, November 13–17). *Rome Declaration on World Food Security and World Food Summit Plan of Action*. Rome: Food and Agriculture Organization of the United Nations. Retrieved December 20, 2014, from http://www.fao.org/ag/againfo/programmes/en/lead/toolbox/Indust/romedec.pdf

Fitznor, L. (2012). Indigenous scholars and writing through narratives and storying for healing and bridging. In J. Hendry & L. Fitznor (Eds), *Anthropologists, indigenous scholars and the research endeavour: Seeking bridges towards mutual respect* (pp. 270–284). New York: Routledge.

Grey, S., & Patel, R. (2014). Food sovereignty as decolonization: Some contributions from indigenous movement to food system and development politics. Agriculture and Human Values. Retrieved from January 20, 2015, from http://rajpatel.org/wp-content/uploads/2009/11/Grey-Patel-2015-Food-Sovereignty-as-Decolonization.pdf.

Hinsley, F. H. (1966). *Sovereignty*. New York: Basic Books.

Hoffman, S. (2008). Engineering poverty: Colonialism and hydroelectric development in Northern Manitoba. In T. Martin & S. Hoffman (Eds.), *Power struggles: Hydro development and Aboriginals in Manitoba and Quebec* (pp. 103–128). Winnipeg: University of Manitoba Press.

Hoffman, S., & Martin, T. (2012). Enduring dreams: Social capital and hydro development in Northern Manitoba. *International Journal of Critical Indigenous Studies*, *5*(1), 31–53.

Holt-Giménez, E., & Altieri, M. A. (2013). Agroecology, food sovereignty, and the new green revolution. *Agroecology and Sustainable Food Systems*, *37*(1), 90–102.

Iseke, J., & Moore, S. (2011). Community-based Indigenous digital storytelling with elders and youth. *American Indian Culture and Research Journal*, *35*(4), 19–38.

Jarosz, L. (2014). Comparing food security and food sovereignty discourses. *Dialogues in Human Geography*, *4*(2), 168–181.

Johansen, B. E. (2013). *Encyclopedia of the American Indian Movement*. Santa Barbara, CA: Greenwood Publishing.

Kamal, A., & Thompson, S. (2013). *Recipe for decolonization and resurgence: Story of O-Pipon-Na-Piwin Cree Nation's Indigenous food sovereignty movement*. Paper presented at Food Sovereignty: A Critical Dialogue at Yale University, September 14–15, 2013, New Haven, CT, USA.

Kamal, A., Thompson, S., Linklater, R., & Ithinto Mechisowin Committee. (2014). Sustainable livelihood approach to achieve food sovereignty in O-Pipon-Na-Piwin cree nation. In F. Deer, T. Falkenberg, B. McMillan, & L. Sims (Eds.), *Sustainable well-being: Concepts, issues, and educational practices* (pp. 139–155). Winnipeg: ESWB Press.

Kickingbird, K. (1977). *Indian sovereignty*. Washington, DC: Indian Legal Curriculum Training Program of the Institute for the Development of Indian Law.

Kuhnlein, H. V., Erasmus, B., Spigelski, D., & Burlingame, B. (2013). *Indigenous peoples' food systems and wellbeing: Interventions and policies for healthy communities*. Rome: United Nations Food and Agriculture Organization, Rome. Retrieved January 20, 2015, http://www.fao.org/docrep/018/i3144e/i3144e00.htm.

Kuhnlein, H. V., & Receveur, O. (1996). Dietary change and traditional food systems of Indigenous peoples. *Annual Reviews*, *16*, 417–442.

Kulchyski, P. (2008). A step back: The Nisichawayasihk cree nation and the Wuskwatim project. In T. Martin & S. Hoffman (Eds.), *Power struggles: Hydro development and Aboriginals in Manitoba and Quebec* (pp. 129–144). Winnipeg: University of Manitoba Press.

Kulchyski, P. (2013). *Aboriginal rights are not human rights*. Winnipeg: Arbeiter Ring Publishing.

Liénafa, K., & Martin, T. (2010). Beyond the conflict: The reconstruction of the O Pipon-Na-Piwin Aboriginal in Manitoba. *Geography Research Forum*, *30*, 50–65.

Loney, M. (1995). Social problems, community trauma and hydro project impacts. *Canadian Journal of Native Studies, 15*(2), 231–254.

Lum, Z. -A. (2014, October 2). Canada is the only UN member to reject landmark Indigenous rights document. *Huffington Post.* Retrieved from January 29, 2015, from http://www.huffingtonpost.ca/2014/10/02/canada-un-indigenous-rights_n_5918868.html.

Martin, T., & Hoffman, S. (Eds). (2008). *Power struggles: Hydro development and first nations in Manitoba and Quebec.* Winnipeg: University of Manitoba Press.

Mason, A. M., Dana, L. P., & Anderson, R. (2009). The Inuit commercial Caribou harvest and related agri-food industries in Nunavut. In R. B. Anderson & R. Bone (Eds.), *Natural resources and Aboriginal peoples in Canada* (pp. 342–361). Concord: Captus Press.

McClullum, H., & McClullum, K. (1975). *This land is not for sale.* Toronto: Anglican Book Centre.

McLeod, N. (2007). *Cree narrative memory: From treaties to contemporary times.* Winnipeg: Purich Publication.

Menser, M. (2014). The territory of self-determination, agroecological production, and the role of the state. In P. Andreé, J. Ayres, M. Bosia, & M-J. Massicotte (Eds.), *Globalization and food sovereignty* (pp. 53–83). Toronto: University of Toronto Press.

Morris, A. (1880). *The treaties of Canada with the Indians.* Reprinted 1971. Toronto: Coles.

Morrison, D. (2011). Indigenous food sovereignty: A model for social learning. In H. Wittman, A.A. Desmarais, & N. Wiebe (Eds.), *Food sovereignty in Canada: Creating just and sustainable food systems* (pp. 97–113). Halifax: Fernwood.

NFA. (1977). Northern flood agreement. Retrieved from January 18, 2015, from https://www.hydro.mb.ca/community/agreements/nfa/t_of_c.htm.

Power, E. M. (2008). Conceptualizing food security for Aboriginal people in Canada. *Canadian Journal of Public Health, 99*(2), 95–97.

Province of Manitoba. (2015). *Manitoba Government issues apology over past hydro development.* Retrieved from March 20, 2015, from http://news.gov.mb.ca/news/index.html?archive=&item=33753.

Public Utilities Board. (2014). *A review of community health issues related to Manitoba hydro's needs for and alternatives to (NFAT) preferred development plan.* Winnipeg: PUB Manitoba.

Robson, R. (1993). Modernization in the Manitoba North: The housing initiative. *Canadian Journal of Native Studies Annual, 13*(1), 105–138.

Rudolph, K., & MacLachlan, S. (2013). Seeking indigenous food sovereignty: Origins of and responses to the food crisis in northern Manitoba, Canada. *Local Environment: The International Journal of Justice and Sustainability, 18*(9): 1079–1098.

Schnarch, B. (2004). Ownership, control, access, and possession (OCAP) or self-determination applied to research: A critical analysis of contemporary aboriginals research and some options for aboriginals communities. *Journal of Aboriginal Health, 1*(1), 80–95.

Shadian, J. M. (2014). *The politics of Arctic sovereignty: Oil, ice and Inuit governance.* New York: Routledge.

Simpson, L. (2004). Anticolonial strategies for the recovery and maintenance of indigenous knowledge. *The American Indian Quarterly, 28*, 373–384.

Simpson, L. (2011). *Dancing on our Turtle's back.* Stories of Nishaabeg recreation, resurgence and a new emergence. Winnipeg: Arbeiter Ring Publishing.

Stédile, J. P., & de Carvalho, H. M. (2011). People need food sovereignty. In E. Holt-Giménez (Ed), *Food movements unite!* (pp. 21–34). Oakland, CA: Food First Books.

Tarasuk, V. (2009). Health implications of food insecurity. In D. Raphael (Ed.), *Social determinants of health: Canadian perspectives (Chap. 14)* (pp. 205–220). Toronto: Canadian Scholars Press.

The Kino-nda-niimi Collective. (2014). *The winter we danced, voices from the past, the future and the idle no more movement.* Winnipeg: ARP Books.

Thompson, S., Gulrukh, A., Ballard, M., Beardy, B., Islam, D., Lozeznik, V., & Wong, K. (2011). Is community economic development putting healthy food on the table: Food sovereignty in northern Manitoba's aboriginal communities. *Journal of Aboriginal Economic Development, 7*(2), 14–39.

Thompson, S., Wiebe, J., Gulrukh, A., & Ashram, A. (2012). Analyzing food-related economic development in indigenous communities in northern Manitoba for impacts on food sovereignty, food security and sustainable livelihoods. *Canadian Journal of Nonprofit and Social Economy Research, 3*(2), 43–66.

Via Campesina. (1996). *The right to produce and access to land.* Position of the Via Campesina on Food Sovereignty presented at the World Food Summit, November 13–17, Rome, Italy. Retrieved January 22, 2015, from http://www.voiceoftheturtle.org/library/1996%20Declaration%20of%20Food%20Sovereignty.pdf.

Waldram, J. B. (1984). Hydroelectric development and the process of negotiation in northern Manitoba, 1960–1970. *The Canadian Journal of Native Studies*, *2*, 205–239.

Waldram, J. B. (1985). Hydroelectric development and dietary delocalization in Northern Manitoba, Canada. *Human Organization*, *44*(1), 41–49.

Waldram, J. B. (1988). *As long as the rivers run: Hydroelectric development and native communities in Western Canada.* Winnipeg: University of Manitoba Press.

Waziyatawin, A. W., & Yellow B. M. (Eds). (2005). *For indigenous eyes only: A decolonization handbook.* Santa Fe: Santa Fe Press.

Wittman, H. (2011). Food sovereignty: a new rights framework for food and nature? *Environment and Society: Advances in Research*, *2*(1), 87–105.

Wittman, H., Desmarais, A., & Wiebe, N. (Eds). (2011). *Food sovereignty in Canada: Creating just and sustainable food systems.* Black Point: Fernwood.

Index

Page numbers in bold refer to tables. Page numbers in italics refer to figures.

For Product Safety Concerns and Information please contact our EU
representative GPSR@taylorandfrancis.com
Taylor & Francis Verlag GmbH, Kaufingerstraße 24, 80331 München, Germany

www.ingramcontent.com/pod-product-compliance
Ingram Content Group UK Ltd.
Pitfield, Milton Keynes, MK11 3LW, UK
UKHW050055200926
475702UK00019B/2846
* 9 7 8 0 3 6 7 1 3 9 2 9 2 *